Advanced Information and Knowledge Processing

Springer-Verlag London Ltd.

Gregoris Mentzas, Dimitris Apostolou,
Andreas Abecker and Ron Young

Knowledge Asset Management

**Beyond the Process-centred and
Product-centred Approaches**

With 76 Figures

KM MADE
IN EUROPE

Springer

Gregoris Mentzas, PhD
National Technical University of Athens, Greece

Dimitris Apostolou, PhD
Planet Ernst Young SA, Athens, Greece

Andreas Abecker, Dipl.-Inform.
DFKI (German Research Centre for Artificial Intelligence), Kaiserslautern, Germany

Ron Young, FBCS
Knowledge Associates, Cambridge, UK

Series Editor
Xindong Wu

British Library Cataloguing in Publication Data
Knowledge asset management: beyond the process-centred
  and product-centred approaches (Advanced information and knowledge processing)
  1. Knowledge management   2. Knowledge management – Computer
  network resources
  I. Mentzas, Gregoris
  658.4'038
ISBN 978-1-4471-1109-2   ISBN 978-1-4471-0069-0 (eBook)
DOI 10.1007/978-1-4471-0069-0

Library of Congress Cataloging-in-Publication Data
A catalog record for this book is available from the Library of Congress

AI&KP ISSN 1610-3947

ISBN 978-1-4471-1109-2

© Springer-Verlag London 2003
Originally published by Springer-Verlag London Limited in 2003
Softcover reprint of the hardcover 1st edition 2003

Typesetting: Gray Publishing, Tunbridge Wells, Kent

34/3830-543210   Printed on acid-free paper   SPIN 10863751

to Lily and Maria
GM

to Tota
DA

to Carin and Flo
AA

to Emma, Benjamin and Nicholas
RY

Foreword

A new economy is emerging. An economy that is transforming the fundamental rules of business. An economy based on exploiting knowledge and innovation. An economy where knowledge is the main source of wealth for regions, nations, enterprises and people.

This new economy is based on economic values far removed from those of the industrial economy. Value has shifted towards intangibles and in particular towards increasing value by incorporating knowledge into services and products.

The advent of this new economy is rapidly changing the role and structure of global business. Winning enterprises are those best able to harness the benefits and opportunities of information and communication technology, capitalize on their knowledge base and move at the speed of the market.

Knowledge management lies at the heart of the European Community's competitiveness strategy. The European Commission facilitates and supports applied research in knowledge management through its Information Society Technologies (IST) programme, a major theme of research and technological development within the European Union's Research and Technology Development Framework Programme. Specifically, the New Methods of Work and Electronic Commerce action of the IST programme supports long-term applied research in areas combining technological innovation with new work practices and advanced business and work models.

Organizational knowledge management is a critical component of this action of IST. The Commission supports a plethora of applied research and technology development work in the knowledge management area by funding projects that aim at the development and validation of multidisciplinary solutions and practices for the acquisition, sharing, trading and delivery of knowledge in order to leverage individual and collective knowledge, and support worker and business innovation and entrepreneurship.

This book presents an innovative knowledge asset-centric solution to knowledge management that helps companies to tap into their corporate knowledge and enhance their competitiveness. The solution was developed and validated within two highly successful industrial research projects that were cofunded by the European Commission: the Know-Net (EP-28928) and the LEVER (IST-1999-20216) projects.

Applied research on the concepts and approaches proposed within the book is further elaborated by the authors in two additional projects supported by the European Commission: the DECOR (IST-1999-13002) and the INKASS (IST-2001-33373) projects.

The book outlines a conceptually rigorous yet pragmatic approach for managing knowledge assets in order to enable organizational growth, foster innovation and create responsiveness to market demands. The explicit development, nurturing and facilitation of knowledge assets presents tremendous opportunities for organizations of the future that will operate and thrive in the knowledge economy.

Rosalie Zobel
Director, New Methods of Work and Electronic Commerce
Directorate-General Information Society
European Commission

"One of the rare books today on Knowledge Management that addresses the leveraging of an organization's intellectual assets by using an integrative and holistic approach. Well worth reading!"

Michael Stankosky, Professor of Knowledge Management and
Co-founder/co-director of the Institute for Knowledge Management, The George Washington
University

"This book is a useful illustration of Knowledge Management implementation principles: it synthesizes theoretical and pragmatic approaches to the subject and does a competent job of embracing the various dimensions of a Knowledge Management initiative."

Daniele Chauvel, Director, European Center for Knowledge Management; Business School
Marseille-Provence

"For those organisations who wish to take a strategic view of knowledge management, this book shows how they can take KM to the next level – not driven by a technology solution but based on the strategy and needs of the business."

Marc Auckland, Chief Learning Officer and Head of the BT Academy, BT

"The KM method proposed in this book enables enterprises to exploit their knowledge more effectively by making it easily available to employees and by facilitating the exchange and integration of information used by knowledge workers in a variety of business situations"

Ciro Maddaloni, SOGEI S.p.A., Gruppo Telecom Italia

Contents

Introduction

Organizations of all kinds are coming to the realization that knowledge is their greatest competitive asset. As knowledge becomes the key strategic resource of the future, the need of organizations to develop a comprehensive understanding of knowledge strategies, processes and tools for the creation, transfer and deployment of this unique asset is becoming critical.

The task of developing and applying "knowledge management" (KM) as a new discipline is a challenging endeavour. This new discipline must respond successfully to the diverse needs of companies in a timely fashion. For businesses that must compete in a daily changing world, superior management of knowledge is the key to innovation, productivity and growth.

This book presents an innovative and holistic solution to KM that is theoretically sound, yet practical and easily applicable. The approach is explicitly based on managing an organization's knowledge assets in order to create value. It includes a management framework, a knowledge transformation methodology and an intranet-based tool. The solution was developed after 3 years of applied research and practical experimentation in eight companies in the financial services sector, the IT sector and the professional services sector.

Our motivation to write the book was the realization that practical KM efforts in organizations adopt one of two approaches: the *process-centric* approach, which mainly treats KM as a social communication process; and the *product-centric* approach, which focuses on knowledge artefacts, their creation, storage and reuse in computer-based corporate memories. We found evidence of this distinction not only in KM implementations in companies, but also in supporting methodologies and tools.

However, it is our true belief that in order for organisations of the twenty-first century to add value to their product and service "offerings", a holistic perspective is required that would fuse these two approaches. The presentation of a practical framework, method and a tool that provides a balanced fusion of these two KM views is the aim of this book.

About This Book: The Know-Net Solution

This book presents the Know-Net solution, an innovative KM solution, which is based on leveraging the knowledge assets of an organization, be it a profit business or a not-for-profit institution. The Know-Net solution is the result of a major multipartner industrial research project that was cofunded by the European Scientific Programme of Research in Information Technology (ESPRIT) of the European Commission within the theme of IT for Learning and Training in Industry (under contract ESPRIT EP28928), the Swiss BBW and the participating companies.

The Know-Net consortium comprised the following companies: Planet, a Greek management consultancy company active in south-east Europe (now Planet Ernst & Young); Knowledge Associates, a UK-based global company specializing in knowledge management; DFKI, the German Research Centre for Artificial Intelligence; the Centre for Advanced Learning Technologies of the INSEAD business school; NAI Gooch Webster, a UK-based chartered surveyors firm; the Greek Institute of Communication and Computer Systems, a research institute of the National Technical University of Athens; Fachhochschule bei der Basel, a Swiss academic institution; and the Credit Risk Valuation Department of UBS, the global financial institution. The Know-Net project started in October 1998 and was finalized in March 2000. The world-wide web address of the project is *http://www.know-net.org*

The Know-Net solution presented in this book was further validated and enhanced in a second project entitled LEVER (Leveraging Knowledge in the Software Industry). The objective of LEVER was the customization and validation of the Know-Net solution to companies in the IT services sector. LEVER was funded by the Information Society Technologies (IST) programme of the European Commission under contract IST-1999-20216.

The LEVER partners included: Planet Ernst & Young and Knowledge Associates, which were also participating in Know-Net; Singular, the leading company in Greece in the areas of designing, developing, implementing and supporting integrated business software packages; AlphaNova, a UK-based global developer of collaborative customer relationship management (CRM) solutions; Debus, an ERP development and localization centre based in the Czech Republic; MDA, a Turkish software development company; the Software Research and Development Center of the Middle East Technical University of Turkey; and the Federation of Hellenic Information Technology and Communication Enterprises (SEPE), a non-profit organization with more than 350 members. The LEVER project started in November 2000 and was finalized in October 2001. The website of the project is *http://www.kmlever.com*

The Know-Net solution is based on the principle that the foundation of KM in contemporary enterprises lies on managing and leveraging knowledge assets. In Know-Net's view, KM is not an abstract proposition for the future. Its full realization is, indeed, a long-term goal, but implementing the practical solutions that are available today is not a case of following the latest management fad; it is a vital aspect of world-class management in today's business environment.

Know-Net is a *total* KM solution, which includes three components. The first component is a conceptual *framework* that can be used by managers as a roadmap for ensuring integrity of the KM effort. The second component is a modular *method* that helps organizations to define and document their knowledge management strategy, audit and design business processes that enhance and facilitate corporate learning, establish related organizational roles, facilitate knowledge sharing between people in the organization, and explicitly measure and evaluate the quality and business value of the organization's intellectual capital. The third component is an intranet-based *tool* that supports the collection and categorization of internal and external information, the reuse of stored knowledge using flexible and customizable knowledge navigators, advanced search, both keyword based and concept based, and collaboration facilities via on-line workspaces that allow knowledge workers to work together from different locations.

Structure of the Book

The first chapter outlines the process- and product-centric approaches to KM. The chapter analyzes the differing perspectives adopted by these two approaches in three different issues: in KM-related software, in KM methods and consulting services, and in real-world KM implementations in various companies. Moreover, the need is identified for a consistent and coherent fusion of the two approaches.

Chapter 2 describes the Know-Net conceptual framework that aims to help consultants and implementers of KM to tie all of the different initiatives and different components into one holistic system. The main building blocks of the framework are the knowledge assets of the organization, but knowledge assets need a strategy to develop them, distribute them, store them, measure them and so on. These knowledge assets need KM processes to facilitate capturing new learning and ideas and building new knowledge assets. They also need communications and collaboration technologies to support them and organizational structures, that is, roles and responsibilities, to leverage them. So, around the knowledge assets we need to ensure that we have a strategy, processes, systems and structure, adequately in place. In addition to that, for KM to be successful, we have to be quite clear how it affects the individual, the team and the entire organization, where the power of collective and systematic application of knowledge assets begins. Finally, we have to look at the interorganizational dimension, which is the relationship between the organization and its customers, suppliers and strategic partners, and how we can better manage the knowledge assets across this whole community and not just within an organization.

Chapter 3 outlines the Know-Net method, which is modular so an organization can choose to start at different levels depending on its readiness, needs and requirements. In "Stage I: plan", an organization determines the vision and readiness for a KM initiative, and the scope and feasibility of the project. In "Stage II: develop", the structure and the design of a holistic solution (that covers processes, people and technology) are iteratively developed, tested and reviewed. "Stage III: operate" is the company-wide implementation of the KM initiative, while the measurement part of the method aims to provide consistent support for measuring the creation, sharing and use of knowledge assets within the company.

Chapter 4 provides an overview of the Know-Net tool, a KM software infrastructure that has been designed to be fully scalable, in order to support and enable either a small team of knowledge workers or a global enterprise-wide KM effort. The tool aims to help companies to collect and categorize internal and external information by allowing knowledge workers to capture knowledge assets and link them to their context into a knowledge repository, to reuse knowledge assets using customizable knowledge navigators, to find knowledge assets using both textual and graphical searching mechanisms, and to collaborate and share knowledge assets via on-line workspaces.

Chapters 5 and 6 give an account of our efforts to test the applicability of the Know-Net solution. We focused on organizations that exhibit high knowledge intensity (the knowledge-intensive organizations or KIOs). Such organizations usually adopt network organizational structures, they are customer centric and their most critical asset is their people. Examples of KIOs can be found in sectors such as advertising, consulting, financial or legal advice, nursing care and software programming.

Chapter 5 presents the application of the Know-Net solution in four companies in the IT services sector (Delta-Singular, AlphaNova, Debus I.T. and MDA). These descriptions are relatively short and highlight how our methodology has addressed specific but different KM undertakings in companies of the same industry sector.

Chapter 6 summarizes the application of Know-Net in the case of the consulting firm Planet. This description covers the application of all aspects of the Know-Net methodology and aims to be a full example of our approach.

Chapter 7, Knowledge Asset Management and Beyond, starts by giving an account of how the presented KM solution truly integrates the product-centric and process-centric approaches, and continues by discussing how the explicit treatment and leveraging of knowledge assets opens up a wealth of both basic research and action-oriented directions for further exploration.

Acknowledgements

We had the opportunity to interact with many people during the development of the Know-Net knowledge management solution as well as during the preparation of this book. As mentioned above, this book, to a large extent, is the product of two European research projects. We would like to thank the European Commission not only for partially funding our efforts, but also for helping us to shape our ideas and work. We thank Agnes Bradier, Khalil Rouhana, Paul Hearn and Anne Jubert of the European Commission. We are also grateful to the reviewers of these projects: Ann Macintosh from the International Teledemocracy Centre of Napier University, Thorsten Schwarz from TESSAG Technical Systems & Services AG, Basilis Masoulas from Shell International, Daniele Chauvel from EcKM Groupe ESC, and Ciro Maddaloni from Sogei. Their comments and recommendations have been extremely constructive and beneficial for the successful completion of the projects.

This book would have not been written without the interaction with many colleagues and friends from the companies we work for, as well as from companies we worked with. Maria Legal from Planet Ernst & Young, Pooja Goyal and Jill Atherton from INSEAD and Joanna Lee from Knowledge Associates deserve particular recognition for their significant work on the development and application of Know-Net. In addition, we would like to thank Raphael Koumeri, Mamina Amourgi and Rania Vrettou from Planet Ernst & Young; Britt-Marie Young, Andy Burnett, Graham McEwan, Darren Hodges, David Foulds, Nick Young and Alex Carr from Knowledge Associates; Joachim Hackstein and Jamel Zakraoui from the German Research Center for Artificial Intelligence (DFKI); Albert Angehrn, Thierry Nabeth and Hubert Poulhes from INSEAD; Colin Manders and Ermina Topintzi from NAI Gooch Webster; Spyros Dioudis and Giorgos Papavassiliou from the National Technical University of Athens; Michael Wolf and Gabriele Sonnenberger from UBS; Marco Bettoni, Rolf Todesco and Robert Ottinger from FHBB; Andreas Oikonomopoulos, Kyriakos Kassis and Evelina Peristeri from Delta-Singular; George Zachariades and Keith Shonfeld from AlphaNova; Thomas Seitl and Anatoly

Gafurov from Debus I.T.; Aral Ege from MDA; Asuman Dogac, Yildiray Kabak and Gokce Banu Laleci from the Middle-East Technical University; and finally Christina Troumpetari from the Federation of Hellenic Information Technology Enterprises.

We would like to acknowledge Mary Ondrusz and Rebecca Mowat, the editors for Springer Verlag with whom we worked. We are appreciative of their interest, persistence and feedback.

A warm thank you to our families for their support and continuous encouragement during the writing of this book.

1 Process and Product Approaches in Knowledge Management

1.1 Knowledge and Knowledge Management

The twenty-first century marks the beginning of an era in which the traditional pillars of economic power – capital, land, materials and labor – are no longer the main determinants of business success; instead, achievement will be essentially determined by our ability to use knowledge, a precious global resource, wisely. This is due to the constant and overwhelming change in the business environment, from one in which the market assumptions were stable, the business rules were rigid, the command-and-control management model was adequate, competitors and customers were known and the future was almost predictable, to an environment in which the only thing that can be predicted is unpredictability itself.

Most companies of today are primarily run on the basis of insights gained from the successes of the manufacturing-based, capital-intensive industrial economy of the past. These companies have fallen or are rapidly falling out of alignment with the evolutionary direction of the future, as the economy transits from the post-industrial era to what is rapidly becoming a global knowledge economy.

In this knowledge economy most organizations depend for their value and competitiveness on the development, use and distribution of knowledge-based competences. As knowledge increasingly becomes the key strategic resource of the future, the need of organizations to develop a comprehensive understanding of knowledge strategies, processes and tools for the creation, transfer and deployment of this unique asset is becoming critical. The challenge is to seek fundamental insights, to help organizations to nurture, harvest and manage the immense potential of their knowledge; to help them to create new maps and measures and reinvent themselves in order to innovate and excel in the context of the knowledge economy.

The task of developing and applying knowledge management (KM) as a new discipline is a challenging endeavour. This new discipline must respond successfully to the diverse needs of companies in a timely fashion. However, despite a wealth of books, reports and studies, neither researchers nor practitioners have an agreed definition of "knowledge management". The term is used loosely to refer to a broad collection of organizational practices and approaches related to generating, capturing and sharing knowledge that is relevant to the organization's business. There are many different interpretations as to what exactly it means and how best to address the emerging questions about how to use its potential power effectively (see for example Nonaka and Takeuchi, 1995; Davenport and Prusak, 1998; Edvinsson and Malone, 1997; Wiig, 1995). Some would even argue that "knowledge management" is a contradiction in terms, being a hangover from an industrial era when control modes of thinking were dominant.

Whatever the term and the definition employed to describe it, KM is increasingly seen not merely as the latest management fashion, but as signalling the development of a more organic and holistic way of understanding and exploiting the role of organizational knowledge in the processes of managing and doing work.

But what would "knowledge" be in an organizational setting? Debates and discussions about the definition of knowledge abound. In everyday language, it has long been the practice to distinguish between information, i.e. data arranged in meaningful patterns, and knowledge, i.e. something that is believed, that is true (for pragmatic knowledge, that works) and that is reliable. The interchangeable use of information and knowledge can be confusing if it is not made clear that knowledge is being used in a new and unusual sense, and can seem unscrupulous insofar as the intent is to attach the prestige of knowledge to mere information. It also tends to obscure the fact that while it can be extremely easy and quick to transfer information from one place to another, it is often very difficult and slow to transfer knowledge from one person to another.

In the West, intuitive knowledge has often been devalued in favour of rational scientific knowledge, and the rise of science has even led to claims that intuitive knowledge is not really knowledge at all. However, recognition of the difficulties inherent in transferring knowledge from one person to another has tended to highlight the importance of tacit knowledge, notably in the writings of Polanyi (*The Tacit Dimension*, 1966) and Nonaka and Takeuchi (1995). In the East, the tradition has been to celebrate the importance of the intuitive, in comparison with the rational. The Upanishads, for instance, speak about a higher and a lower knowledge, and associate lower knowledge with the various sciences. Chinese philosophy has emphasized the complementary nature of the intuitive and the rational and has represented them by the archetypal pair yin and yang.

Similar debates about the meaning of knowledge have continued for thousands of years, and seem likely to continue for some time to come. In this book we do not intend to examine the various epistemological definitions of knowledge, nor to analyse the various perspectives taken by philosophers in this field. Our interest is not focused on what knowledge is, rather it is on what knowledge can do. Hence the focus of this book is not on discovery and truth, rather it is on effective business action and organizational performance.

A definition that is suitable for our purposes is the one given by Davenport and Prusak (1998), who define knowledge as "a fluid mix of framed experience, values, contextual information, and expert insight that provides a framework for evaluating and incorporating new experiences and information. It originates and is applied in the minds of knowers. In organisations, it often becomes embedded not only in documents or repositories but also in organisational routines, processes, practices, and norms". This definition highlights two important types of knowledge: explicit knowledge and tacit knowledge (see also Nonaka and Takeuchi, 1995).

Tacit knowledge refers to that knowledge which is embedded in individual experience such as perspective and inferential knowledge. Tacit knowledge includes insights, hunches, intuition and skills that are highly personal and hard to formalize, making them difficult to communicate or share with others. Tacit knowledge is also deeply rooted in an individual's commitment to a specific context as a craft or profession, a particular technology or product market, or the activities of a work group or team. In other words tacit knowledge is deeply ingrained into the context, i.e. the owner's view and imagination of the world, and into his or her experience, which is previously acquired knowledge.

Explicit knowledge is knowledge that has been articulated in formal language and can be easily transmitted among individuals. It can be expressed in scientific formulae, codified procedures or a variety of other forms. It consists of three components: a language, information and a carrier. The language is used to express and code knowledge. Information is coded externalized knowledge. It is potential knowledge, which is realized when information is combined with context and the experience of humans to form new tacit knowledge. The carrier is capable of incorporating coded knowledge and storing, preserving and transporting knowledge through space and time independent of its human creators.

Both explicit knowledge and tacit knowledge are important for the organization. Both must be recognized as providing value to the organization. It is through the conversion of tacit to explicit knowledge and explicit to tacit knowledge in the organization that creativity and innovation are released and the potential for value creation arises. The goal, then, is to leverage both explicit knowledge and tacit knowledge and to reduce the size of the organizational knowledge gaps.

The business and popular press abound with real-world industrial examples of initiatives that attempt to address these goals. Such initiatives may be classified within three strands. First, some companies, such as Dow Chemical, address innovation in product development initiatives, either by making sure that knowledge is embedded in their products, or by identifying and reusing knowledge. Second, organizations such as Texas and Chevron develop process and operational improvement initiatives that focus on the transfer of best practices by creating best practice databases and organizing best practice sharing events. Third, many companies (e.g. in the telecommunications and the banking sectors) develop customer and market initiatives, in which they mine customer data to make sense of who buys and why, and how to keep clients buying.

KM has moved from an early premature phase, characterized by considerable hype and confusion, to a state of relative maturity, in which the value it brings to business and government organizations is not disputed. The adopters of this new discipline have followed different approaches with varying emphasis on technology, cultural, organizational and managerial issues. Nevertheless, if one looks into the research landscape as well as into the business applications of KM, it is easy to notice that two main perspectives for KM are usually employed (see e.g. Hansen *et al.*, 1999; Kühn and Abecker, 1997; Spek and Spijkevert, 1997). We will call them the *"product"* and the *"process"* approaches.

1.2 The Process and Product Approaches in KM

The "product" approach implies that knowledge is a thing that can be located and manipulated as an independent object. Proponents of this approach claim that it is possible to capture, distribute, measure and manage knowledge. This approach mainly focuses on products and artefacts containing and representing knowledge; usually, this means managing documents, their creation, storage and reuse in computer-based corporate memories. Examples include: best practice databases and lessons-learned archives, case-bases which preserve older business-case experiences, knowledge taxonomies and formal knowledge structures. This approach is also referred to as "content-centred" or "codification" approach.

Adopting a product-centric approach to KM means treating knowledge as an entity rather separate from the people who create and use it. The typical goal is to take documents with explicit knowledge embedded in them (memos, reports, presentations, articles, etc.) and store them in a repository where they can be easily retrieved. Companies that aim at a continual enhancement of their knowledge base, in the collection of best practices, methods and reusable work products, include General Motors, Glaxo Wellcome and DaimlerChrysler.

The "process" approach puts emphasis on ways to promote, motivate, encourage, nurture or guide the process of knowing, and abolishes the idea of trying to capture and distribute knowledge. This view mainly understands KM as a social communication process, which can be improved by collaboration and cooperation support tools. In this approach, knowledge is closely tied to the person who developed it and is shared mainly through person-to-person contacts. The main purpose of Information and Communication Technology (ICT) in this case is to help people to communicate knowledge, not to store it. ICT tools in this case comprise e-mail, video-conferencing, workflow management systems, systems for the distributed authoring of hypertext documents, group-decision support systems, etc. This approach has also been referred to as the "collaboration" or "personalization" approach.

Firms adopting a "process-centric" approach in their KM initiatives focus on the creation of communities of interest or practice (self-organized groups that "naturally" communicate with one another because they have common work practices, interests or aims), to address knowledge generation and sharing. The emphasis in this case is on providing access to knowledge or facilitating its transfer among individuals. For example, companies such as British Petroleum, Skandia, Buckman Laboratories and Matsushita strive to create corporate environments that nurture knowledge communities, in order to facilitate the exchange of ideas and collaboration across the organization.

The existence of these two approaches in KM can be attributed no less to its different origins. Artificial intelligence (AI) and knowledge engineering, for instance, have historically focused on technologies for codification and organization, in contrast to organizational theory which has always treated knowledge independently for the people that own it. Table 1.1 groups the origins of KM according to the two approaches.

Table 1.2 summarizes the basic characteristics of the two approaches in terms of their strategic, technological and human resource-related directions.

Table 1.1 The origins of KM Based on Sveiby (1997a)

	Knowledge as a product	Knowledge as a process
Organization	Systems theory Computer science Business process re-engineering	Organizational theory Sociology
Individual	Artificial intelligence	Psychology Philosophy Pedagogy

Table 1.2 Characteristics of the process- and product-centric KM approaches

	Product-centric approach	Process-centric approach
Focus	Knowledge is represented as objects. The emphasis is on capturing, organizing and sharing knowledge objects. Utilization of products and systems that contain codified knowledge	Knowledge is associated with the individual that owns it. Knowledge sharing is accomplished through human contacts and relations
Strategy	Exploitation of organized, codified and easily reusable knowledge. Linking of people with systems that capture and disseminate knowledge	Exploitation and empowerment of individual and team knowledge. Development of networks for linking people, promotion and facilitation of discussions so that tacit knowledge can be shared
Human resources	Employment of professionals who are well suited to the reuse of knowledge. Training is facilitated passively (through courses, presentations and computer-based courses). Rewarding focuses on using and contributing to the organization's knowledge base	Employment of highly creative professionals who work in teams. Training is facilitated through on-the-job learning, group brainstorming sessions and one-to-one mentoring. Rewarding focuses on group performance and knowledge sharing between professionals
Information technology	Heavy investment in IT. Tools include document repositories, search and retrieval tools	Moderate investment in IT. Tools include discussions databases, real-time communication and collaboration tools, net conferencing and push technologies

The following sections examine further the particularities of the two approaches in the software tools that support KM efforts, in the consulting methodologies and services usually employed for the implementation of KM projects and in the specific directions of the KM initiatives themselves of early-adopter organizations.

1.3 The Process and Product Approaches in KM Software

KM-related software can be classified according to the type of approach (product or process centric) for which it is most suited for (Figure 1.1). As is evident from the figure, not all software tools can be classified as supporting only one or the other approach; rather they exhibit characteristics and functionalities that may be closer to the process or the product perspective.

Process-centric KM software tools provide rich, shared, virtual workspaces in which interactions occur between people who share a common goal. For example, groupware products provide a basic messaging infrastructure for ad hoc forms of information exchange in the form of e-mail services, and a range of collaborative features, such as discussion groups, shared folders or databases, and calendar and scheduling functions. While groupware products provide an informal environment for collaboration, other products have been used to create more formal collaborative applications. Workflow and document management systems have brought greater control to processes that require many people to work on a set of documents. Workflow, for example, has been used in the insurance industry to control the claims assessment process. In the pharmaceutical industry, document management

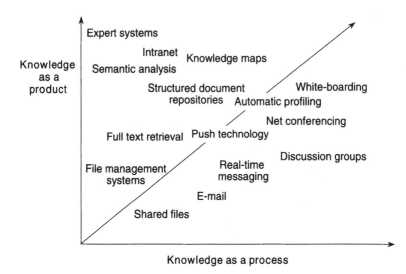

Figure 1.1 Process and product approaches in KM software. (Based on Ovum, 1998.)

applications have brought greater control over the submission of new drugs to regulatory authorities.

For well-defined, structured business applications, workflow and document management vendors have supported coordination between knowledge workers. In weakly structured business processes groupware tools have provided more ad hoc forms of information exchange, mainly through e-mail services. In both cases, collaboration software provides the virtual space, within which participants can share experiences and knowledge. Collaborative environments usually include facilities for both synchronous and asynchronous communication. Synchronous communication tools allow users to set up a conversation, hold conferencing and white-boarding sessions and work together on documents in real-time via an intranet or over the Internet. Concerning asynchronous communication, e-mail is still the dominant tool.

Of significant importance for the "knowledge as a process" approach are also technologies that facilitate the creation of communities of interest and/or practice. Recent improvements in the integration of directory services, based on the take-up of Lightweight Directory Access Protocol (LDAP) and improved automation of expert profiling and discovery, make it easier to find the right person across the network. Expert discovery systems have the goal of suggesting the names of persons who have knowledge in a particular area. Expert discovery systems work either based on user profiles or by automatically associating users with documents based on authorship. User profiling can be maintained manually or automatically. The problem with manual creation of user profiles is that users may not be motivated to keep their profile up to date. Automatic profiling of users is usually supported by creating explicit profiles based on evidence mined from existing databases and inferred from associations of persons and documents.

Software tools that mainly aim to support the "knowledge as a product" approach provide facilities for storing knowledge encapsulating artefacts to multiplatform, heterogeneous sources, including Internet and intranet sites, file servers, databases and legacy information systems. Within such tools search facilities are essential for finding information relevant for some tasks.

Search has become important in the business environment because the total amount of potentially relevant information, including what is on the Internet and company intranets and what is available from commercial on-line publishers, has grown significantly in the past few years. The keyword searches that are provided by most Internet search engines offer a simple and easy way to access a wide range of documents. The effectiveness of such searches is inherently restricted to a relatively simple statistical analysis of the searched document, based on the occurrence of those key terms. The main problem with keyword searches is that not all documents are using the same words to refer to the same concept. Most information-retrieval vendors offer the capability of assigning metadata to documents. Metadata describe the concepts that the documents refer to in a controlled vocabulary. Metadata therefore allow the transition from keyword searching to concept searching. Thesaurus capabilities enable search terms to be expanded to cover a series of related terms. Expansion of a query with synonyms is known to improve the recall in a text search, but thesaurus-based searching is only effective in well-defined domains where the ambiguity of words, and the validity of term relationships, is not an issue. Improving precision in domain searching by reducing the ambiguity of ordinary words is also facilitated by the use of taxonomies, classification schemata and ontologies. These mechanisms allow for the organization of concepts based on a schema of concepts and relations between concepts. The value of these mechanisms is two-fold. First, it allows a user to navigate to pieces of information of interest without doing a search. Second, these mechanisms allow documents to be put in a context, which helps users to assess their applicability to the task in hand.

Manually assigning documents to the terms of an ontology requires significant effort and cost, but in recent years automatic document classification has helped in this direction. The two major techniques that are used to automate document classification are pattern matching, with tools using mainly AI-based techniques to provide comparisons of documents and grouping of documents, based on the similarity of the concepts used, and semantic analysis, which enables an understanding of the semantic relationships characteristic of a specific language and often of a specific domain, such as the medical or legal domain. These techniques are also used to enable large-scale automatic document classification (often called document clustering or document mining). Clustering can identify prevailing themes within a set of documents and then group the documents in relation to those themes. Automatic clustering does not replace the need for human understanding of the patterns identified, but it does help users to find patterns that may be overlooked within large volumes of information.

Expert systems and other knowledge-based systems that aim to replace human reasoning with AI are typical product-centric KM software tools. Such tools are used in stable, concentrated and well-defined domains. In such environments they can enable the knowledge of one or a few experts to be used by a much broader group of workers who need this knowledge. The user normally engages in a dialogue with the system, entering information about the problem or process in order to train the system so that it can act independently of the human. In this sense, expert systems reflect the product approach because their role is to substitute (partially at least) humans and human knowledge in performing specific tasks. It should be noted, though, that the current capability of machine intelligence is such that, for the great majority of business applications, human knowledge will continue to be a valuable resource for the foreseeable future (Marwick, 2001).

1.4 The Process and Product Approaches in KM Methods and Services

The global consulting firms were among the first businesses to make heavy investments in the management of knowledge, their core asset, and are primary KM services and methodology providers. In their internal KM initiatives the bias towards the process or the product approach is evident (see e.g. the reviews of Hansen et al., 1999, Apostolou and Mentzas, 1999). In selling KM services to clients, most global consultancy firms are taking a long-term "programme" approach to implementation. In their KM assignments all major consultancies address strategy, people, process and technology issues, all considered as key factors that need to be altered so that they are aligned with the KM principles.

Nevertheless, despite the holistic consideration of KM, individual approaches show to a lesser or greater extent some bias towards the product or process approach (Figure 1.2). Ernst & Young (E & Y), for instance, considers community enablement as a key solution that runs across most of the company's KM implementations (Ovum, 1998). The firm focuses on the creation of communities of interest or communities of practice (self-organized groups that naturally communicate with one another because they have common work practices, interests or aims) to address knowledge generation and sharing. In contrast, although KPMG also claims the use of a holistic approach covering all "seven key knowledge processes" (creation, application, exploitation, sharing, encapsulation, sourcing and learning), its technology implementations are mainly based on knowledge repositories, such as document management systems for storing captured knowledge assets and data warehousing for knowledge discovery and decision support (Ovum, 1998, 1999). Similarly, PricewaterhouseCoopers' solutions, which target KM at key business areas within the organization, are often implemented as part of a wider Enterprise Resource Planning (ERP) or data warehouse project (Ovum, 1999).

In specialist knowledge consultancies, which usually provide expertise on niche areas, the focus on either the process or product view is relatively clear. For instance, Collaborative Strategies and NetForm are firms with expertise and methodologies for facilitating KM through collaboration and informal people-to-people interaction.

Figure 1.2 classifies the consulting methods of major consultancies as well as some knowledge analysis and modelling techniques. All these methods and techniques are described in the following sections. It should be noted that the analysis is based on data available before the recent mergers of consulting firms Cap Gemini and E&Y (which formed Cap Gemini Ernst and Young).

1.4.1 The KM Method of Ernst & Young

The KM practice of E&Y (pre-merger) provides a range of knowledge services and solutions that focus exclusively on strategy, process and change management. It does not cover system integration or development services, which are usually out-sourced to another part of the organization.

As shown in Figure 1.3, E&Y advocated a "pilot-first" approach consisting of three delivery phases: architect, integrate, operate (Ovum, 1999). The "architect" phase aligns the KM strategy and architecture with the organization's business objectives.

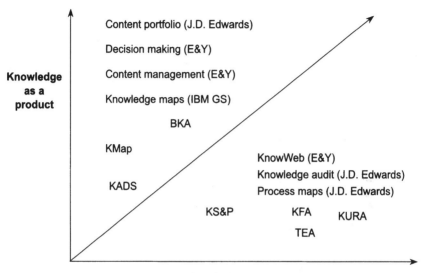

Figure 1.2 The process and product approaches in KM methods.

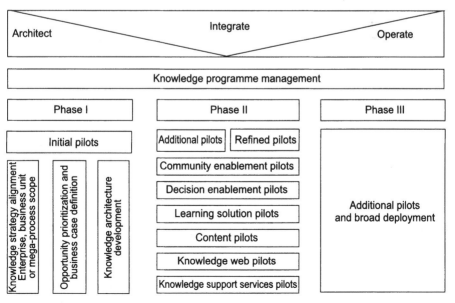

Figure 1.3 The KM method of Ernst & Young.

To a large extent, the services in this phase are aimed towards providing a blueprint for piloting and implementing KM solutions. It reflects making choices about where, when and how each type of available solution must be applied in order to realize the intended benefit.

The "integrate" phase involves piloting specific knowledge-based solutions. Community enablement is a key solution that runs across most of E&Y's knowledge management implementations. It focuses on the creation of communities of interest (COINs) or communities of practice (COPs) to address knowledge generation and sharing. Typically, these types of community are self-organized groups that naturally communicate with one another because they share common work practices, interests or aims. E&Y aimed to formalize the internal dynamics of the community by establishing a regular system of interchange. This includes not only the definition of community roles and responsibilities, but also important issues surrounding content design and management and technology enablement for collaboration. E&Y maintains prepackaged community enablers that can be used quickly to pilot new communities or enhance existing communities. The community enablement pilots are easily replicated to address other business problems in other organizational contexts, or they can be evolved into an enterprise standard for community enablement with links to the broader knowledge infrastructure.

Depending on the scope of the KM project, other distinct knowledge solutions can also be piloted. Examples include: content, which focuses on managing content generated externally (typically, this solution addresses the need to match content with business needs for research, analysis and business intelligence capabilities); decision, which addresses the needs of selected high-level decision-makers and is achieved through a combination of content management and the development of explicit decision models, decision workflow processes and data warehouse integration; and KnowledgeWeb, which provides a user-centric knowledge brokering system.

Finally, the "operate" phase involves wide-scale deployment of the KM system throughout the enterprise, and the development of additional pilot solutions outlined in the integrate phase.

1.4.2 The KM Method of Cap Gemini

The management consulting company Cap Gemini offered knowledge management services based on the Applied Knowledge Management Framework (Figure 1.4) (Cap Gemini, 1999a, b). This framework distinguishes between phases of operation and focused streams of activity.

The phases of operation provide the logical structure upon which the phases of the KM programme may be built. These can be effectively divided into two dominant phases of activity: the initial or "scoping" phase includes the business vision and business readiness phases; the second or "delivery" phase includes the iterative phases of solution design, solution development and solution deployment plus operation and evaluation. In "scoping" the business vision phase helps to identify the scale of the opportunity for a client and create a vision for a knowledge-enabled organization. The business readiness phase helps to establish the ability of an organization to deliver the vision, and determines the effective ambition level for delivery phases to implement elements of the vision. In solution design, the struc-

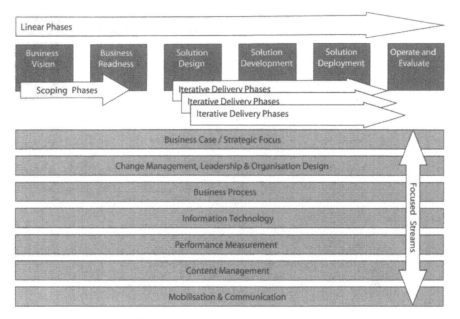

Figure 1.4 The KM method of Cap Gemini.

ture and design of the solution is finalized, building upon the design outlines in the scoping phases. Solution development creates the new functional capabilities laid out in the design phase. Key issues in solution deployment are to ensure that the dependent functional streams deploy their solutions in a logical sequence to ensure that the programme maintains its desired impact. In solutions operation and evaluation the impact of the delivery is measured against the forecast benefits and any insights or new knowledge captured during the programme are evaluated and measured.

The focused activity streams help to define the activities of the KM programme. Each stream exists in every phase of the programme; however, the influence of a stream can be more or less dominant depending on the phase of the programme and the needs of the user. Streams exist to address the key functional elements. In addition, streams convey the means to overcome issues created when dealing with a business programme on this scale. For each intersection of a phase and stream there is a number of activities. Each activity specifies the appropriate action to be taken at this point, together with hints and warnings arising from the experience of KM practitioners.

1.4.3 The KM Method of KPMG

KPMG focuses on optimizing the seven key knowledge processes within an organization: creation, application, exploitation, sharing, encapsulation, sourcing and learning (KPMG, 1999). Its services cover awareness raising, strategy, systems integration and development, business process engineering and change management.

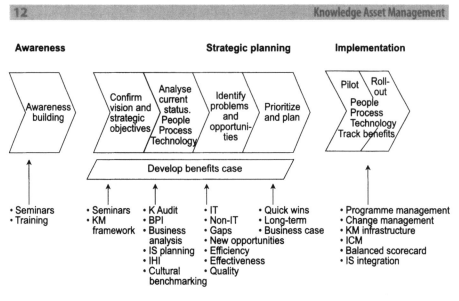

Awareness   **Strategic planning**   **Implementation**

- Seminars
- Training

- Seminars
- KM framework

- K Audit
- BPI
- Business analysis
- IS planning
- IHI
- Cultural benchmarking

- IT
- Non-IT
- Gaps
- New opportunities
- Efficiency
- Effectiveness
- Quality

- Quick wins
- Long-term
- Business case

- Programme management
- Change management
- KM infrastructure
- ICM
- Balanced scorecard
- IS integration

Figure 1.5 The KM method of KPMG.

KPMG regards KM as an ongoing process, consisting of a number of integrated projects, phased over time, rather than a single discrete project. KPMG favours a programme-management approach that involves the three principal service components (Figure 1.5).

During strategic planning the company uses a mixture of standard, in-house and specialist techniques:

● to confirm strategic objectives and the vision for KM using its KM framework tool

● to analyze and benchmark the current status of the organization's KM infrastructure, using knowledge audit and other analysis techniques

● to identify problems and opportunities, and agree on a measurement system for evaluating the effectiveness of, and the business benefits associated with, KM.

● to plan a series of quick win projects and longer term initiatives based on a clear business case.

KPMG's implementation activities cover information technology (IT) implementation and change management. KPMG does not develop its own software products for KM. Rather, its KM solutions are built using tools from Microsoft, with whom the company has a formal alliance, and from several specialist KM tool vendors.

1.4.4 The KM Method of IBM Global Services

The relation of Global Services to the rest of IBM and its position as a relative newcomer in the management consultancy business give it a different perspective to its main competitors. It has no single prescriptive method for KM projects, but it uses several techniques and metrics to help an organization to understand and develop its knowledge assets and intellectual capital (Figure 1.6) (Ovum, 1999).

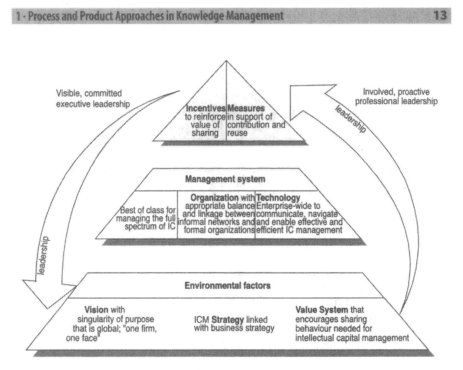

Figure 1.6 The KM method of IBM.

A key concept promoted by IBM is the knowledge map. The principle behind knowledge maps is that a company needs a high-level view of its existing knowledge before it can decide on a programme of business improvement. The overall approach is based on identifying an organization's key tacit and explicit knowledge assets and its current approaches for managing knowledge processes. These approaches are mapped to types of knowledge in order to identify knowledge "gaps". KM solutions, processes and tools are then clearly prioritized with reference to each approach and type. The result is an overall knowledge performance study that serves as the basis for system design. IBM Global Services uses KnowledgeX, a specialized software tool for the automatic creation of knowledge maps from data warehouses and database management systems.

1.4.5 The KM method of JD Edwards

Applehans et al., (1999) developed a KM method based on practical experience gained from the development of Web-based KM systems for J.D. Edwards. Their approach focuses on the design and development of "content centres" as the corner-stone of the knowledge architecture. The method supports the translation of content centres into a networked organization, including navigation strategies and other issues surrounding the deployment of people, content and technology. Concepts and tools used in this approach include the audit, the content portfolio and the knowledge architecture.

The purpose of the audit is to help to break KM down into manageable projects without losing sight of the "big picture". It supports the identification of the success factors of the organization and the relevant business processes, the important points in these business processes where actions or decisions are taken, the people that act or use content and the content itself.

The content portfolio represents the specific pieces and types of content that the organization must effectively package and deliver to people who can act on them as knowledge. This may include documents, competitive intelligence, product specifications, case studies, etc.

The knowledge architecture represents the organization's formal recognition that it has important experience and expertise that it must preserve and use to its advantage. The knowledge architecture identifies the scope of the investment that will be made in managing knowledge in terms of people, technology and content.

These concepts and tools are used to design an infrastructure that organizes around knowledge by combining content and people. Two additional concepts that are key to this approach are knowledge storyboarding and knowledge networks. The purpose of knowledge storyboarding is to identify the relationships among people, processes and knowledge. It consists of four steps: specification of a business process and related steps within the process, identification of information leveraging points within the business process, identification of organizational roles and people that use information in each step, and identification of detailed content used in each step. An essential objective of this tool is to identify the information needs of users within specific business processes. This is accomplished with user-profiling techniques.

The objective of mapping the knowledge networks is to visualize the organization's knowledge and to assign responsibilities to people who maintain different kinds of content. It consists of three steps: identification of high-level centres of information, identification of content satellites (lower level centres), and staffing and assigning ownership to content.

1.4.6 Other KM Methods and Techniques

There exists a large number of techniques for auditing, surveying, eliciting, analyzing and modelling knowledge. Although these techniques are not stand-alone or complete methodologies they are widely used during KM implementations mainly for field knowledge analysis and modelling purposes. Wiig (1995) provides an extensive overview of such methods. Table 1.3 presents a summary of the most characteristic knowledge analysis and modelling techniques.

1.5 The Process and Product Approaches in KM Projects

Real-life KM projects are usually a combination of objectives and vary in terms of business focus, strategy direction and technological orientation. Most KM initiatives, especially in large organizations, consist of a number of smaller, clear-targeted subprojects. Subprojects typically develop experts' networks, document repositories or lessons-learned databases, or focus on rewarding and compensation schemes for knowledge-sharing and try to create knowledge-sharing cultures among employees.

Davenport and Prusak (1998) categorized KM projects and they consider that companies often pursue more than one type of subproject. For instance, the main

Table 1.3 Knowledge analysis and modeling techniques

Method	Key characteristics
Task Environment Analysis (TEA) (Wiig, 1995)	TEAs consist of in-depth investigations of how knowledge workers perform business tasks and the conditions under which they work. The focus is on knowledge, its presence and use of knowledge, how the task is performed at present, what its inputs are and what its deliverables are. TEA provides the added perspective of knowledge flows and uses
Basic Knowledge Analysis (BKA) (Wiig, 1995)	BKA refers to an analysis and a characterization of the knowledge in the task environment. It focuses on how knowledge is held, and used in decisions and other knowledge-intensive tasks
Knowledge Mapping (Kmap) (Newbern and Dansereau, 1995)	Kmap is used to develop concept maps as hierarchies or networks. Kmap systems are used for identifying relevant information from workers, displaying this information and presenting it for training, communicating, planning, problem-solving or decision-making purposes
Knowledge Use and Requirements Analysis (KURA) (Wiig, 1995)	KURA is performed to explicate knowledge use and proficiency requirements. The focus is on the use of knowledge in problem-solving, decision-making and other knowledge-intensive processes within the target business area
Knowledge Scripting and Profiling (KS&P) (Wiig, 1995)	KS&P is used for the detailed description of knowledge-intensive processes, tasks and scripts
Knowledge Flow Analysis (KFA) (Wiig, 1995)	KFA is used to gain overview of knowledge exchanges, losses, or inputs to the business process or the whole enterprise. It also determines characteristics, strengths and weaknesses of existing and potential knowledge exchanges
CommonKADS (Schreiber, 1999), Knowledge Metaprocess (Staab et al., (2001)	These methods focus on the application-oriented development of ontologies and support all phases from the early stages of setting up a KM project to the final roll-out and maintenance of the ontology-based KM application

focus of a project may be the development of a best practices database, but the project may also address rewarding mechanisms and market knowledge organization. Indeed, careful examination of the types of KM subprojects reveals that they fall in one of the two main approaches: product and process (Figure 1.7).

Davenport and Prusak's categorization of KM projects includes four broad categories: creation of knowledge repositories, improvement of knowledge access, improving the culture and environment for knowledge exchange, and focus on knowledge as a corporate asset.

In KM projects that focus on the creation of knowledge repositories much of the energy has been spent on treating knowledge as a "product", an entity separate from the people who create and use it. The typical goal is to take documents with knowledge embedded in them, such as memos, reports, presentations and articles, and store them in a repository where they can be easily retrieved. Another less structured form of knowledge is the discussion database, in which participants record their own experiences on an issue and react to others' comments. Three common types of repository are for:

● external knowledge, e.g. competitive intelligence. External knowledge repositories range from information delivery "clipping services" that route articles and reports to executives to advanced customer intelligence systems

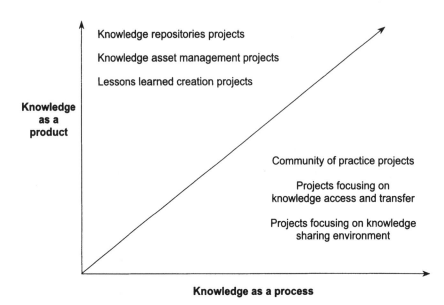

Figure 1.7 The process and product approaches in KM projects.

- structured internal knowledge, e.g. research reports, product-oriented marketing materials, and techniques and methods
- informal internal knowledge, e.g. discussion databases full of know-how, sometimes referred to as "lessons learned". This is softer, more experiential knowledge that must be interpreted and adapted by the user in a new context.

The second type of project focuses on providing access to knowledge or facilitating its transfer among individuals. Whereas knowledge repositories aim at capturing knowledge itself, knowledge access projects focus on the possessors and prospective users of knowledge. These projects recognize that finding the person with the knowledge one needs, and then successfully transferring it from one person to another, are difficult processes. If the metaphor of a library is useful for conceptualizing knowledge repository projects, then the Yellow Pages represents the purpose of knowledge access projects. The underlying strategy here is to facilitate connections between those people who possess and those who need knowledge. Technological implementations on these types of project focus primarily on databases of internal and external experts, who vary from company employees to outside consultants and collaborators.

The third type of KM project involves attempts to establish an environment conducive to more effective knowledge creation, transfer and use. In this category some projects intend to build awareness and cultural receptivity to knowledge, to change behaviour relating to knowledge and to improve the KM process. A large consulting firm was making significant inroads towards changing employee perceptions of their jobs, from deliverers of consulting services to creators and distributors of management knowledge. One way they did this was by making significant changes to the performance appraisal system so that contributions to the firm's structured knowledge base became a significant factor in compensation decisions.

The fourth type of project focuses on managing knowledge as a corporate asset. One way this is being done is by treating knowledge like any other asset on the organization's balance sheet. This approach focuses the organization's attention on how it is increasing or decreasing its effective use of knowledge assets over time.

1.6 The Need to Integrate the Two Approaches

The previous sections of this chapter have clearly shown that KM efforts may fall under one of two approaches: the product-centric and the process-centric approaches to KM. These two approaches are distinct in the sense that they imply different strategic focus, the use of different software tools, and so on.

The question that arises then is: which companies should adopt one or the other approach, and when? The choice of the overall approach to be followed by a KM initiative should be neither arbitrary nor ad hoc; it depends on the company characteristics, the ways in which the company delivers its products and services, its financial characteristics and its organizational culture.

A solution proposed in the literature is to relate the choice of the most appropriate approach to the vital characteristics of a company's product or service (Table 1.4). (Hansen et al., 1999).

The product-centric approach is more likely to be followed by those companies with a business strategy based on standardized and mature products. The processes for developing and selling such products involve well-understood and well-organised tasks, and the product knowledge is relatively rigid and thus more easily codified. In such cases, developing a strategy around the "knowledge as a product" approach seems more suitable.

The process-centric approach is more likely to be followed by those companies with a value proposition based on developing highly customized and/or extremely innovative products or services that meet unique customer needs. Because these needs vary dramatically, codified knowledge is of limited value. In those cases, adopting a "knowledge as a process" approach, which mainly supports the sharing of knowledge, expertise and judgement, seems more appropriate.

Such a roadmap may be useful for some extreme cases, but seems to be of limited value in supporting the decisions of companies that operate within the constantly challenging e-business world in which there is a clear need for delivering product–service hybrids with distinct characteristics: their lifetime is linked to the life of the customer need; their major cost element is the cost of design; their main revenue model is subscription and user fees; and their marketing objective is building communities of satisfied clients.

Hence the challenge faced by modern firms is to exploit effectively the intangibles that add value to these "offerings": technical know-how, design of the offering, marketing and presentation, understanding of the customer need, etc., so that they can

Table 1.4 Relation of the KM approach to product characteristics

	Standardization of product or service	Maturity of product or service
Knowledge as a "product"	Standardized	Mature
Knowledge as a "process"	Customized	Innovative

integrate knowledge in their offerings and create new value by designing and developing new offerings.

These challenges call for the integration of the "knowledge as a process" approach (which will facilitate the leveraging of tacit, intangible knowledge) with the "knowledge as a product" approach (which will enable the consistent management of explicit knowledge, e.g. best practices). So there is a real need for a balanced fusion of the two KM views. Such a fusion should clearly focus on the knowledge assets of the company, link strategic and operational issues in a consistent manner, and enable the key knowledge of the firm to be averaged at the individual, team and organizational levels.

The next chapter outlines the conceptual framework of the Know-Net KM solution, which aims explicitly to provide for such a fusion.

2   The Know-Net Approach and Framework

2.1 A Strategic Perspective to Knowledge Assets

The methodological and technical architecture of the Know-Net knowledge management solution should ensure the fusion of the product-centric knowledge management (KM) approach with the process-centric KM approach. What is needed is a conceptual, theoretical foundation that will guarantee this fusion and that will underlie every aspect of the solution (software tool, consulting methodology, measurement system, etc.).

Both the process- and the product-based approaches aim to support the identification, managing and leveraging of knowledge, through better management of the organization's knowledge assets. Knowledge assets are the resources that organizations wish to cultivate. In essence, KM works to manage better the content, quality, value and transferability of knowledge assets.

The focus of the Know-Net solution is on knowledge assets as the critical strategic resources of the firm. Such a focus is in line with the recent trend in the strategic management literature to leverage the internal resources of the firm in order to create value. The following paragraphs briefly outline two commonly used approaches to strategic management: the competitive strategy approach and the resource-based view, and proceed with analyzing the knowledge asset-centric approach as the proposed theoretical solution to integrating the product- and process-centric approaches.

2.1.1 The Competitive Approach to Strategy

The competitive strategy perspective posits that competitive advantage is derived from the firm's environment, more precisely from the industry in which it competes. In fact, the goal of competitive strategy for a company or business unit is to "... find a position in the industry where the company can best defend itself against ... competitive forces (new entry, threats of substitution, bargaining power of buyers, bargaining power of suppliers, and rivalry among existing competitors) or can influence them in its favour" (Porter, 1980).

The competitive strategy perspective can be seen as an "outside–in" approach to understanding the basis of competitive advantage. This approach stresses that an effective competitive strategy calls for the firm to take offensive or defensive action to create a defendable position against competitive forces. Thus, industry conditions determine the rules of the game when it comes to the nature of competition and the strategies available to firms.

A major assumption of this perspective is that all relevant, industry-specific resources are distributed homogeneously and are perfectly mobile. That is, the basis for competition is not derived from the firm as such, but rather from the characteristics of the industry. Consequently, superior performance in an industry or a strategic group results from this environmentally derived competitive advantage.

A second assumption of this approach is that both demand and supply conditions are known and, consequently, market conditions are relatively stable. In a stable demand environment, competition is viewed as a zero-sum market share rivalry between existing and potential firms. In addition, because the demand side of the market is known or predictable, competitive advantage stems from the supply side.

Consequently, selecting the competitive advantage that yields the highest levels of economic performance requires intensive analysis of the industry structure, of suppliers, buyers, new entrants and threats from substitutes, as discussed in depth by Porter (1980) and other authors within the industrial organization paradigm.

Thus, the essence of formulating a competitive strategy is to relate a company to its environment, analogous to the opportunities and threats part of the classical SWOT (strengths, weaknesses, opportunities, threats) analysis. The essence of this approach was expressed by Porter (1980) as: "Worship the environment – not the inside [of the firm]".

The two assumptions mentioned above (i.e. homogeneous distribution of resources and already known demand and supply conditions) have been raised in the resource-based view.

2.1.2 The Resource-Based View to Strategy

From the resource-based perspective the firm is seen as a portfolio of resources. What a firm can do to create competitive advantage is not a function simply of the opportunities in the environment (industry) but also of what resources the firm can assemble (Wernerfelt, 1984). The resource-based perspective is an "inside–out" approach to understanding the basis of competitive advantage.

The resource-based view (RBV) of the firm focuses attention on how firms achieve and sustain advantages and contends that the answer to this question lies in the possession of certain key resources. Sustainable competitive advantage can be obtained if the firm effectively deploys these resources in its product markets. The list of resources in any given firm is likely to be a long one.

One of the principal insights of the resource-based view is that not all resources are of equal importance or possess the potential to be a source of sustainable competitive advantage. Much attention has focused, therefore, on the characteristics of advantage-creating resources and various approaches have been followed in analyzing the characteristics of advantage-creating resources. For example, Barney (1991) proposes that advantage-creating resources must meet four conditions, namely, value, rareness, inimitability and non-substitutability, while Grant (1991) argues that the levels of durability, transparency, transferability and replicability are important determinants.

Strategic, advantage-generating resources comprise three distinct subgroups: namely tangible assets, intangible assets and capabilities.

Tangible assets refer to the fixed and current assets of an organization, which have a fixed long-run capacity. Examples include plant, equipment, land, other capital goods and stocks, debtors and bank deposits. Tangible assets have the properties of ownership, their value is relatively easy to measure and they are relatively weak at resisting duplication efforts by competitors.

Intangible assets include intellectual property such as trademarks and patents, as well as brand and company reputation, company networks and databases. The presence of intangible assets accounts for the significant differences between the balance sheet valuation and stock market valuation of publicly quoted companies. Intangible assets have relatively unlimited capacity and firms can exploit their value by using them in-house, renting them (e.g. a licence) or selling them (e.g. selling a brand). They are relatively resistant to duplication efforts by competitors.

Capabilities have proved more difficult to delineate. Capabilities encompass the skills of individuals or groups as well as the organizational routines and interactions through which all the firm's resources are coordinated (Grant, 1991). Typical of the latter, for example, are teamwork, organizational culture, and trust between management and workers. Capabilities have limited capacity in the short run owing to learning and change difficulties but have relatively unlimited capacity in the long run.

Although the RBV recognizes the importance and role of knowledge in firms achieving a competitive advantage, it may be argued that the RBV does not go far enough. Specifically, the RBV treats knowledge as a generic resource, rather than having special properties, and subsequently, does not make any distinction between different types of knowledge-based capabilities.

2.1.3 Intrinsic Characteristics of Knowledge Assets

Knowledge assets are different from other firm resources (Glazer, 1991; Day and Wendler, 1998).

Knowledge assets are not easily divisible or appropriable. This means that the same information and knowledge can be used by different economic entities at the same time. Moreover, knowledge assets are not inherently scarce (although they are often time sensitive). This implies that they are not depletable.

Knowledge assets are essentially regenerative. This means that new relevant knowledge may emerge from a knowledge-intensive business process as additional output besides products and services.

Knowledge assets may not exhibit decreasing returns to use, but will often increase in value the more they are used. This characteristic is of crucial importance for senior management (den Hartigh and Langerak, 2001). Most assets are subject to diminishing returns, but not knowledge. The bulk of the fixed cost in knowledge products usually lies in creation rather than in manufacturing or distribution. Once knowledge has been created, the initial development cost can be spread across rising volumes. Network effects can emerge as knowledge assets are used by more and more people. These knowledge users can simultaneously benefit from knowledge and increase its value as they add to, adapt and enrich the knowledge base. In traditional industrial economics, assets decline in value as more people use them. By contrast, knowledge assets can grow in value as they become a standard on which others can build.

As knowledge assets grow, they tend to branch and fragment. Today's specialist skill becomes tomorrow's ticket to play, as fields of knowledge grow deeper and more complex, or as Drucker (1997) puts it "knowledge constantly makes itself obsolete, with the result that today's knowledge is tomorrow's ignorance". While knowledge assets that become standards can grow more and more valuable, others, such as expiring patents or former trade secrets, can become less valuable as they are widely shared. A successful company must therefore continually refresh its knowledge base. The rapid and effective re-creation of knowledge can represent a substantial source of competitive advantage.

2.2 Conceptual Foundation of Know-Net

The focus of this book is not on what knowledge is, rather it is on what knowledge can do. Hence for the purpose of having a definition of knowledge, the definition given by Nonaka (1991) is extended, according to which "knowledge is justified belief that increases an entity's capacity for effective action".

The definition of knowledge used herein is: The ideas, or understandings, which an entity possesses that are used to take effective action to achieve the entity's goal(s). The focal point is the business domain and individuals, teams, organizations and interorganizational settings (e.g. virtual enterprises) are examined as entity types that leverage knowledge to create business goals and achieve commercial values.

KM may be considered to be a new discipline of enabling individuals, teams and entire organizations collectively and systematically to create, share and apply corporate knowledge assets to better achieve organizational efficiency, responsiveness, competency and innovation".

KM encompasses the identification and mapping of knowledge assets within the organization, the generation of new knowledge assets for competitive advantage, making knowledge assets accessible and sharing them across an organization.

Know-Net tackles the fact that KM should be implemented as an ongoing business task with two primary aspects:

● treating the knowledge component of business performance, reflected in strategy, processes, structure and systems at all levels of the organization.
● making a direct connection between the organizational knowledge assets, both explicit and tacit, and improved business performance.

From a conceptual abstract point of view, for the integration of the process and product views this section follows the work of Cook and Brown (1999), who strive to explain how knowledge is connected to the actions of individuals and groups. Their concept of knowing, i.e. putting knowledge into practice, is close to the concept of knowledge as a process. Cook and Brown (1999) call "what is 'possessed' knowledge and what is part of action 'knowing'" (p. 383). In other words, knowing is putting knowledge into practice while knowledge is knowing at rest. They admit that "this does not mean that knowledge of abstract concepts and principles is useless to action, only that it is not the same as enacting the skills associated with it" (p. 19). Cook and Brown (1999) also add that knowledge itself does not underlie or enable knowing, just as having a hammer may not mean that one knows how to use it.

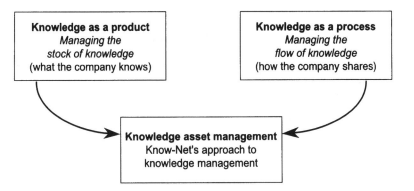

Figure 2.1 Knowledge asset management fuses the product- and process-centric approaches.

In this way a static ("knowledge as a product") mode, and a dynamic ("knowledge as a process") mode may be introduced in KM. Knowledge represents the static mode, as what we possess we do not always use, and knowing is the dynamic mode, as it represents a concrete, dynamic human action and it focuses on the interactions with the social and physical world. This approach is interested in managing both the stock of knowledge (that covers the "knowledge as a product" approach) and the flow of knowledge (that addresses the "knowledge as a process" approach) within the organization (Figure 2.1). It is based on explicitly treating knowledge assets and knowledge objects in such a manner as to integrate both approaches that were presented in Chapter 1.

This perspective is that *"knowledge assets"* can be human (e.g. a person or a network of people), structural (e.g. a business process) or market (e.g. a brand name of a product).

Naturally, the product-centric approach is more concerned with accessing and organizing knowledge assets, while the process approach makes direct connections between the organizational knowledge assets, both explicit and tacit. Both approaches, however, are using some form of knowledge representation as a means of packaging and transferring knowledge either from a person to a system and vice versa, or between people.

If the means of representing knowledge are defined as "knowledge objects" then the following statement outlines the relation between knowledge assets and knowledge objects:

A knowledge asset creates, stores and/or disseminates knowledge objects.

For example:

- a person is a knowledge asset that can create new ideas, learnings, proposals and white papers (knowledge objects);
- a community of interest is a knowledge asset that can create new ideas and best practices (knowledge objects);
- a process is a knowledge asset that can create and/or store and disseminate best practices, company standards and R&D material (knowledge objects);
- a vision is a knowledge asset that can create a new mission statement, strategic plan and goals (knowledge objects).

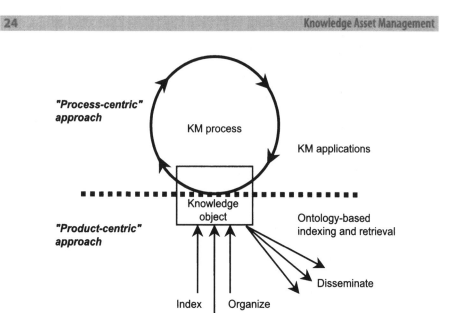

Figure 2.2 Knowledge assets and knowledge objects.

A knowledge object represents the information required to be processed by humans and transformed into knowledge (Figure 2.2). Knowledge derives from information through knowledge-creating activities that take place within and between humans. The following are typical knowledge-creating activities (Davenport and Prusak, 1998).

● Comparison: how does information about this situation compare to other known situations?
● Consequences: what implications does the information have for decision and actions?
● Connections: how does this bit of knowledge relate to others?
● Conversation: what do other people think about this information?

The knowledge objects aim to facilitate and leverage such knowledge-creating activities by providing to humans the information needed. A knowledge object has the following characteristics.

● It acts as a catalyst, enabling the fusion of knowledge flows between people, with knowledge content discovery and retrieval, through technology. That is, a knowledge object acts, amongst other things, as the primary connecting node for all key components in a KM system (strategy, people, process, content, technology): the "KM glue".
● It facilitates the knowledge transfer from person to person, or from information to person.
● It is created and maintained by a KM process.
● It is used to search, organize and disseminate knowledge content.

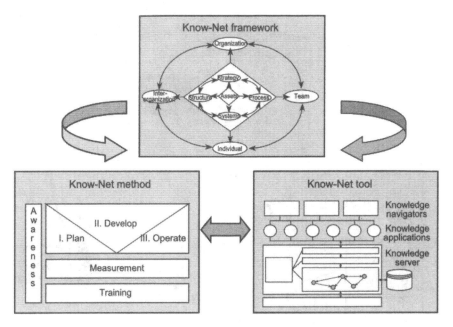

Figure 2.3 The three components of the Know-Net solution.

Knowledge assets and knowledge objects are the common unifiers of the holistic Know-Net KM solution that incorporate and integrate process and content. These concepts have been used as the resultant manifestation in the design of the Know-Net solution that fuses the process-centric approach with the product-centric approach.

Know-Net is a total KM solution, which includes three components (Figure 2.3):

- a holistic conceptual *framework* that can be used by managers for creating awareness about KM, as well as a roadmap for ensuring the integrity of the KM effort. The Know-Net framework is presented in Section 2.3.

- a KM *methodology* that helps organizations to develop their knowledge leveraging strategy and business processes and explicitly evaluate the business value of the KM effort. The Know-Net method is presented in detail in Chapter 3.

- an *intranet-based tool* that supports the collection, organization and sharing of corporate knowledge using flexible and customizable knowledge navigators. The functionalities and characteristics of the Know-Net tool are presented in Chapter 4.

2.3 Overview of the Know-Net Framework

This section describes in greater detail the Know-Net framework (Figure 2.4), which represents the following types of element:

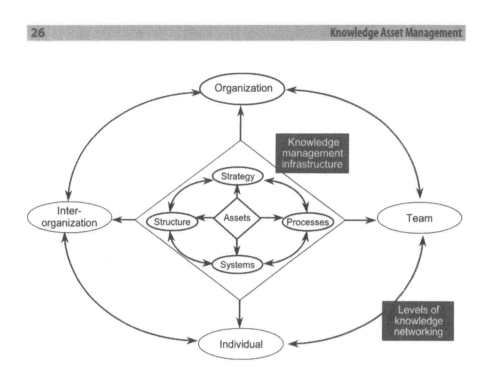

Figure 2.4 Overview of the Know-Net framework.

- the business-related *knowledge assets* of the company. Three types of knowledge asset are examined: human assets, structural assets, and market assets.
- the *knowledge networking levels*, the interdependencies of which facilitate the leveraging and flow of knowledge assets. Know-Net identifies four levels of knowledge networking: individual level, team level, organizational level, and interorganizational level.
- the *KM infrastructure* that should be established within a company in order to facilitate knowledge leveraging initiatives. Four components of the KM infrastructure are examined: strategy, structure, processes and systems.

Before proceeding with the analysis of the various elements of the Know-Net framework, it is shown how the framework guarantees consistency with the definition of KM. In the previous section KM was defined as the "new discipline of enabling individuals, teams and entire organizations collectively and systematically to create, share and apply corporate knowledge assets better to achieve organizational efficiency, responsiveness, competency and innovation".

Three important keywords of this definition are reflected in the Know-Net framework: knowledge assets, collectively and systematically.

The emphasis on *knowledge assets* is reflected on the clear focus of the framework on knowledge assets. The emphasis on the creation, sharing and application of knowledge assets in a *collective* (versus an individualistic) manner is evident from the focus on network organizational forms and the definition of the levels of knowledge networking. Finally, the focus on a *systematic* (versus an ad hoc) approach to managing knowledge assets is evident in the Know-Net framework, with the explicit inclusion of the four elements of the KM infrastructure.

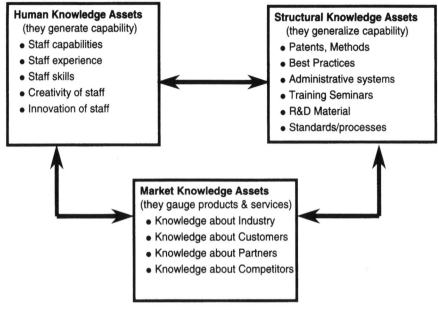

Figure 2.5 Types of knowledge asset.

2.4 Knowledge Assets

Know-Net focuses on three types of knowledge asset, which are dynamically interwoven: human knowledge assets, which generate organizational capabilities; structural knowledge assets, which generalize the human capabilities; and market knowledge assets, which gauge the products and services of the company (Figure 2.5).

Human knowledge assets are the capabilities of the individuals that are required to provide solutions to the customers of the company. People are the "owners" of human knowledge assets; they "rent" their knowledge assets to the company. Human assets grow when the working environment fosters and facilitates knowledge creation and sharing; when more people know in depth what knowledge is actually useful to the organisation and when the company uses more of what people know. As human assets grow the results are a higher concentration of skills in what is important for the company, increased innovation and participation, and an increase in people working in areas that are critical for the business.

Structural knowledge assets are the organizational capabilities to meet market requirements. They comprise what is left when people go home and they provide the structure and continuity that people need to perform within the business environment. To build structural knowledge assets an organization must provide knowledge-related leadership, i.e. policy and strategy that take explicitly knowledge leveraging into account, build the necessary structure and culture for knowledge creation and sharing, and provide information technology (IT) support (e.g. communication systems and documentation systems). As structural knowledge assets grow individual capabilities turn to grow and become organizational capabilities, the company's performance is improved and people are better supported and become more productive in the business context.

Market knowledge assets refer to knowledge about the market, the company's clients, partners, competitors, etc., i.e. knowledge about the value created from the company's relationships with the people and organizations with which business is conducted. Market knowledge assets gauge, evaluate and value the company's products and services. They are the final outcome of investments in human and structural knowledge assets. To build market assets an organization must deliver customized solutions more quickly, involve partners in all phases of product development, and provide feedback that customers can use practically. As market assets grow the results will include higher trust levels in the company's supply chain and clear customer value.

2.5 Knowledge Networking Levels

Networks of people and networked organizations are emerging because the classic hierarchy of the bureaucratic model is slow to respond to the recent changes in the business environment. In the network, activities still need to be coordinated and integrated, but this integration relies on knowledge and relationships and a clear common sense of purpose. This has led to ideas about "work as a network of conversations" and the "hypertext organization" (Nonaka and Takeuchi, 1995). Networks may take various organizational forms, ranging from communities of practice between individuals with similar experiences and purposes to supply chains of companies that exchange knowledge within their industry.

The Know-Net levels of knowledge networking correspond to what Nonaka (1994) calls the "ontological dimension" in his model of organizations as knowledge creating mechanisms. This ontological dimension refers to the social interactions, which begin at the individual level and then by communication between organizational boundaries let knowledge expand and grow.

According to Nonaka and Ray (1993), if new knowledge is relevant to the needs of the organization, it is likely to permeate through groups and divisions and thereby extend the community of interaction dealing with that knowledge. New knowledge that has a potential to support more advantageous ways of doing things is likely to be retained as a subject for further debate within the network and may also lead to an extension of the network. For example, what eventually proves to be a successful product might emanate from an R&D department and gradually acquire a greater circle of interested parties within the organization as the dimensions of its potential impact become clearer. As news of the emerging product travels beyond the organization, the circle will grow still wider, embracing competitors, customers, firms dealing with complementary technologies, and so on. Thus the network will go beyond the original hard core of knowledge creators to include those that are in some way affected by the exploitation of that knowledge.

However, there is no reason to suppose that there will be a linear sequence of expansion, starting from the individual, progressing to the group and subsequently to the organization and beyond. The knowledge network could span departmental and organizational boundaries from the outset. Possible members of this community, such as suppliers, customers and competitors, might all enter the knowledge networks at any time.

Knowledge networks, between individuals, teams or even organizations, are seen as the principal organizational form for collective knowledge asset creation, sharing and application.

Knowledge networks are relationships among entities (individuals, teams, organizations) working on a common concern and they embed dynamism for collective and systematic knowledge asset creation and sharing. The structure of a knowledge network implies principles of coordination that not only enhance the individual capabilities of member entities, but themselves lead to capabilities that are not isolated to the network's members. Cooperation can also engender capabilities in the relationship itself, such that the members develop principles of coordination that improve their joint performance, or they may involve more complex rules governing the process by which innovations are collectively produced and shared. In this sense, the network is itself knowledge, not in the sense of providing access to distributed information and capabilities, but in representing a form of coordination guided by enduring principles of organization.

Knowledge networks have five critical characteristics that differentiate them from other similar organizational structures and mainly from communities of practice (Wenger, 1999; Wenger and Snyder, 2000). These characteristics are: knowledge networks are responsible for creating, sharing, protecting and cultivating common knowledge assets; knowledge networks are working networks and they are purpose-driven; knowledge networks require organizational commitment beyond the commitment of their participating members; knowledge networks are built on expertise, not just interest or common practice alone; and knowledge networks aim at the development and strengthening of the learning capacity of all members.

Within Know-Net four levels of knowledge networking are distinguished: individual, team, organization and interorganization (Figure 2.4). The individual level refers to the capabilities, experience, competences and personal development issues treated at the individual level of the knowledge worker. The team and organizational levels include the internal company networks, i.e. the informal, self-organizing or the formal networks of people involved in related activities (e.g. project teams) that are built within an organization. The level of interorganizational networks refers to interenterprise relationships, value networks where each focuses on core competences, as well as on the accessibility to external, developed capabilities. Hence, networks with customers, competitors, subcontractors, partners, etc., are included in this level.

2.6 KM Infrastructure

To guarantee a systematic approach to leveraging knowledge assets, a company has to define, develop and consistently nurture four issues related to KM: a *knowledge strategy*, i.e. the strategic issues of knowledge management as they are embodied in the company's vision, mission and values; a *knowledge structure*, i.e. the organizational structures required for facilitating knowledge management, e.g. chief knowledge officers and knowledge analysts; *knowledge processes*, i.e. the business processes dedicated to the capture, organization, transfer and application of knowledge assets; and *knowledge systems*, i.e. all the information and communication technology systems that support knowledge processes. These four issues comprise the elements of the knowledge management infrastructure (KMI) of the Know-Net framework (Figure 2.4).

2.6.1 Knowledge Strategy

The strategy component of the KMI refers to the company's values and mission, i.e. the knowledge-related strategic values of the company, the specific knowledge-related business objectives, and the explicit and/or implicit links of knowledge strategy to business strategic objectives and goals.

KM is meaningless without the old-fashioned objectives of serving customers and beating competitors. If a company does not have its fundamentals in place, all the corporate learning, IT or knowledge databases are mere costly diversions. As Manville and Foote (1997) put it: "the old truth is still the best truth: a company has to know the kind of value it intends to provide and to whom. Only then can it link its knowledge resources in ways that make a difference: serving customers around the world in a coordinated, consistent manner; responding quickly and effectively to changing competitive conditions; and offering its products or services to customers more quickly, cheaply, efficiently, and innovatively".

Realizing the complete vision of an innovative, knowledge-sharing organization is probably a long-term objective for most companies. Organizations should focus on both obtaining real benefit through "quick-win" projects and the long-term vision. Complete realization of the vision of KM depends on organizational maturity in terms of having the right culture as well as on technological sophistication.

2.6.2 Knowledge Processes

The knowledge processes component of Know-Net framework can be classified within the following five groups (Figure 2.6): acquisition, organization, sharing, use and creation of knowledge assets. For a similar analysis see also Romhardt and Probst (1997).

Knowledge acquisition processes include the identification of knowledge needs, the capture and collection and the import of knowledge assets. Before investing heavily in the development of new capabilities, companies should know what

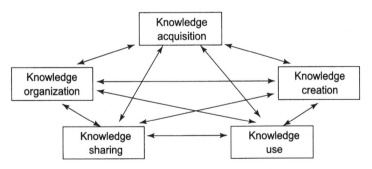

Figure 2.6 Knowledge processes.

knowledge and expertise exist both inside and outside them. One way to increase internal knowledge transparency is by creating knowledge maps, which support systematic access to parts of the organizational knowledge base. Knowledge import is also critical. The explosive growth and simultaneous fragmentation of knowledge have made it all but impossible for companies to build up all the know-how they need for market success by themselves. Instead, they have to buy critical capabilities, often from many knowledge markets, using focused acquisition strategies.

Knowledge organization includes the interpretation, analysis, codification, indexing, aggregation, filtering, synthesizing, packaging, archiving and linking of knowledge assets to their context. Critical tasks include the maintenance and knowledge purging functions. After knowledge has been acquired or created, it must be carefully organized and preserved. Many companies complain that in the process of reorganization they have lost part of their corporate memory. This collective amnesia is often the result of the destruction of informal networks, which steer important but little-observed processes. To avoid the loss of valuable expertise, companies must shape the processes of selecting valuable knowledge for preservation, ensuring its suitable storage and regularly incorporating it into the knowledge base. Companies should identify core areas of their organizational knowledge base and establish a pragmatic selection process for knowledge to be saved.

Knowledge sharing includes mechanisms for knowledge asset distribution (proactive distribution, event-based distribution, subscription-based distribution, etc.), schemes such as targeted push and/or pull sharing, the commercialization of available knowledge and the development of trust in corporate knowledge. In making knowledge assets available and usable across the whole organization, the critical questions are: who should know what, to what level of detail, and how can the organization support these processes of knowledge distribution? IT-supported knowledge-sharing infrastructures can facilitate the efficient exchange of knowledge within the business environment and connect formerly separated experts through an electronic network. Efficient knowledge sharing can generate not only time and quality advantages, but also a direct rise in customer satisfaction.

Knowledge creation consists of all activities intended to produce new knowledge both at the individual and at the collective level. The main processes for individual knowledge creation rely on creativity and on systematic problem solving. Creativity may be called the chaotic component of the knowledge development process and the capability of problem solving the systematic component. A KM system must support both components, for example through traditional tools such as corporate proposal systems that may be revitalized or reused. Collective knowledge creation involves the learning dynamics of teams. Management must ensure that team members have complementary skills and that each group as a whole has defined realistic goals. Moreover, cultural issues such as an atmosphere of openness and trust play significant role and allow the intensity of communication that makes collective learning results superior to individual ones. The establishment of internal think tanks, learning arenas or centres of competence may support these processes. In a process of self-reflection, every team should identify critical "lessons learned" at the conclusion of each project and pass the information on to future teams in the form of a short, clear report that allows others to learn from that experience.

Knowledge use includes the application of knowledge assets in corporate services or products and in supporting the delivery of value to customer. The productive deployment of organizational knowledge assets in the actual delivery of products and/or services is the heart of KM. Successful identification and distribution of critical knowledge do not ensure its daily use. Without consistent use, there is a high probability that any KM effort will decay in quality and the investment will be wasted. The potential user of knowledge has to see a real advantage in order to change his or her behaviour and adopt the knowledge assets provided.

2.6.3 Knowledge Structure

The need for an explicit, formal organizational structure that directs, facilitates and supports the KM-related activities within a company has been identified and discussed in recent academic as well as business literature. There exists a variety of job titles related to leveraging knowledge assets, such as knowledge architect and knowledge manager, as well as more traditional titles such as VP customer care and manager of systems and applications. However, one can analyze various jobs at three levels: leadership-level positions (e.g. CKOs), management positions (e.g. knowledge managers) and technical positions (e.g. knowledge analysts).

Whatever the role and responsibilities of leadership related to knowledge leveraging, few doubt that it is an essential ingredient of competition. Leadership in KM is not about tools and technologies. It is about the fast-rising influence of a new generation of managers tasked with leveraging the collective mind and the know-how of intellectually driven companies. One significant issue is related to whether organizations have mistakenly applied a very traditional, hierarchical organizational model to the practice of knowledge leveraging. Research has shown that a common belief is that the CKO may be an anomaly, a hierarchical construct applied to what is naturally a diffuse process (Delphi Group, 1998). A general observation is that since KM is being applied in line of business applications, a single knowledge leader, across all lines of business, is a tough sell to the business managers. In addition, there have been concerns that the CKO becomes just another layer of unnecessary bureaucracy. A fundamental concern that is associated with putting a CKO into place is the potential for suboptimization; that the company may end up with someone whose vision of KM dilutes the effectiveness of managing knowledge in each of the particular business units, projects or teams. Forward-thinking companies have accepted that, without regard to what it is called, the importance of better leveraging enterprise knowledge is a permanent fixture of the organization; a new way to look at how you organize your people or your information, or both. However, knowledge leadership may be viewed as a temporary role. For many companies, positions of knowledge leadership are considered an interim measure, which would take KM to critical mass.

Research on the unique qualifications of knowledge leaders has shown that there is no single profile, but there are some general characteristics. The most notable include: hybrid IT/business experience; at least 10 years (and often much more) of line of business experience, an entrepreneurial attitude and a fair amount of interest in building careers for the future (Delphi Group, 1998). Knowledge leadership positions should provide vision, awareness of purpose, standardization of best practices and stewardship. However, most organizations have already identified ownership for at least the first two categories of responsibility. What remains is the need for best practices and stewardship. These are not necessarily well suited for hierarchical ownership in the case of knowledge-based practices. Hence knowledge leaders should be educators of best practices, stewards of the frameworks that facilitate knowledge creation and sharing, but they are not the owners. Knowledge leadership will build the bridges and the culture, but it is ultimately the knowledge workers themselves who will build their own reasons to use knowledge management. Leadership-level positions should combine an orientation to structured, explicit knowledge with an intuitive feel for precisely how cultural and behavioural factors may impede or enable the leveraging of knowledge in an enterprise. Measurement and economic return should also be key points of focus.

The responsibilities of leadership-level management roles usually include:

- leading the development of the knowledge strategy, focusing the firm's resources on the type of knowledge it needs to manage most
- planning and executing KM initiatives as well as designing, implementing and overseeing the firm's knowledge infrastructure
- directing the development and management of processes and technologies that enable staff to leverage organizational knowledge toward business goals
- managing the firm's knowledge managers, giving a sense of community, establishing professional standards and managing their careers.

In addition to the knowledge leadership position, at least two other positions are needed: the knowledge (initiative) manager and the knowledge analyst. Davenport (1996) claims that the knowledge manager is analogous to the leader of a re-engineering project or a strategic planning group. KM initiatives are similar to these more familiar types of projects insofar as they are process oriented and advance some strategic goal. Hence knowledge initiative managers should have facility with project, change and technology management. Good candidates may have led successful research, re-engineering or behaviour-changing IT projects in the past. They should also have a strong sense of their own limitations. There is, however, a critical issue to be tackled: when those who lead such initiatives learn a great deal about the knowledge domain being managed, they may come to feel that they know more about the field than anyone in the company. The resulting arrogance is detrimental to the initiative's success.

The responsibilities of knowledge manager positions include:

- promoting and educating staff on knowledge-sharing processes, technologies and resources
- identifying and sharing external information from research groups, marketing publications, Internet websites, etc.
- collaborating with firm experts to write detailed learning histories and capture best practices
- developing new formats and mechanisms to share knowledge assets effectively, and monitoring and measuring the use of knowledge bases and tools
- coordinating with other KM team members to ensure consistency and synergy.

Knowledge analysts are people able to capture knowledge assets, organize them into a form anyone can use, and periodically update and edit those knowledge assets. These skills are not really taught anywhere, but the closest approximation may be found in journalism schools. Davenport (1996) claims that an alternative source to journalists is the group that was called "knowledge engineers" in the heyday of expert systems. Knowledge analyst roles require a combination of hard elements (structured knowledge, technology and tangible benefits) with softer traits (a sense of the cultural, political and personal aspects of KM). It is not easy to find all this in one person; at a minimum, KM teams should combine these hard and soft orientations, and each member must respect all required skill sets.

The responsibilities of knowledge analyst positions include:

- capturing and organizing knowledge assets and supporting the use of knowledge-oriented software packages
- managing and monitoring knowledge tools (e.g. discussion databases)
- making knowledge assets appealing and persuading by designing and implementing target group-based distribution facilities and informative displays.

2.6.4 Knowledge Systems

One role of technological systems is to enhance human capability. Such systems should free the members of knowledge networks (be they individuals, teams or organizations) and facilitate the creation, sharing and application of knowledge assets. In an effort to provide a framework that is generic enough to support any organization but at the same time provide clear and concrete directions for the implementation of a KM initiative the *core services* that need to be offered for systematic KM are defined, rather than examining the technologies available. The services should span the whole knowledge life cycle, from knowledge acquisition to knowledge use. At the centre of the Know-Net knowledge *systems* are six core services (Figure 2.7).

Indexing, mapping and classification services are usually facilitated by knowledge maps that define the channels and the mechanisms available for knowledge asset categorization. When put to work, the knowledge map will provide a representation of available knowledge assets and knowledge objects (document bases, topics, sources, narrative summaries, higher level descriptions, etc.). Automated indexing routines can be facilitated to ensure complete synchronization of indexes and data sources.

Search and retrieval services should provide transparent access to multiplatform, heterogeneous sources, including Internet and intranet sites, file servers, databases, popular proprietary formats and legacy information systems. Various types of search service should be accommodated: hierarchical (e.g. traversing hyperlinks),

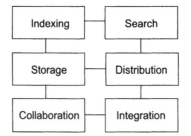

Figure 2.7 Core services of knowledge management systems.

attribute (query-type searching) and content (e.g. crawler-type searching of popular world-wide wed (www) search engines).

Storage and metadata handling services are core services that are facilitated by the use of technologies that span from relational database management systems and document management systems to AI-based corporate memories. No matter what technology is being used, such services have layered storage capabilities that provide different abstraction levels and provide assistance to users for the execution of knowledge organization processes. Metadata services should define and insert new knowledge elements into the different layers of the storage system.

Distribution, publication and filtering services may include: subscription-based approaches on internal (such as bulletin boards) and external (such as www sites) information sources, and push and smart-pull approaches coupled with intelligent, selective mechanisms of content relevance assessment that will provide useful knowledge while preventing information overload.

Collaboration services are offered by technologies providing rich, shared, virtual workspaces in which interactions occur between people who share a common goal. Indicative collaboration services include e-mail, messaging, on-line discussions, electronic scheduling and meeting, video and audio conferencing, virtual workshops and just-in-time workgroup alerting.

Integration services provide for integration with application and tools that are currently used within the organization (e.g. word-processors, spreadsheets and databases). In this way, the infrastructure will tap into the flow of information that is already happening in the organization, and therefore will improve acceptability by the users.

2.7 Using the Framework in an Integrated Manner

The Know-Net framework can be a valuable tool in creating awareness for KM within a company. It can be used as an integrated and consistent approach for thinking and discussing about KM initiatives since it can guarantee an efficient treatment of the linkages between all the interrelated components of a KM effort.

Take, for example, the definition of what knowledge is crucial for a company (strategy). This issue has major implications for the directions of an IT system to be developed (systems), e.g. whether it should be based on strict document management or on looser collaboration facilities, as well as on organizational issues (structure), e.g. how the company promotes organizational changes and roles that facilitate the capture of such knowledge, and even on knowledge-related process issues (process), e.g. how the specific tasks and activities of knowledge capture are integrated within the normal flow of work.

Other examples may be linking skills management (individual) to overall company directions (strategy) for leveraging knowledge assets may have implications for the design of an IT system (systems), as well as on the organizational roles of executives overseeing the company-wide effort (structure); while making the most of customer knowledge (interorganizational) within the company's crucial knowledge (assets) may generate a number of strategic questions (strategy) of how the company views its supply chain and its relation to clients, as well as technological questions (systems) of how the company might interact with its clients to capture their knowledge.

The Know-Net Method

3.1 Introduction

This chapter presents the main elements of the Know-Net methodology. This methodology was designed as a supporting tool to help the design, development, and deployment of a holistic knowledge management (KM) infrastructure that is aligned with the business strategy, to facilitate in planning the organizational changes required for KM to succeed, and to show ways to evaluate the impact of the KM initiative on the overall performance of the organization.

The Know-Net methodology exploits the theoretical approach of integrating the process and product views using the knowledge assets and objects as the unifying elements, as presented in Chapter 2. In addition, it supports the customization and configuration of the Know-Net tool, which is presented in Chapter 4, however, it could be equally applied to the customization of other software that supports the development of a KM initiative.

The method is complete in the sense that it covers the design, development, implementation and measurement of the KM initiative, and holistic in the sense that it addresses all components of KM (strategy, people, processes, and technology) as presented in the Know-Net framework in Chapter 2.

Finally, a significant characteristic of the method is that it is modular, with each module being a self-contained and value-adding component. This modularity permits an organization to choose to start at different levels depending on its readiness, needs and requirements.

The Know-Net method consists of six stages (Figure 3.1):

- "**Awareness**" about the benefits of KM and its relationships to strategic as well as operational and day-to-day issues in the corporate environment. The Know-Net framework, as presented in Chapter 2, may be used for creating awareness about the specific issues of KM.

- "**Stage I: plan**" refers to the KM strategic planning phase, during which an organization determines the vision and readiness for a KM initiative and the scope and feasibility of the project.

- "**Stage II: develop**" is the phase in which an organization transforms itself into a knowledge-intensive company based on the company-specific KM value proposition derived in stage I. Here, the holistic KM solution (that covers processes, people and technology) is iteratively developed, tested and reviewed.

- "**Stage III: operate**" is the phase in which an organization rolls out a company-

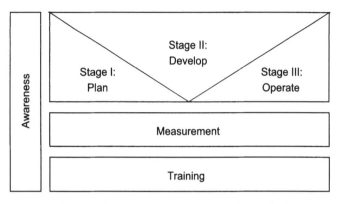

Figure 3.1 Building blocks of the Know-Net method.

wide implementation plan with a holistic approach to KM. This stage concerns the actual day-to-day operation of a KM environment, so no specific methodology is provided for it; change management and project management methods may be used for that effect.

● **"Measurement"** provides consistent support for measuring the creation, sharing and use of knowledge assets within the company, using the Know-Net knowledge asset measurement process (KAMP).

● **"Training"** of both the knowledge workers in the new processes and technologies and the staff to take up new knowledge-related roles (e.g. chief knowledge officers, knowledge analysts).

3.2 Strategic Planning for KM (Stage I: Plan)

The implementation of any KM initiative calls for a comprehensive understanding of the context in which the KM project is being undertaken. The task can be overwhelming because of the complexity involved.

Stage I aims to break down a KM initiative into manageable projects without losing sight of the big picture. Stage I comprises a series of separate, value-adding activities, each of which can be managed independently of the others. (Figure 3.2, Table 3.1). The sequence and the emphasis on the activities of the methodology may differ from organization to organization. Some activities may seem elementary or abstract for some organizations because of their strategic orientation. However, the importance of the activities is that they set the high-level direction for a KM project.

The goal of strategic planning is to focus quickly on knowledge that counts and delivers value to the firm. Based on the corporate strategy and objectives a clear KM strategy needs to be defined to help the firm to set forth the criteria for choosing the knowledge assets that it plans to pursue and how it will go about capturing, sharing and using them.

A key deliverable of this stage is the creation of a business case, which sets the scope of the project by designating critical knowledge assets for the business and identifying the sources of those knowledge assets. The focus of this stage is to

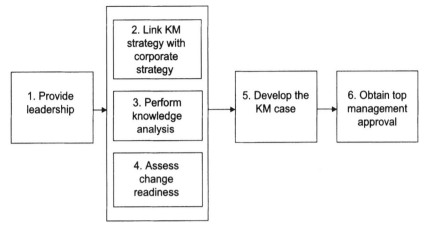

Figure 3.2 Overview of stage I.

Table 3.1 Activities and tasks in the implementation of stage I

Activities	Tasks
1. Provide leadership	Meet the CEO and top management Form and educate a KM initiation team
2. Link KM strategy with corporate strategy	Organize workshops/conduct interviews ● Analyze vision, strategy, objectives and critical success factors ● Link strategy to critical success factors, improvement needs, key people and processes Select key business area and process of focus
3. Perform knowledge analysis	Determine knowledge orientation; current and desirable Identify critical knowledge assets Analyze KM infrastructure
4. Assess risk and change readiness	Change readiness assessment Stakeholder analysis
5. Develop the case for KM	Explain the need for KM Project description Provide solution detail ● Develop performance measurement and evaluation plan ● Determine resource and funding requirements ● Develop awareness generation and education plan ● Determine implementation schedule
6. Obtain top management approval	Improve awareness of the executive group Present the KM proposal Form the KM project implementation team

convince top management of the need for and benefits of KM and to gain their full commitment to the initiative.

3.2.1 Provide Leadership

Apparent in successful KM cases is a visible evidence of knowledge leadership with one or more people actively championing the knowledge agenda. However, the first critical task for a knowledge champion is to understand corporate thinking and garner the full commitment of the senior management for the initiative. Since KM influences almost everyone in the organization and affects specific programmes and policies, top management support is indispensable.

Top management should have a common understanding of what KM is and of the need for a KM initiative. A preliminary approval to explore the possibility of undertaking such an initiative is needed. This would help an external consultant or an internal change agent to gauge the extent of support available from senior management and to plan the project accordingly.

The role of the CEO can vary from one of passive support, through active stimulation to knowledge leadership, where the CEO personally takes a leading role in making the knowledge initiative happen. This could significantly affect the strategic planning for the KM project. For example, if there is only passive support from the CEO then the knowledge champion would have to invest significant time and resources in demonstrating the value of KM and helping senior management, middle management and employees to understand the need for the organization to turn to KM and the payoffs that exist. However, if the senior management has already bought into the idea then effort can be concentrated on planning the project and drawing up the project detail.

Having obtained an initial commitment from senior management, the next important step would be to assemble a small team who would lead the KM effort in the organization. The KM initiation team should be made up of a cross-section of the organization. The number of members in the team will depend on the size of the organization. However, the size of the team should be kept small and may vary from one person to four people. A key member of this team will be the "change agent". A change agent is the person responsible for the process of change and incorporating the principles and tools of change management into an organized and systematic plan of implementation. The onus is on the change agent to set the direction and create general awareness about KM and how it can benefit the organization.

3.2.2 Link Corporate Strategy with the KM Strategy

KM strategy sets forth the criteria for choosing which knowledge assets a firm plans to pursue and how it will go about capturing and sharing them. For the successful implementation of a KM programme the strategic thrust of the initiative has to be closely aligned with the overall vision, strategy and objectives of the organization. Hence, this activity will help the KM initiation team to focus on the business area or the process that adds the greatest value.

Traces of the overall strategy of the organization can be found in the annual business plan of the company, vision statements, annual reports, press releases and executive interviews with the press, long-range planning statements, SWOT (strengths, weaknesses, opportunities, threats) analyses, submissions to stock exchanges, and any other documents in which future direction and market position are discussed. Table 3.2 lists a set of indicative questions that can be used alternatively to elicit the key strategic directions of the organization.

The SWOT analysis put forward by Michael Porter is a useful technique that can be used at this stage to identify the organization's strengths (core competences), weaknesses and opportunities (improvement needs) and threats (critical success factors).

Table 3.2 Indicative strategy elicitation questions

Where are we now as an organization?

Where do we want to be? What are our strategy, mission and values?

What are the priorities?

What are the key drivers and critical success factors?

What measures will best capture the success for each of these critical success factors?

For each of the critical success factors, who are the key people involved?

What are the processes involved with achieving these critical success factors?

In which areas are competitors performing better or catching up with the organization?

What are the major problems facing our organization?

What are the key skills that our organization needs to adopt during the next three years to gain and/or maintain competitive advantage?

What are the organization's key knowledge assets?

What measurement will best capture the success for each of these critical success factors?

How do these correlate to the knowledge asset categories?

The objective is to sustain the company's strengths, mitigate its weaknesses, avoid threats and grab opportunities. Such a technique is in good accordance with the competitive approach to strategy, described in brief in Chapter 2. As mentioned in Chapter 2, Porter's five forces model, though much respected, has recently been criticized for its focus on entire industries instead of individual companies.

In contrast, the approach presented here focuses on a company's core resources, and especially on knowledge as the main strategic resource for achieving competitive advantage. Therefore, to articulate the overall strategy, a company must explicate its strategic intent, identify knowledge required to execute that strategic choice, and reveal its strategic knowledge gaps by comparing these to its actual knowledge assets.

The KM initiation team should link each of the salient features of the firm's strategy to the opportunities and improvement needs of the company, the critical success factors (CSFs), key processes and the key people in the organization (Figure 3.3).

Based on the data collected, the KM initiation team should attempt to link each of the CSFs with a measurable parameter. A successful knowledge management programme requires clearly defined links to the value proposition, its bottom line being a contribution to business benefits. Therefore, it is important that the right measures are identified at the outset of the project.

3.2.3 Perform Knowledge Analysis

Embarking on a KM initiative is very much like setting out on a journey. Before you begin, you need to know where you are and where you want to go, and plan out the path and alternative routes. Appendix A provides a simple knowledge orientation matrix to help to determine an organization's current coordinates and map the desirable ones.

Knowledge analysis aims to identify the state of the KM infrastructure from two perspectives: what currently exists and what is missing. As already outlined in

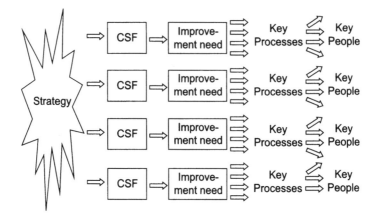

Figure 3.3 Linking strategy and improvement needs to processes and people.

Chapter 2, there are four essential and interrelated elements of the KM infrastructure: strategy, systems, processes and structure.

KM Strategy

The KM initiation team needs to understand the strategy for KM in the company if there is one, or work at developing it based on the business analysis of the organization. Skyrme and Amidon (1997) classify the strategies for knowledge management into four broad categories based on KM initiatives in the business world:

- *managing knowledge as a core asset*: knowledge in whatever form is an organizational asset that is to be leveraged and protected. This is most evident in companies that depend on high intellectual capability, e.g. pharmaceutical companies;
- *managing knowledge to enhance product or service capability*: in industries where knowledge adds value to products by making them smarter, e.g. high-tech manufacturing industries such as automobile, computer and aerospace;
- *managing knowledge as a business*: the modus operandi of the management consultancies and also pursued by market research and analysis companies;
- *managing knowledge to enhance business and management processes*: the focus here is on having the right knowledge at the right place at the right time to improve the efficiency and effectiveness of an organization's processes. This is most evident in service industries or global manufacturing.

These are distinct but not exclusive strategies and organizations that are effective at managing their knowledge assets should be aware of these multiple facets.

KM Systems

The KM initiation team should develop a broad understanding of the current and desirable use of technology enablers in the organization for KM.

KM Processes

An important indicator of the level of knowledge awareness in a company is whether there are institutionalized systematic processes for KM. Are there processes that identify and share existing organizational knowledge and processes for the creation of new knowledge and its conversion into new products and processes? Is there easy access to classified knowledge bases by people throughout an organization? Are there KM processes at all three levels of the organization: the coordinating strategic level, the level of specific tools and methods that underpin major processes, and the level of skills and techniques to perform knowledge work?

KM Structure

Successful knowledge-based companies depend on how successful individual knowledge workers are at creating and applying new ideas productively and efficiently. This requires an organizational structure to facilitate and support these processes. An understanding of the formal or informal organizational structure, which directs, facilitates and supports KM-related activities within the company, is rendered as absolutely essential for a successful KM initiative.

3.2.4 Assess Change Readiness

KM involves extensive cultural and behavioural changes in the organization. Change readiness assessment is an invaluable tool for determining the potential hurdles and pitfalls of implementing change. A change readiness assessment is a survey of employees at various levels to determine whether they understand the need to change, the direction of change, and the benefits of change and how willing they are to change. The objectives of the change readiness assessment techniques are:

- to raise the overall awareness of the organization regarding change, fundamentals of successfully managing the change process and likely impacts
- to reveal hidden agendas and key resistance issues that might prove troublesome later if not discovered
- to provide focus on later changes of the change effort.

Change readiness assessment can help the KM initiation team to develop a clear organizational change management plan which forms an integral part of a KM effort and should be covered in extensive detail in developing the business case.

Another business analysis technique that can be used at the beginning of a KM project is stakeholder analysis. Stakeholders are individuals or groups who, at some time during the KM programme, will affect and be affected by what is happening. The stakeholders will have to be identified based on the scope and objectives of the KM programme. Depending on the scope of the project the stakeholder population could include customers, employees, owners, suppliers and other business partners. It is important to analyze these stakeholders because, on one hand, motivated stakeholders can have a multiplier effect on the KM initiative and, on the other, demotivated stakeholders can seriously hinder the progress of the project.

A simple table, listing for each area of change the potential impact, stakeholders, anticipated reactions and issues, planned response and communication strategy, can be used for a simple stakeholder analysis. The overall purpose is to identify possible problematic points and plan actions to overcome them.

3.2.5 Develop the case for KM

A business case in the context of a KM project primarily serves three purposes.

1. *It is an effective planning tool for the KM initiation team.* The writing of the business case forces the KM initiation team to reflect on the work they have done and the work they have to accomplish in the coming months. It provides a vehicle for the team to step back and subjectively review their facts and assumptions.
2. *It serves as a communication vehicle* for sharing the project goals with the rest of the organization. The KM business case is one place where all relevant facts are documented and linked together into a cohesive story. The story tells people about the what, when, where, how and why of the KM project.
3. *The development of the business case simplifies the financial justification for the KM initiative.*

The KM business case is a powerfully persuasive justification for the initiative and includes a preliminary detail of the need for KM, the scope of the project, resource requirements, implementation schedule, and awareness generation and change management plan. The outline of a typical business case for a KM project is summarized in Table 3.3. Not all projects will require all of the sections; they should be tailored to meet the needs and expectations of the audience and the case.

3.2.6 Obtain Top Management Approval

Given the changes to corporate culture, behaviour and processes and high resource requirements that usually characterize KM, corporate leaders cannot be lukewarm about it and have it succeed. They must be fully committed, realizing that they too will probably be required to learn new skills and new ways of running their functions. The time and resource requirements for obtaining fully fledged top management support will depend on their awareness and commitment.

Senior management needs to understand the concept, the resources required to implement it and more importantly the benefits of the project. This can best be accomplished by providing an executive seminar of what KM is all about. The introductory chapters of this book can be used as a reference point to begin with.

The strategic thrust of the whole KM initiative could be summarized in the form of the template shown in Figure 3.4. The KM business case is the main vehicle for obtaining top management approval. Based on the selection of the key business area or process that has been identified in the business case, a team of people who will be involved in carrying out the implementation stages of the project must be formed. The members of this team should have a good understanding of the functions of the business area or processes. It may be important to have the head of the business area or function as part of the team along with the KM initiation team.

Table 3.3 Indicative outline of a KM business case

Executive summary	This provides management with a snapshot of the business case. The focus of the executive summary should be on the bottom-line benefits to the organization. The remainder of the business case provides the detail and analysis to support the statement made in the summary
The need for KM	This presents the main benefits from the KM initiative, preferably in both qualitative and quantitative terms, and the ways in which the initiative will help the organization in the achievement of its goals. The benefits could span a big range, with typical examples being reduced cycle time, reduced costs, enhanced functional effectiveness, increased organizational adaptability, increased value of existing product and services, and the creation of new knowledge intensive products, processes and services. This section should provide the situational assessment and problem statement, which will draw heavily from steps 2 and 3 of stage I
Project description	This describes the desired end state for the KM initiative. The end state provides the framework for the solution definition. Things to include are KM strategy or goals, a high-level description of the solution – it should paint a picture for the reader of what the end state will look like, a description of the key business area or process selected to begin the project and the justification for doing so
Solution detail	● **Performance measurement and evaluation plan:** measures the business value of the KM initiative ● **Resource and funding requirements,** needed to control the resources expended and minimize duplication of effort. The KM initiation team should draw up a detailed cost structure for the KM team, including development, testing and any ongoing maintenance or administrative costs ● **Awareness generation and organizational change management plan:** a review of how organizational change management plan is going to be used to support the KM initiative should be included in the business case. The KM initiation team should describe their plan of action depending on the change readiness assessment and stakeholder analysis ● **Implementation schedule:** having identified the best value future state solution, the KM initiation team must set its sights on developing an implementation plan. Part of this implementation plan will be an organizational change management plan, which is designed to minimize the resistance to change and prepare the organization to embrace the future state solution. Each major step in the implementation of the solution is depicted on the timeline. Major steps should include development, testing, training, initial implementation and roll-out

3.3 Developing the Knowledge Organization (Stage II: Develop)

"Develop" is the phase in which an organization transforms itself into a knowledge-intensive company based on the organization-specific KM value proposition derived in the "stage I: plan" phase. Here, the structure and design of a holistic solution (that covers processes, people and technology) are iteratively developed, tested and reviewed.

Three simple steps underlie the proposed iterative approach. First, diagnose the most critical problems and opportunities facing the organization with respect to KM and sketch out a possible solution. Second, quickly, over a few weeks or months, translate the sketch of a solution into new work processes and systems; include new

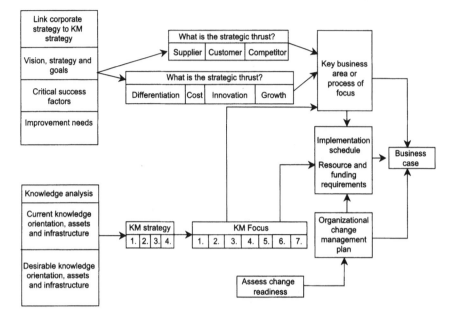

Figure 3.4 Presenting the KM business case.

ways of working as well as new computer systems, and begin using both for real. If, for example, the problem at hand is customer KM, use the new process to manage some important customers at several offices (or business areas). Given this real-world experience, determine where these new processes and systems succeed or fail, and quickly fix the failures. In other words: do it, *then* fix it. Third, scale up systems for roll-out across the whole organization. Communicate the proven success of the trials in order to build momentum for change.

The essence of the iterative prototyping approach is rapid learning from doing. Speed ensures that change is always relevant, it forces trade-offs so that limited resources are devoted to pursuing goals of real value, it allows top people to participate in change and it builds unstoppable momentum. Trying out new ideas in the real world allows their shortcomings to be rooted out by the harshest of tests – real-world experience – and their successes to be proven beyond challenge from the most cynical critics. By stressing speed of change and using the real world as a laboratory to learn from, the iterative prototyping approach makes change and improvement a constant fact of corporate life.

This second stage of the Know-Net method is based on the analysis and the information technology (IT)-based leveraging of knowledge assets that can be found within business processes, as well as between networks.

A structured, modular representation of this stage comprises three audit-leverage pairs of modules (one pair for business processes, modules 1 and 2; one for people networks, modules 3 and 4, and one that focuses on technology issues, modules 5 and 6), a core module that focuses on the development of the knowledge asset schema of the organization (module 7), and a module that synthesizes the changes

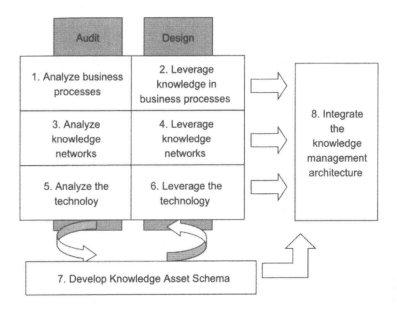

Figure 3.5 Modules of stage II: developing the knowledge organization.

that the organization is implementing, documents them, guarantees their consistency and makes sure that all synergies are exploited and all possible conflicts in the development of the initiative are resolved (module 8, Figure 3.5, Table 3.4).

3.3.1 Analyze and Leverage Business Processes

Project teams in knowledge-intensive business processes are used to deal with a huge amount of information, documents, etc. Lessons learned in previous engagements, insights from prior projects and notes for subsequent process steps are scattered among manifold knowledge containers, from personal memory, through paper, to different electronic systems. Even if there are mechanisms explicitly to capture and store bits and pieces of best practice, these are seldom used in a coordinated manner, and at best take into account document content, but not so much document context, i.e. neither the creation situation nor the potential usage situation.

However, business processes are a context-giving, structuring element prevalent in a company, often even formally modelled for some purpose such that it would make sense to exploit the usage of business processes to organize knowledge archives. The goal is to enable context-sensitive storage, more purposeful access to information, and better integration with the process-oriented, day-to-day work of the employee with the knowledge system.

Knowledge-oriented business process analysis as a central KM objective examines which knowledge and information sources are required for, or created in the organization's business processes, which information flow happens within and

Table 3.4 Overview of stage II modules of the Know-Net method

Module	What is it used for?	Comment
1. Analyze business processes	To audit the knowledge requirements of business processes	Modules 1 and 2 are useful: 1. in relatively structured environments 2. when there is a need to manage knowledge better in specific business processes
2. Leverage knowledge in business processes	To design and implement additions and modifications in business processes to improve KM within the process	
3. Analyze knowledge networks	To understand the informal flow of knowledge within networks of people in the organization	To be used mainly in environments where there already exist informal networks of people that focus on a specific knowledge asset or business area
4. Leverage knowledge networks	To design and moderate knowledge networks within the organization	To be used by organizations that wish to build communities that will be collecting, storing and advancing key knowledge assets of the organization. Particularly important for dispersed organizations
5. Analyze the technology	To assess the current state of IT in the organization	Supports the integration with existing enterprise systems
6. Leverage the technology	To analyze the technology element in KM	
7. Develop the knowledge asset schema	To design the knowledge asset schema, knowledge objects and attributes, and the ontology	Provides essential input for the design of the knowledge repository
8. Integrate the KM architecture	To integrate people, process and technology changes into one holistic solution	Gives practical tips on integrating the people, process and technology changes. Addresses cultural issues

between knowledge-intensive processes, and how process-intrinsic parameters influence information needs.

Approaching knowledge-oriented business process analysis is a central enabler for KM because it builds the basis for process-oriented knowledge archives and efficient access to such archives. Analysis and leveraging of business processes help to show how business processes, people, systems and content are related, identify the knowledge gaps within the execution of the business process and elicit requirements for KM within the business process.

Based on the high-level identification of strategic knowledge assets and business areas, here the method reviews key business processes that support them. This area examines whether it is possible to enhance management of a particular knowledge asset by improving existing business processes or by designing completely new processes explicitly to support management of the specific knowledge asset.

In doing so CSFs for the new process and potential barriers to implementation of the new process are identified, stakeholder analysis is performed, and the cultural and organizational changes required are facilitated. We base the design of the new processes on the knowledge asset schema. In any additions or modifications to the designed business processes, it is ensured that the related knowledge objects have all of the metadata, classification and indexing information required by the IT system.

Appendix B presents in detail the methodological steps for analyzing and leveraging knowledge in business processes.

3.3.2 Analyze and Leverage Knowledge Networks

Knowledge networks, informal networks of knowledge workers who share similar goals and interests, are instrumental in facilitating knowledge sharing and knowledge creation within any organization. This part of the Know-Net method helps to identify, cultivate and sustain existing knowledge networks as well as to facilitate the creation of new ones. The objective is to build knowledge networks to cultivate and nurture the organization's key knowledge assets, not to replicate the existing departments and organizational structures.

Typically, knowledge networks are self-organized groups, which naturally communicate with one another because they share common work practices, interests and aims. Nevertheless, the Know-Net methodology aims to formalize the internal dynamics of the community by defining community roles and responsibilities, recognizing the fact that the essence of these networks is their members. Members are self-organizing and participate because they get value from their participation. Participation is voluntary and employees are encouraged to participate only if they see the network purpose to be meaningful and believe that they could gain from or contribute to the community.

An additional objective of this part of the method is to provide the knowledge networks with suggested tools to help to create, capture and share knowledge. A tool, in this instance, does not refer to automated systems for transferring information. Rather, these tools are techniques or forums for thinking, e.g. techniques for generating ideas and building relationships, or forums that promote knowledge flow and transfer.

Finally, this part is designed to help knowledge networks facilitators to assess progress, recognize the natural evolution of network interactions, recognize and reward both individual and community contributions, and continuously foster innovation and growth.

Appendix C presents in detail techniques and tools for analyzing and leveraging knowledge networks.

3.3.3 Analyse and Leverage Technology

In an effort to provide a framework that is generic enough to support any organization but at the same time provide clear and concrete directions for the implementation of a KM platform, the Know-Net method defines the *core services* that need to be offered for systematic KM (distribution, collaboration, indexing, storage, integration, search and retrieval; see also Chapter 2).

This section outlines a generalized technical architecture (Figure 3.6) based on several layers that may alternatively be considered for the KM project. The knowledge technical architecture in general is a federation of technologies running on top of existing networks and IT systems. This generalized architecture provides a framework for positioning existing, disparate technologies for KM and a blueprint guide for the development of the new KM system in the organization.

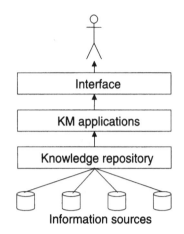

Figure 3.6 Layers of the knowledge technical infrastructure.

Layer 1: The Interface

The interface or portal is the first level aiming to present simplicity to the user. As KM software brings together the resources of the corporate memory, the interface becomes a portal to those resources. Although many of these resources may lie outside the KM architecture, it is the KM software that provides the organization, indexing and search capabilities. The interface is the universal view of the organization, a window to the repository of organizational knowledge. Technically speaking, the interface will typically be based on web technology, allowing the widest possible access and greatest integration of services.

Layer 2: The KM Applications

Knowledge-enabling applications provide users with productivity enhancements and improved ways of doing their jobs. This layer may include authoring and publishing tools, document management, discussion databases, competitive intelligence knowledge bases, calendars, employee Yellow Pages, sales force automation, and executive balance scorecard applications. This list of applications provides just a starting point for the kind of functionality that the organizational infrastructure should provide to meet the specific needs of the organization and the people and teams within it.

Groupware is a core technology to be used for KM applications. KM collaborative software must support the creation of knowledge networks, communities of interest within the organizational network and beyond. This requires an environment that supports knowledge sharing and capture. While groupware products provide an informal environment for collaboration, there exist products that create more formal collaboration applications. Workflow and document-management systems provide greater control of processes that require many people to work on them.

However, large-scale collaborations, involving document-management or workflow systems, are expensive to implement and difficult to roll out to the organization.

Another core technology that should be exploited in KM applications is information retrieval. The information retrieval component of a KM architecture provides basic search techniques for finding resources in a distributed, heterogeneous environment and more advanced requirements for classifying and analyzing large volumes of information. The keyword searches provided by most Internet search engines are a simple way of providing easy access to a wide range of documents. The effectiveness of such searches is inherently restricted to a relatively simple statistical analysis of the searched document based on the occurrence of those key terms. Specialized information retrieval products provide some improvements on keyword search. The most common addition is elementary linguistic analysis, which enables words to be "stemmed" (so that the search includes both the singular and plural forms of a word). A further refinement is to provide thesaurus capabilities, so that search terms can be expanded to cover a series of related terms.

Layer 3: The Knowledge Repository

The knowledge repository is a key component of any KM framework. It provides for the administration, management and manipulation of the knowledge being captured. The basic functions of the knowledge repository include:

- classification and indexing of sources stored in the repository as well as external sources, such as websites or other databases and file systems
- a corporate thesaurus, so that common definitions can be defined and accessed, and automatic substitutions can be made
- metadata management, including simple metadata such as author, last edit date, annotations and comments on documents.

A repository can be implemented in a number of ways, e.g. in a RDBMS, in a Lotus Notes database or in a document management system. The knowledge repository does not have to store all of the items included in the corporate memory, it should rather act as an "umbrella", keeping them all connected and making them available to the KM applications. A knowledge repository may sit on top of several existing databases and file systems; It is used in indexing and metadata management but usually does not store the actual information, just the links. Metadata are information on information. They can have many levels. For example, a document may have some basic metadata on the author, time of last edit, current version number and so on. More complex metadata might include annotations on the value of the document or keywords that are used to identify the document with particular topics.

3.3.4 The Knowledge Asset Schema

A knowledge platform may consist of several repositories, each with a structure that is appropriate for the particular type of knowledge assets that it represents and the content that it stores. Such repositories may be logically linked to form a cohesive, consolidated repository.

The knowledge asset schema helps maintain a logical, integrated view of the content stored in the various repositories. This part of the Know-Net methodology also deals with the design and maintenance of the logical taxonomy of the knowledge resources available to the user via the KM system.

A detailed description for developing the knowledge asset schema is presented in Appendix D.

3.3.5 Integrate the KM Architecture

The knowledge architecture identifies the scope of the investment that is made in managing knowledge. More than a technical solution, it encompasses issues related to people, processes and technology. This part of the Know-Net methodology brings together these elements into a working relationship.

An erroneous assumption that many organizations make is that the intrinsic value of a change programme such as a KM initiative will lead to its enthusiastic adoption and use by the employees. On the contrary, encouraging use and gaining employee support require integration of business processes with KM system use, and new reward structures that motivate employees to use the system and contribute to its infusion, championing and training.

As part of this last step in designing the KM infrastructure, one should:

● understand the different types of potential users of the KM system and make sure these map to people in the organization
● integrate the KM system within the working environment by enabling business process triggers for specific KM applications
● understand the function of the new organizational roles and decide what are the exact responsibilities of these roles, and how these map to the KM systems and KM-related business processes
● manage and implement cultural changes as well as reward mechanisms that motivate knowledge workers to participate in the common effort.

3.4 Operating the Knowledge Organization (Stage III: Operate)

This stage involves the wide-scale deployment of the KM architecture. Companies at this stage go beyond initial, small-scale pilots into an operational and continually evolving KM infrastructure.

This stages addresses the company-wide deployment of knowledge processes, roles and systems as they were developed in stage II: develop, the development of additional pilots, as well as the full-scale development of knowledge support services within the organization.

Such support services may include the implementation of an organizational infrastructure by setting up and staffing roles such as knowledge analysts and knowledge editors, the introduction of KM-induced cultural changes, the establishment of networks such as communities of practice, and the large-scale integration of KM tools with legacy IT systems. All of these constitute small steps toward a continuous knowledge journey.

3.5 Measurement of Knowledge Assets

3.5.1 The Know-Net Measurement Model

Measuring the knowledge assets of a company has been a challenge for many researchers who devoted a lot of effort to present a concrete system that will clearly portray the invisible assets of a company; see for example the Intangible Assets Monitor of Sveiby (1997b), the Navigator Approach of Edvinsson and Malone (1997) or the Balanced Scorecard of Kaplan and Norton (1996a). The Know-Net knowledge assets measurement model has been developed by taking into account the above-mentioned research approaches.

The Know-Net measurement approach provides a framework for systematic measurement of business performance indicators linked to the organization's market, human, structural and financial assets(Figure 3.7). The reason for including financial assets, besides the four categories of knowledge assets (which were described in Chapter 2), is to remind managers of the importance of the financial or accounting bottom line, since any knowledge-related improvement should somehow translate into an improvement in a financial indicator.

The Know-Net measurement approach also treats assets both from a "stock" and from a "flow" perspective (which enables a transformation from one type of asset to another).

The bathtub metaphor may be used to illustrate the difference between asset stocks and flows: "At any point in time, the stock of water is indicated by the level of water in the tub; it is the cumulative result of flows of water into the tub (through the tap) and out of it (through the leak)."

In the example of R&D the amount of water in the tub represents the stock of know-how at a particular moment in time, whereas the current R&D spending is represented by the water flowing in through the tap; the fact that know-how depreciates over time is represented by the flow of water leaking through the hole in the tub" (Dierickx and Cool, 1989).

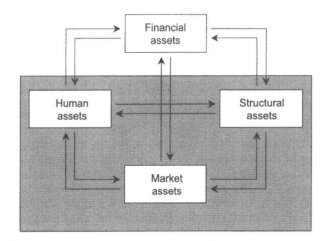

Figure 3.7 The Know-Net knowledge assets measurement model.

Table 3.5 Examples of stock indicators

Financial assets	Human assets	Market assets	Structural assets
Return on Investment Return on Assets Cost of capital	Average years in the industry Revenue per employee Employee turnover compared to industry average Percentage of staff with graduate degrees	Market share Customer satisfaction Customer penetration Percentage of profits from new business	Patent citation count Key process efficiency indicators (e.g. order filling, error rates, R&D efficiencies) Organizational culture indices

Table 3.6 Examples of flow indicators

From	To Human assets	Structural assets	Market assets	Financial assets
Human assets	Hours spent coaching Internal training expenses	Learning captured Hours spent codifying processes R&D man-hours Best knowledge codified and easily available	Man-hours spent on a relationship/ customer profit contribution	Consulting fee per man-hour (net of administrative costs)
Structural assets	Utilization of best practices Attractiveness indices for recruiting Employee retention indices		Profitability of uninvited contacts	Licensing fees Revenues from database sales Price premium over competition
Market assets	Assessment by employee of personal development through external relations	Organizational learning from partners (joint ventures, suppliers, customer, etc.)		Brokering fees Profitability of referrals
Financial assets	Investment in training	Advertising and marketing investments R&D investments Improvements in working environment	Investment in relationships	

Table 3.5 lists some examples of indicators that may be used for measuring the stock perspective of the four asset categories.

Table 3.6 gives some examples of the indicators that capture the flows through which an asset is transformed from one category to another. For example, assume that it is critical to the success of a strategy that some particular human knowledge asset should be transformed into a structural knowledge asset. Initially, just capturing, codifying and making available that knowledge to the key people it affects could be a measure of success. What one needs to consider measuring, however, is not only the "stock" of the human asset or the "stock" of the structural asset involved, but also the "flow", focusing on how efficiently this transfer was.

A factor making it difficult for companies to understand and measure asset flows is the existence of long and uncertain delays between the time of investment and the time of rewards. For example creating a strong brand may well take years, and the same can be said about increasing the human capital of the organizational members, or generating enough goodwill around the company to have customers and suppliers participate in the improvements of internal process efficiencies. What is worse, this time delay is variable and uncertain, so that managers cannot ever be completely certain whether a given investment is a failure, or the pay-off just has not manifested yet. Still, the pay-off of monitoring both asset stocks and flows is important.

3.5.2 The Performance and Asset Measurement Process

The previous section described the Know-Net measurement model and gave examples of measurements that might be developed. In this section a process for developing these measurements is described. In developing this process, it was borne in mind that these measurements cannot be developed independently of the rest of the Know-Net method and that the development of metrics is an integral part of drilling down from the strategic view of any organization to a single critical knowledge asset.

To proceed with the definition of the metrics a well-planned workshop is the most effective means of gaining common understanding and agreement amongst the organization's executives. The process of agreeing and defining measurements is important because this is when shared understanding and common language are developed and the links are made to strategy so that communication throughout the organization is consistent.

It is also important to recognize that as the understanding of the knowledge assets of the company and industry grows so does the ability to fine-tune the measurement systems. At the most pragmatic level, the idea is to start measuring "something". Quite often this will start with the simple counting of things, followed by a need for a quality dimension to be introduced. Insights about interactions between variables, combinations of measures and redundancy of some measures form the basis of longer-term improvements to the measurement system.

The process for developing the measurements is shown in Table 3.7. It starts top–down: identifying the organization's vision, strategy, CSFs, the business performance measurements for those CFSs and the key knowledge assets that should be associated with the CSFs. The CSFs and their business performance measurements can then be cross-referenced to the Know-Net asset categories. The process then switches to a bottom–up one: starting with the knowledge assets identified for each of the key CSFs and developing the knowledge asset measurements for them. These are then again cross-referenced to the Know-Net asset categories (Figure 3.8). The process is described below in more detail.

Not all indicators in the measurement system will be equally important to an organization. The best way to prioritize indicators is through strategy: this should give a single, clear statement of which knowledge assets are to be considered more important. Thus, the top management team should spell out in clear terms the long-term strategy for the organization. Suffice it to say that for the purposes of the measurement process the strategy could be a statement of the company's long-term objective, as well as an indication of how to achieve it. The strategy statement should also make very clear what knowledge assets are most important for the organization and its success, thus supplying a way to prioritize asset categories first, and indicators afterwards.

Table 3.7 The Know-Net performance and asset measurement process

Evaluate your strategy
> *Ask*: How do you achieve above normal returns?

Identify your critical success factors
> *Ask*: What are the CSFs to succeed in your strategy?

Document measurements for these CSFs
> *Ask*: How do you measure these CSFs?
> *Ask*: What should you be measuring for these CSFs?
>> Document high-level snapshot of measurements?

Identify your key knowledge assets
> *Ask*: What are your intangible and knowledge assets?
> *Ask*: What are the assets associated with your CSFs?
> *Ask*: Do your existing assets match those needed to support your CSFs?

Develop knowledge asset measurements
> *Ask*: How do you best measure these assets?
>> Agree and document bottom-up developed details of measurements

Implement/pilot the measurement systems
> Enhance and integrate reporting systems

Establish a continuous review cycle
> Introduce a review cycle for the measurement system

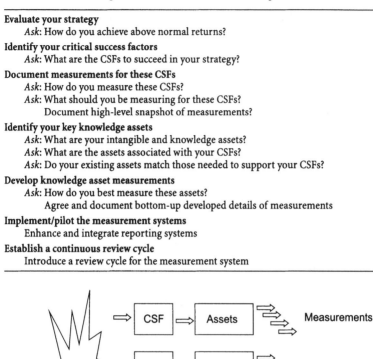

Figure 3.8 Linking strategy, critical success factors (CSF), asset categories and measurements.

Once the strategy is clear and shared by the whole top management team, it is possible to move to the next steps. At this point, two activities must be carried out, relatively independently: the identification of CSFs and the identification of key knowledge assets.

Identifying CSFs means identifying the most important activities and processes that the organization has to get right to reach the goals outlined in the strategy. Note that CSFs are not yet pure indicators: they only outline the special activities and processes, but do not yet give concrete measures to identify the degree of success (although these measures can be obvious). Thus, examples of CSFs are product development, inventory reduction, time-to-market and customer service. There is no numerical limit to CSFs, and indeed complex strategies may require good performance in a high number of different activities. All the same, parsimony should guide this phase, as the enumeration of many separate CSFs will cause the company to spread its attention thinly, with predictable negative consequences. Thus, it is essential to boil down the list to a manageable number (five to seven CSFs is a good benchmark).

At this point, the CSFs can be translated into concrete indicators that measure the company's performance. Each CSF should generate multiple indicators, though the specific numbers will vary greatly from one case to the next. Again, a rule of thumb is that there should be between three and ten indicators per CSF, with the average being around five or six. Quite often the main actors of this step can include middle and operating managers with front-line experience. Senior management can be, by its very nature, too detached to indicate the specific performance indicator for concrete processes. Often the measurements defined at this point will be financial and profit oriented.

As mentioned above, there is a second activity to be independently performed once the CSFs are identified: the identification of the company's knowledge assets that are linked to the CSFs. This involves assessing the present situation of the knowledge assets of the company. The purpose of this is clear: the desired position of the company (expressed by the strategy) should be tempered and matched by the current situation of the company, as expressed by its stocks of assets and their utilization (its flows). The identification of all knowledge assets requires broader participation than simply top management. Workshops may be used with representatives of various functions or business units, to identify the knowledge assets present in each unit and their use.

Once the knowledge asset audit is finished, then the assets identified should be matched with the CSFs. In case an evident mismatch is present, top management should be encouraged either to change their strategy to fit the knowledge asset in, or to stop investing in the specific knowledge asset, which is draining resources without being of any use to the completion of the strategy.

To develop low-level knowledge asset measurements, more detail is required. For example, "new product development" may become "speed in developing new products". This further specification and limitation of the focus is of immense help in finding the measurements. Implementing the measurements requires integrating any requirements generated through defining them into the requirements and systems specifications being developed. Once the measures are defined a snapshot of the current state should be taken and flow through of these measurements to any new reward practices should be identified and communicated.

Finally, once the system is in place, management should make sure that the effort spent in creating it does not go to waste. All too often, measurement systems are created and then not used, bringing about a considerable waste of resources. Instead, leveraging the system can generate considerable gains. As time passes, the knowledge asset measurement system should be constantly reviewed, with new measures being added and old measures dropped, to reflect refinement of the understanding of the organizational dynamics, but also reorientations in strategy and CSFs. Note that this maintenance of the momentum requires the company not to just implement an IT system, but also to change the culture and climate, encouraging employees at all levels to add their contribution to the refinements.

4 The Know-Net Tool

4.1 Introduction

In order to link the design goals and architectural choices that were made in the development of the Know-Net tool, this section briefly examines the information and communication technology support for knowledge management (KM) using as a basis the knowledge conversion processes of Nonaka and Takeuchi (1995). This process distinguish between four modes of knowledge transformation and knowledge flow between tacit and explicit knowledge: socialization (from tacit to tacit); externalization (from tacit to explicit), combination (from explicit to explicit), and internalization (from explicit to tacit) (Figure 4.1). What kinds of software tool could be useful to support these kinds of knowledge transfer?

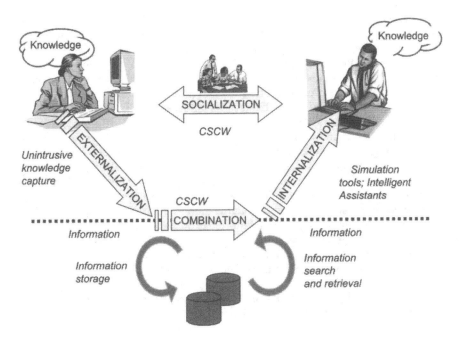

Figure 4.1 Modes of knowledge conversion and types of software support.

Socialization happens when people closely work together, so building up a shared understanding and context, even without words and explanations. Normally this is the case in a real-life, face-to-face collaboration. This kind of collaboration can be enabled in a wide-distance network via high-performance communication and computer-supported collaborative work (CSCW) tools, using technologies such as videoconferencing, white-boarding or application sharing.

Externalization means that people explicate their personal knowledge and encode it to the most possible extent in some form of *information*, such as a text document or a drawing showing some interesting relationships between topics to be talked about. The fact that the whole of human culture and science is based on the possibility of encoding knowledge to some extent in information shows that information technology (IT) does indeed affect KM. The quest is, however, for ergonomically and economically adequate tools which help the user and chase him to articulate his knowledge in a comfortable and not very intrusive or time-consuming manner, yet explicating as much *context* and *background knowledge* to make possible a later reuse. In the ideal case, machine learning techniques and expert system knowledge acquisition methods would come into play here to work fully or semi-automatically. In today's practice, more realistic ways are comfortable editors for describing knowledge objects, such as lessons learned or best practices, and for easily attaching to the appropriate metadata.

Internalization maps explicit knowledge into internal knowledge; it happens when individuals, exposed to other's people knowledge, make it their own. People internalize knowledge by doing, but also by looking at what other people have done in a similar context and by example. This process could be fostered by intelligent assistant systems, such as critiquing systems (Kühn et al., 1994), which apply formalized explicit knowledge to find problems in human decision making and confront the user with the respective knowledge item; or it could be facilitated by simulation tools which operationalize some portion of knowledge about system behaviour to help the user to experiment and learn with artificial decision problems to internalize the underlying principles. Simpler ways of software support could be context-oriented automatic retrieval of stored knowledge objects since the alleviation of the burden for a precise information search will also improve the acceptance of knowledge use and reuse and the level of understanding of stored knowledge objects (Abecker et al., 1998a).

Combination generates new knowledge by combining pre-existing explicit knowledge and bringing it together to produce new insight. It is the process of exchanging explicit knowledge, i.e. knowledge represented by some information items, between several partners. While communication support such as e-mails or real-time chats seems to be the nearby solution to allow combination in spite of geographical barriers, there is also great potential in communication asynchronous in space and time, i.e. by storing knowledge objects in a knowledge database and later retrieving them whenever appropriate. Here, one main challenge is to find appropriate forms of representing knowledge objects such that enough context is retained to make possible the later assessment of the potential usefulness in other situations, and the concrete application of the knowledge in a new situation. The other challenge is to design retrieval mechanisms that exploit this knowledge description format such that in a given new situation the user will easily find the appropriate knowledge objects stored.

Besides the fact that the above description of potential software support in the different scenarios of knowledge transfer also shows *innovative* approaches that have not yet been investigated very deeply, the integrated use of the *well-known* techniques is already challenging enough. Even if business managers do not make the mistake of thinking that IT support only concerns database-like approaches, represented in Figure 4.1 by the area below the dashed line, and that above this dashed line is only the area of non-technical, human factor-oriented KM, even if they think about the use of CSCW technologies to support socialization and communication, they normally do not think about the integrated, synergetic use of techniques for each of the transfer modes. Usually they do not think about a methodologically embedded use of these technologies that should pay special attention to systematic employment of processes which foster externalization and internalization, such that closed networks of knowledge flow arise; and they normally do not think about a seamless integration of these KM processes into the existing everyday work processes that should be disturbed by a KM initiative as little as possible (see also Kühn and Abecker, 1997). These points are exactly the design goals underlying the Know-Net tool development to be discussed below.

As a first step toward an integrated KM tool consider Figure 4.2, which presents an abstract system architecture, slightly changed from the one proposed by Ovum (1999). Some ideas realized in this approach are: (1) manifold different data formats and legacy systems are combined, linked together and uniformly accessible via an intranet middleware; (2) discovery services and collaboration services represent what we call the two complementary approaches to KM: product approach and

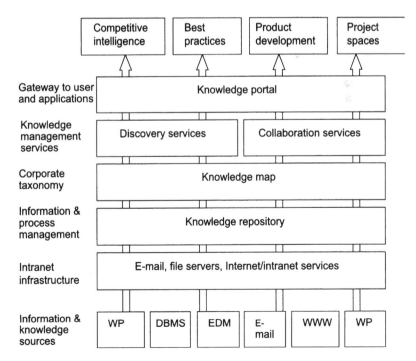

Figure 4.2 The OVUM abstract KM system architecture.

process approach, which shall be combined; (3) Intranet knowledge portals feed the KM services into knowledge-enriched processes in the company.

In the following sections the Know-Net architecture is described as a concrete instantiation of this abstract system design.

4.2 Design Goals of the Know-Net Tool

The design of the Know-Net integrated set of tools and applications is based on the Know-Net holistic KM framework and aims to support the whole range of tasks and activities required for introducing and operating a KM solution. Keeping in mind the Know-Net framework and method presented in the previous chapters, this leads to the following basic design goals, which were targeted with the Know-Net tool infrastructure.

4.2.1 Support of the Know-Net Method

Figure 3.1 in Chapter 3 shows the six stages of the Know-Net method. The following four stages are explicitly supported by the tool. Stage I: plan; stage II: develop; stage III: operate and measurement. The Know-Net tool supports the chief knowledge officer (CKO) or KM consultant in planning and developing the knowledge organization, it supports the knowledge workers using the tool operationally helping them to do their everyday knowledge-oriented work, and it helps to prepare and enact the measurement in the knowledge organization. All of these parts are seamlessly integrated, both on a conceptual basis and regarding the software realization.

4.2.2 Integration of the Product-centric and the Process-centric Approaches

As Figure 2.2 in Chapter 2 shows, the common denominator of the product-centric and the process-centric approaches to KM is the *knowledge object*. In the conceptual architecture and in designing the technical architecture for fusing the two complementary approaches, the knowledge objects are the "glue" between them. A technical implementation that exploits the consideration of the knowledge object being the common unifier of information retrieval (product) and groupware (process) technologies is, at the architectural level at least, relatively simple and straightforward. Applications that support the process view of KM, such as groupware applications, should use knowledge objects that are also accessible by applications and tools that support the product view, such as searching and indexing tools. Therefore, knowledge objects have to be independent from the applications that create or use them in order to be accessible also by other applications. To achieve this, a three-tier architecture is suitable, with a separate repository, a "place holder" for the knowledge objects. The knowledge repository does not have to store knowledge objects, but it should know where they reside and point to them. In fact, owing to the heterogeneity and variety of information systems and sources existent in any organization, it is more meaningful for the knowledge repository to act as a knowledge broker than actually to store information. The knowledge repository can serve requests for information, and use whatever mechanisms are necessary to retrieve and deliver the results to the user.

4.2.3 Support all Levels of Knowledge Networking

The Know-Net tool has been designed to be fully scalable, from supporting and enabling a small team of knowledge workers, as a project or a KM pilot, to supporting and enabling a global enterprise-wide knowledge management system. Typically, the Know-Net tool can support a team of people connected by intranet, but based in different locations, people in a department, a company or organization, or a global group of companies or organizations. As mentioned above, this design goal is achieved by designing an intranet/internet-based solution accessible world-wide through standardized browser technologies. The solution is to settle on the Lotus Notes and Lotus Notes Domino approach, and thus scaling up to support new communities or to extend the underlying databases is not a problem. It is easy to include new knowledge networks whenever necessary. Nevertheless, to keep simple the unique point of access for the end user, all services are offered in an integrated manner in one web browser/navigator for the individual knowledge worker.

4.3 Fundamental Elements of the Know-Net Tool

The Know-Net tool has three fundamental layers and associated components, as listed below and shown in Figure 4.3.

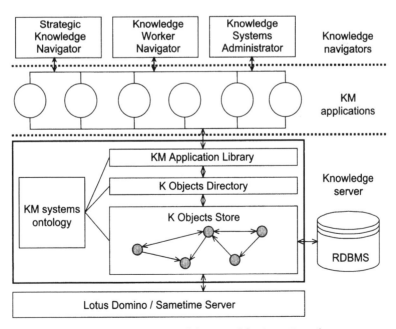

Figure 4.3 Fundamental elements of the Know-Net tool.

The Know-Net knowledge navigators provide role-specific views and perspectives on the Know-Net system services and give a unique point of access to all processes and applications relevant for a given KM role. In particular, the *Strategic Knowledge Navigator (SKN)* shows the Know-Net system from the perspective of a CKO, a director of knowledge management, and/or a KM consultant. The *Knowledge Worker Navigator (KWN)* takes the perspective of the individual knowledge worker undertaking projects, being involved in operational business processes, who will be integrated in the corporate-wide knowledge network. The *Knowledge Systems Administrator Navigator (KSAN)* offers the system administration tools.

The Know-Net KM applications provide the processes that create and manipulate knowledge objects. Essentially, these are Lotus Notes (technically, non-Notes applications would also be possible) applications that realize some KM process or incorporate the basic KM learning process into other operational business processes.

The Know-Net knowledge server is the one place, accessed by the knowledge navigators from anywhere, to store persistently the software provided (*KM Applications Library*), the basic structures and schemata underlying the other applications and services (*Knowledge Objects Directory, KM Systems Ontology*), and the concrete instances of these schemata and mass data to be dealt with [*Knowledge Objects Store, Metadata Store* (MDS), *Mail Knowledge Base* (MKB)]. The knowledge objects created are kept in a relational database management system (RDBMS).

The same architecture applies from the personal portfolio level to the enterprise-wide level.

As the integration and programming platform of the tool, Lotus Domino and the Lotus Sametime server were used, which offer much of the basic functionality required, such as basic file handling and archiving, web programming functionalities, user authentification and security issues. In the following sections, the three layers of the Know-Net tool are discussed in more detail.

4.4 The Knowledge Server

In order to foster knowledge networking in the entire organization for creating, retaining, leveraging, reusing, measuring and opti-mizing the use of the organizational knowledge assets, a centralized knowledge server is required that will manage the communication and collaboration between *networks of people* as well as the creation and sharing of knowledge between them. This is supported to some extent by the integration of the Lotus Sametime commu-nication technology; furthermore, it leads to the creation of network-specific virtual collaboration spaces where people exchange explicit knowledge in discussion groups, shared libraries, etc.

To organize and facilitate this knowledge creation and exchange, a centralized knowledge server will manage the "*processes*" that generate and disseminate knowledge assets. Having installed the appropriate processes, the knowledge networks as key knowledge assets will continuously produce and manipulate knowledge objects. To create, retain, leverage, reuse, measure and optimize the use of the knowledge objects of the entire organization requires a centralized knowledge server will manage the "*content*" to:

● receive explicit knowledge objects from all business processes performed in the organization into a knowledge object store

- maintain and develop explicit knowledge objects in one central place, avoiding duplication and fragmentation of knowledge
- allow for enterprise-wide navigation, searching, filtering and dissemination of explicit knowledge objects.

The knowledge objects that are created by the knowledge assets, through key processes, are then automatically written directly into a knowledge objects store, which is based on an RDBMS. Whenever knowledge objects are created, edited, modified, developed or deleted in the key processes, they are automatically created, edited, modified, developed or deleted in the RDBMS. In other words, the knowledge objects are both embedded in the application documents and written to a relational engine.

Besides hosting of applications, provision of CSCW functionalities and storing the knowledge objects, it is also part of the knowledge server to hold all **metadata**, which are suited to support retrieval and reuse of a knowledge object. This issue is elaborated in Section 4.9 on the Know-Net Advanced Search Interface. At least, one can think about the following minimum set of metadata: (a) document title, (b) authors, (c) creation date, (d) date of last modification, (e) document short description, (f) status of the document, (g) lifetime of the document, (h) index categories.

4.5 The KM Applications

Underpinning every enterprise is a set of processes to per-form the business. Key business processes, for example, are typically the sales and marketing processes, the manufacturing and distribution processes, and the human development processes. Each of these business processes is typically automated, and many software applications perform these processes, e.g SAP, PeopleSoft. Much knowledge about how to perform the process and how to manage the information the process requires is embedded in the software application itself.

However, business processes not only contain the knowledge of performing the process, but also contain the knowledge to manage the information and *knowledge content*. The process manages and generates knowledge objects. A business process is, therefore, a key knowledge asset to be managed. Hence, the better the quality of business process design and automation, the better the quality of this knowledge asset and the knowledge objects generated.

Know-Net recognizes the importance of identifying and managing the knowledge assets and knowledge objects of an organization through high-quality and innovative process design and execution. To improve process design, the following generic KM process is embedded in it (Figure 4.4): perform a task or activity and learn from the experience; review the learnings and document them (capture and make explicit); develop new learnings into improved codified "best practices" and share them; and develop from "specific" cases of best practice the best knowledge, which is "generally" applicable.

The Know-Net tool embeds this KM process into the organization in two ways:

- At a high level learnings may be captured and entered into best practice databases contained within libraries of documents, which are freely configurable by the system administrator for specific knowledge networks and/or topics.

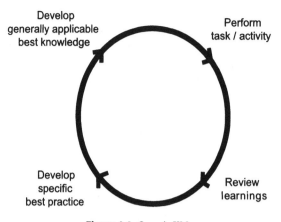

Figure 4.4 Generic KM process.

● The KM process can also be embedded within each business process application. For example, a normal bid management process would also become a KM-enhanced bid management process.

Further pursuing the second approach, one of the ideas behind the Know-Net applications library is to define and build gradually a library of "knowledge-enhanced" business processes, define them as knowledge assets, define the knowledge objects they create by executing the processes, and define measurements for both the knowledge assets and the knowledge objects.

Knowledger, a commercial KM tool developed by Knowledge Associates, is provided to the Know-Net tool as an optional initial set of business process applications developed to execute through web browsers. Over a period of time, other business process applications could be created and/or modified likewise to write their knowledge objects directly into the Know-Net knowledge object store and utilize the knowledge objects directly from the Know-Net knowledge objects store. The following Knowledger applications are available as plug-in modules to Know-Net:

● Knowledger.objectives: performs a process to capture, maintain and share the organization's values, vision, mission and objectives (part of the business planning and review process)

● Knowledger.contacts: performs a sales automation process, including client relationship tracking, proposals repository, presentations repository and sales focused discussions

● Knowledger.bidmanagement: embeds the KM process into an automated bid management process

● Knowledger.project: embeds the KM process into an automated project management system

● Knowledger.pdp: embeds the KM process into an automated personal learnings and competence management system

● Knowledger.ideas: embeds the KM process into an automated creativity and innovation system

- Knowledger.bestpractices: implements a best practices process (also integrated with Knowledger.pdp)
- Knowledger.bestknowledge: implements a best knowledge process
- Knowledger.capital: captures performance and intellectual capital measures, in a simple form, and analyzes them into human capital, structural capital and customer capital reports
- Knowledger.who'swho: a simple Who's Who directory in the organization
- Knowledger.discussion: a modified discussion template to allow dynamic creation and listing of multiple discussions
- Knowledger.libraries: a modified document libraries template to allow dynamic creation and listing of multiple libraries of documents

Furthermore, Know-Net can link any other Notes-based application to its navigators, including Lotus Team Room and Lotus Learning Space.

4.6 The Strategic Knowledge Navigator

The purpose of the Know-Net Strategic Knowledge Navigator (SKN) is to help the CKO or KM consultant doing the analysis and planning activities presented in the previous chapters for analyzing and developing the knowledge-based organization. To this end, a navigator was designed that, either in the sidebar navigation bar or via hotlinks in the graphical presentation of the Know-Net framework (see Figure 4.5), offers applications (or processes), which help to enact the several steps required. This help usually means that the system guides and documents this enactment by:

- the provision of *input forms* for the relevant information to be gathered, created or changed in this step. Filling in these forms leads to the automatic creation of corresponding knowledge objects (or, as a more concrete example, Lotus Notes documents) stored in the Know-Net knowledge server;
- provision of *structured views* on the knowledge objects already created, e.g. the list of knowledge objects describing the company's knowledge networks organized according to their scope (group, company, interorganizational);
- preparation for representing the main required *links and relationships* between the several elements of the framework and method, e.g. the input mask for KM processes offers the list of already represented knowledge objects as a pulldown menu, in order to specify which ones are created or modified by this process; or, when newly creating a knowledge asset there is a pulldown menu to link it to the respective knowledge asset type (market asset, people asset, etc.) to which it belongs. Figure 4.6 gives an overview of the several links and relationships represented in the Know-Net tool.

Going through the several steps of the Know-Net method, the following way of working is enabled. Stage I of the Know-Net method identifies at the highest level the key knowledge assets that need to be better managed in the organization. At this stage some basic ideas are captured into the Know-Net tool about how the knowledge assets are to be defined and measured. Stage II identifies and defines at the deeper level the key knowledge assets that need to be better managed in the organization. At this stage, detailed specifications are captured into the Know-Net

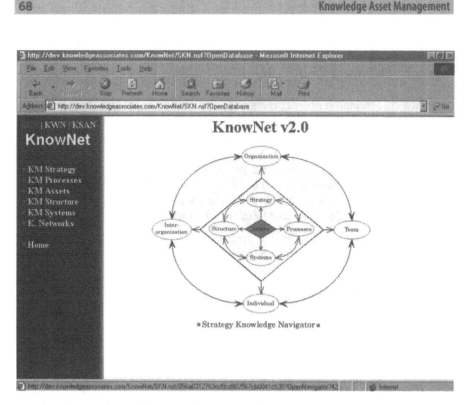

Figure 4.5 Strategic Knowledge Navigator.

tool about how the knowledge assets are to be defined and measured. Stage II also identifies the knowledge objects that are created by the knowledge assets and how they are to be defined and measured. The measurement part of the Know-Net method has the potential to integrate knowledge objects directly into the knowledge measurement system.

Table 4.1 summarizes the different kinds of elements, which can be modelled, organized, surveyed and modified via the respective KM applications accessible through the Know-Net SKN. Figure 4.6 gives an overview of the most important Knowledge Objects automatically created when working with the SKN for an organization analysis and KM planning, as well as the most important relationships between these knowledge objects established by the tool.

To give a better idea of the look and feel of the Know-Net tool, several working steps are documented with some screenshots. From the SKN the user may move to "KM Processes" and view the processes and applications to support the operative business processes; these are listed by their name or application code, by the knowledge objects they create or modify, or by the application category. In other words, these views enable the CKO or KM consultant to develop and maintain simple, but powerful, knowledge process maps and knowledge object maps. Figure 4.7 shows a listing of KM applications, sorted by category.

The KM Applications Library has been designed to be able to list all applications that exist in the organization regardless of their type and location (e.g. IBM Main-

Table 4.1 Tool support via the Strategic Knowledge Navigator

Know-Net method	Comments	Knowledge object created
Develop a KM Strategy and Objectives	Launch the "objectives" application to identify and store the KM vision, mission, values, principles, objectives and critical success factors, determined by the CKO and/or KM consultant	KM vision object KM mission object KM values object KM objectives objects: one per objective Critical success factors: one per CSF
Identify the KM processes	Launch an application to identify, list, manage and execute the KM processes/applications Library determined by the CKO and/or KM consultant	KM process object(s): one knowledge object per process entered
Identify the knowledge assets and knowledge objects	Define and map the knowledge assets critical to the business, and identify the knowledge object(s) the knowledge asset contains	Knowledge Asset object(s): one per asset Knowledge object definition(s): one per object
Determine the KM structure	Identify and list the KM people, roles and responsibilities critical to the KM project: the "KM team"	Person object(s): one per person entered
Determine the KM systems	Identify and describe the KM systems critical to the KM project	KM system object(s): one per system entered
Knowledge networking levels	Launch an application to identify, define and list the knowledge networks determined by the CKO and/or KM consultant	Knowledge network object(s): one per network entered

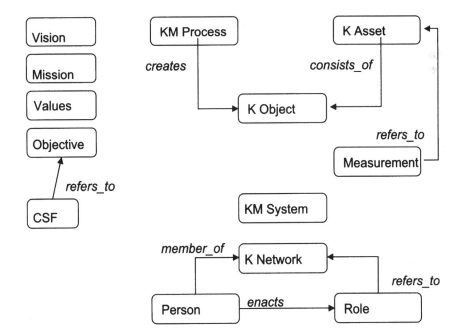

Figure 4.6 Relationships between knowledge objects created with the SKN.

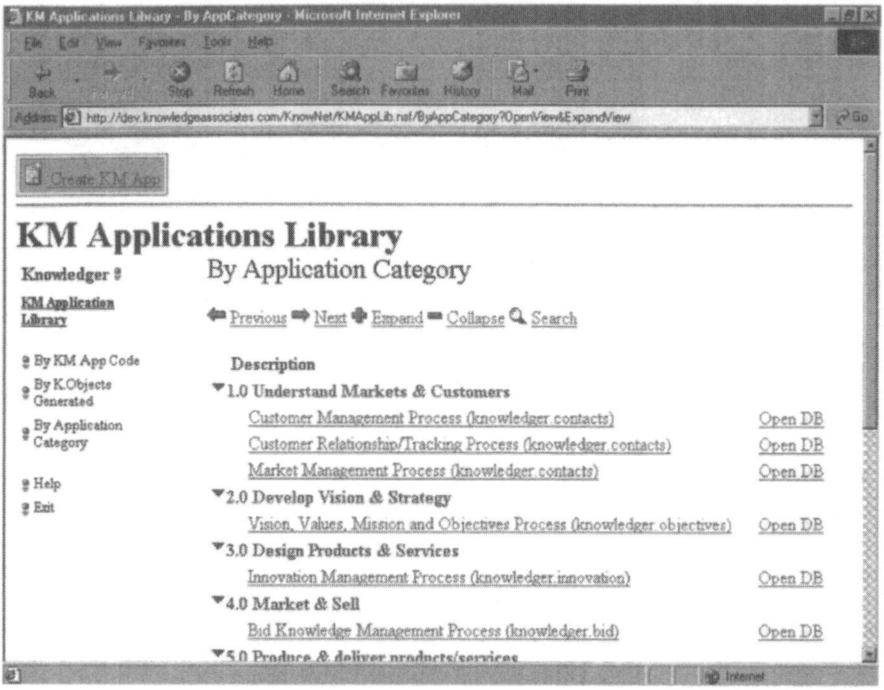

Figure 4.7 KM applications, sorted by category.

frame Sales Order Processing System written in COBOL) and categorize them, so that the CKO or KM consultant can consider the better integration, usage and implementation of all systems across the organization. Furthermore, the KM consultant can also add to the knowledge objects directory knowledge object descriptions that the non-Know-Net applications produce, to ensure even better knowledge asset management and reuse.

The next important entity in the Know-Net framework concerns knowledge assets. A knowledge asset can be composed of a knowledge object or a cluster of knowledge objects. Hence, the Know-Net tool provides means to define and map the knowledge assets critical to the business, and identify the knowledge object(s) that the knowledge asset contains. When creating a new knowledge asset with the appropriate input form, specified as belonging to one of the three types (Figure 4.8), it is also possible to create directly associated knowledge asset measurements.

4.7 The Knowledge Worker Navigator

For the daily work of a professional or knowledge worker the KWN was designed as a simple to use, pragmatic, highly relevant and highly practical navigator (Figure 4.9).

The main design goals for this navigator were:

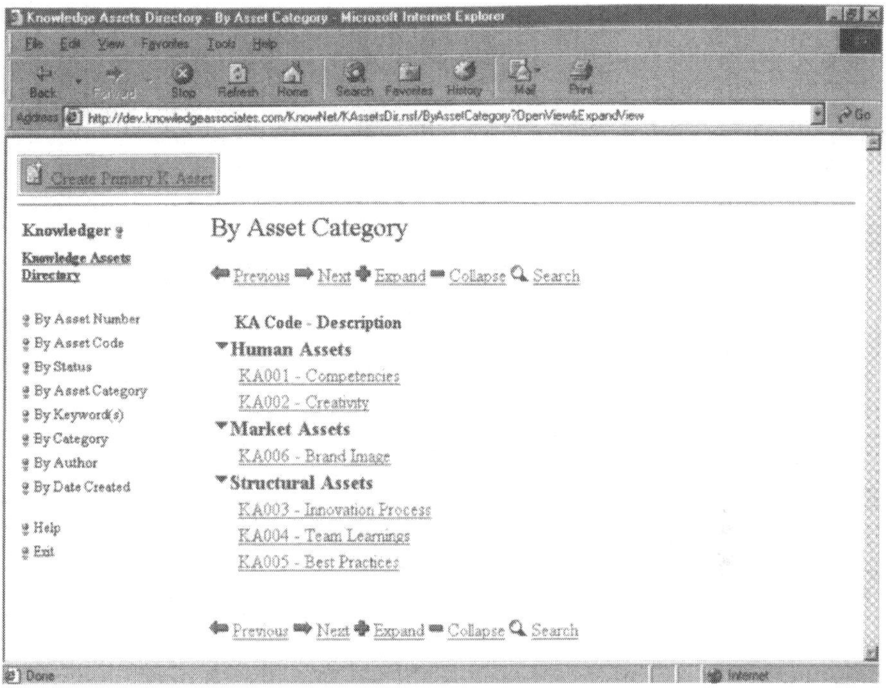

Figure 4.8 Listing of categorized knowledge assets.

- to give easy, powerful and precise access to *explicit knowledge* represented in stored knowledge objects, as well as comfortable means for creating and manipulating explicit knowledge objects. For this purpose, links are provided to discussion and library databases containing documents and discussion contributions, a powerful content-based document search engine was designed, new or changed documents are stored periodically to give a quick overview of what happened in the system, personally configured push services are offered, and all often used input forms are included in one place to make the system faster and easier to use;

- to foster and support frequent and easy access to *implicit knowledge,* knowledge sharing and joint knowledge creation via good communication channels between colleagues. To this end, the system includes a who's who catalogue of people in the organization, described with their respective knowledge areas, and the powerful Lotus Sametime technology for online communication and collaboration is linked into the Know-Net tool;

- to *seamlessly integrate "normal" work support and daily work activities with KM activities and tasks* in order to understand KM as a natural part of everyday work. To reach this goal, a "Projects Work Space" is included, an application that offers specific support for the tasks to be done when starting and running projects, and access is allowed to all applications in the "KM Processes Directory", for other specific business process support. Further, the indexing mechanism in the libraries and discussion databases allows the installation of project- or process-specific document databases.

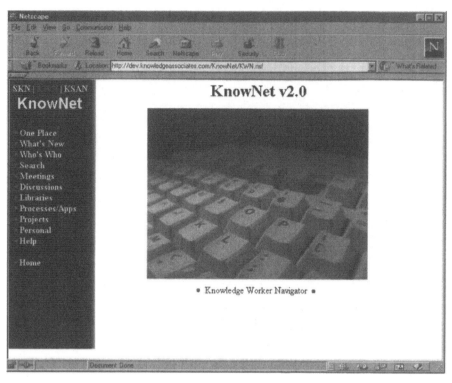

Figure 4.9 Knowledge Worker Navigator.

After this general introduction, we present the Know-Net KWN by going through the several options offered in the navigation sidebar.

4.7.1 One Place

Instead of forcing the knowledge worker to launch a specific application for entering contacts and organizations, to launch another application to enter tasks, project team members, details for a specific project, etc., and another application to enter a good idea, personal learning or a proposal, or to write a specific R&D report or White Paper, or to enter a timesheet, a diary appointment or a personal to-do list item, etc., the user can go to "**One Place**" only, to enter any new information into the system, with a maximum of two mouse clicks to receive the appropriate entry form. This reflects very well the typical style of working of a knowledge worker who is continually switching thoughts in his thinking from say, client/project work, to receiving new telephone calls, contacts and information. New ideas pop up at the least expected times during the day, and tasks are continually being changed and reprioritized. For this reason, **One Place** includes a list of links going to the most frequently used input forms. This list can be configured by the system administrator.

It is possible not only to launch Lotus Notes applications, but also to link arbitrary non-Notes applications into the system.

4.7.2 What's New

At present, many knowledge workers have to spend much time 'trawling' through databases to see whether new items of importance or relevance, and needing attention, have been added to the system. With the use of "What's New", knowledge workers can quickly ensure that they are fully informed and up to date because it provides daily links to all documents or knowledge objects that have recently been entered into the database.

Since it is also possible to mark documents as "mandatory readings", when a very important document is inserted into the system, it has to be decided whether to give an e-mail notification of all users affected *and* insert in the What's New database, or whether to give only an e-mail notification and insert in the What's New database only "non-essential" readings.

4.7.3 Who's Who

A primary function of a good KM system is to connect quickly and easily people to people who have the right knowledge. To assist the knowledge worker with this knowledge networking, a "Who's Who" database (or "Yellow Pages" system) has been developed, which contains details about people in the organization, their location, skills, contact information, etc. A simple search enables the knowledge worker more easily to find and connect to the right people and tacit knowledge. People may be viewed in the "Who's Who", for example, by surname and/or first name, by location or by skill type (e.g. Subject Matter Expert).

Giving the knowledge worker the responsibility to keep his or her personal details up to date, can significantly reduce costs compared with centralized maintenance of a "person/skills/telephone directory and databases" and the information will be *far more up to date*.

This Who's Who application has saved many organizations large amounts of time and money and, as the application is so simple to set up, has provided a "quick win" early on in the KM initiative. People have an opportunity to be better known and they can immediately benefit from better knowing "who knows what".

4.7.4 Search

By clicking on "Search", going to "**one place, to search across the Know-Net system and beyond**", the knowledge worker can quickly retrieve and list any documents on any item(s) used in the search criteria.

The current version of the Know-Net tool offers two links here. First, the "Full Text Search" option links directly to the Lotus Notes facilities to search for text or parts of text in any attribute of the document metadata or in some attachments. This is sufficient when such a simple text search is sufficient to find the desired document and when the document is managed by the Lotus Domino server. Second, if a complex search is expected because the user does not know concretely what they are really looking for, because there may be many possible answers, because we are not aware of a specific keyword definitely contained in the document text, or because the document is not within reach of the Domino server, the Know-Net Advanced Metadata Search Interface can be used. This is discussed in more detail in Section 4.9.

4.7.5 Meeting Space

Knowledge networking is also about connecting people to people in new and more powerful forms. A primary function of knowledge networking, performed in the daily work of the knowledge worker in the increasingly global knowledge-based economy, is to communicate and collaborate through **virtual meetings**. Know-Net is committed to the intranet and extranets as the primary media for communicating and collaborating. Virtual meetings, "same time – different place" via the Internet will become increasingly common and important.

The idea is to click on "**Meeting Space**", which then links directly to the Sametime Server. This lists, executes and manages all of the scheduled real-time virtual meetings through the Internet. Within a virtual real-time meeting, using the Sametime server the knowledge worker can:

- chat real-time, person to person and in groups;
- have real-time threaded discussions, for more focused, facilitated and contextual virtual meetings;
- use electronic white-boarding;
- share applications over the internet.

4.7.6 Discussions Space

The Know-Net tool has identified and integrated the equally important dimension of "different time – different place" virtual meetings, forums, discussions, etc. "**Discussions**" is a link to a list of all discussions taking place, in alphabetical order of discussion "description" or in user-defined "categories". A discussion database contains a series of discussion contributions, represented as text documents (e.g. e-mails), maybe with attachments, categorized according to topic-oriented subthreads of the discussion, or organized according to the nested argumentation structure (which entry answers to which other entry?).

4.7.7 Libraries Space

With the use of "**Libraries**", the knowledge worker is presented with a list of all the libraries of documents in Know-Net, listed in alphabetical order of library "description" or in user-defined "categories". A library database contains a collection of documents and knowledge objects (e.g. technical reports, project deliverables, technical documentation), categorized alphabetically, according to date or author, or by freely defined topical categories that may contain nested subcategories, etc.

Since the Know-Net navigators rely on standard Internet/intranet technologies, non-Notes libraries could also be included in this space for better enterprise-wide document management, as well as non-Notes Discussion spaces in the discussion directory described above.

4.7.8 KM Applications

The "**KM Applications**" space is entered by the knowledge worker to start an operational business process application, for example:

- launching a client tracking application to view all the latest visit meeting reports;
- launching a best practices application to examine how best to serve a client;
- launching a competences management application to view the overall status on personal competence development and examine personal development plans;
- launching an innovation management application to have a discussion about some good ideas and potential new products;
- launching a bid management application to examine competitor strengths and weaknesses.

In other words, this is the space that the knowledge worker enters to execute the application and perform the processes that represent and/or support his or her daily work.

4.7.9 Projects

The "**Projects**" link launches the **knowledger.projects** application from Knowledger which displays the "personal" project desktop, and manages the key aspects of project management, such as project mission and objectives, reports on project status, team members, project definition and scope management, exception reporting, action plans and task management.

4.7.10 Personal

The "**Personal**" submenu is used (1) to define personal search agents as active knowledge push services (see Section 4.9), and (2) to inspect the personal What's New space which is provided by these personal agents.

4.8 The Knowledge Systems Administrator Navigator

The Know-Net KSAN (Figure 4.10) has been developed as a technical navigator to help to maintain and evolve the KM technical infrastructure. Hence, it gives access to the main directories and entry forms already mentioned in the section on the Strategic Knowledge Navigator.

In particular, the following links can be found.

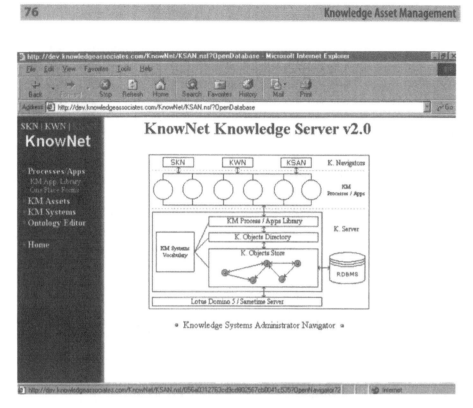

Figure 4.10 The Systems Administrator Navigator.

4.8.1 Processes/Applications

● **KM Applications Library:** the systems administrator can set up and link new software applications to the Know-Net navigator
● **One Place Forms:** the systems administrator can set up and link input forms from applications to the "One Place" navigator in the KWN.

4.8.1 KM Assets

● **K Assets Directory:** the systems administrator can view and maintain the list of knowledge assets that have been created.
● **K Objects Directory:** the systems administrator can view and maintain the list of knowledge objects that have been created.
● **K Objects Store:** this link goes to the administration of the RDBMS underlying the Knowledge Objects Store.

4.8.3 KM Systems

This is an overview listing of the components of technology in the KM system, as initially defined by the KM consultant in the method stages I and II, for the systems administrator to view and maintain.

4.8.4 Ontology Editor

This launches the Know-Net Ontology Editor, a tool for defining the metadata schema and the associated indexing ontologies used for the content-oriented search and indexing. This editor will be discussed later, in the context of the Know-Net Advanced Search Interface (KASI).

Concerning further administration requirements, Lotus Notes has inbuilt functionality to perform the necessary storage administration, archiving and import/export of documents as required for the Know-Net knowledge server.

4.9 The Advanced Search Interface

4.9.1 Basics of the Know-Net Content-centric Approach

For a comprehensive IT infrastructure for KM to give access to the whole wealth of explicit knowledge in an organization, it has to face many aspects of heterogeneity: different versions and multiple storage formats of the same content; geographically dispersed information about the same topic, due to the internationalization of business; organizationally dispersed knowledge about the same topic, due to the division of labour in different departments which may maintain their local organizational memory systems with their specific focus and viewpoints; and logically dispersed information about the same topic, spread over different tools and applications which may deal with new ideas, business bids and proposals, discussion statements, best practices, lessons learned, tips and tricks, project reports, scientific insights, technical documentation, etc.

In order to deal with these manifold dimensions of heterogeneity, the Know-Net content-centric approach is based on two design decisions:

First, a decision was made to rely on the Lotus Notes infrastructure which is capable of storing and managing the usual document types as attachments, replicate them for offline working, support full text search in the attachments, give a URL to each document and enable the basic network services via the Domino server, and host the metadata required without changing the original document. So, the system can easily deal with issues concerning document versioning and multiple storage formats (MS Office formats, PDF, etc.).

In the best case, after introducing the Know-Net system in an organization, the knowledge workers would shift their way of working as far as possible towards working in the integrated, Lotus Notes-based Know-Net tool environment. Maximum benefit is obtained by accepting the philosophy of the tool suite and going over to the collaboration-oriented, networked style of working, in each step settling upon the integrated tool.

Nevertheless, in some situations, you will have to live with external or legacy software solutions. Moreover, Lotus Notes in the current status does not provide the most flexible way of indexing and search facilities needed to cope with the abovementioned phenomenon of knowledge dispersion. So, the second decision was to couple the powerful Lotus Notes-based basic technology with an independent metadata-based annotation and retrieval tool. This is described below.

Comprehensive Metadata Modelling for Knowledge Object Annotation

The KASI aims at a uniform, homogeneous, ergonomically designed and easy to use knowledge portal harmonizing the heterogeneity of representation and storage. To this end, a comprehensive model is proposed, comprising all dimensions of metadata relevant to describe a document or knowledge object, which includes in particular the conceptual structures logically organizing the document content. Based on these metadata, a mixed browsing–searching approach is offered over all underlying information repositories, which are accessible via a uniform search interface.

There is no definite answer as to which metadata should be provided for document description and annotation. Standardization efforts are coming from the digital library community (e.g. the Dublin Core initiative), as well as specific answers tailored for the KM domain (van Heijst et al., 1998; Kingston and Macintosh, 1999; Abecker et al., 1998a). Since no "ultimate solution" is to be expected, the Know-Net system is configurable in the sense that the complete metadata schema can be defined in the **Know-Net Ontology Editor**, described below.

For Notes databases, such metadata are already contained in the documents. For most other document management systems this information is easily available as well, though accessible by other mechanisms. For some other information sources, e.g. company external information providers, such attributes might not be applicable or available.

Further, it makes sense to have some *contextual metadata*, i.e. in which process or context has a document been created? Within the Know-Net tool, such contextual information can mainly be derived from the Lotus Notes database (created by a specific KM application) in which the document is stored. Consequently, this information should be available at the search interface.

The most important question is about the *content of the document*, i.e. the topic(s) it deals with. Graphical representations of concept or topic maps may be built reflecting multiple views and facets of the domain and content of work. These structures can be used for conceptual indexing of documents and for graphically specifying search conditions when querying the system. These concept maps are called index ontologies because they represent important ontological structures underlying the users' work. O'Leary (1998) identified the ontological structures used by the big international consulting companies to organize their KM systems. The industry of the customer (automotive, chemical industry, etc.), the process to be improved (customer relationship management, new product development, etc.), and the tools and methods applied, are examples of the ontological dimensions used to index best practices there. A similar approach for indexing ontologies for categorizing each knowledge object was followed in the Know-Net system (see Section D.4, Development of the Knowledge Ontology, in Appendix D).

4.9.2 Elements of the Know-Net Advanced Search Solution

Figure 4.11 gives a rough, schematic overview of the software architecture behind the Know-Net ontology-based indexing and retrieval approach.

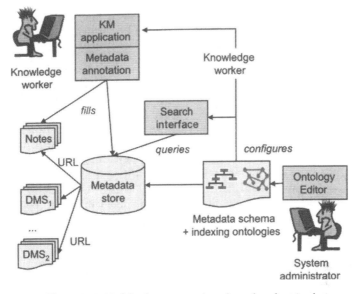

Figure 4.11 Modules for content-oriented search and retrieval.

The whole approach is based on a freely configurable metadata schema defined with the Know-Net Ontology Editor. Here, one can specify a simple hierarchical schema of metadata to be attached to each document for later retrieval. When specifying the ranges of allowed values for a metadata attribute, not only is provision made for simple data types such as strings, dates or enumeration types, but also there is the opportunity to describe the set of possible attribute values by a graphically denoted model of some domain ontology structure. The result of this metadata definition is then used for three purposes.

The first use is the database schema describing allowed instances of document descriptions in the annotated document database which is a part of the Know-Net knowledge server. This database contains an entry for each document or knowledge object, which specifies its metadata values and contains a link (the URL) to the original document source. Currently, it relies completely on the Lotus Domino server for holding documents, but technically it is no problem to link arbitrary document management systems into the metadata management, provided the single documents are accessible via a URL.

Second, the metadata schema is used to configure the user input forms for documents and knowledge objects. Normally, such an input interface could be dynamically created depending on the current metadata schema and indexing ontologies. However, since the current version of the tool already has a powerful enough backbone with the Lotus Domino server, without additional external sources, and since the overall metadata schema usually remains quite stable at the top level, which describes what attributes are used, it is sufficient to have a fixed input mask in Lotus Notes which provides the metadata structure. This input mask then links into the dynamically generated index ontology visualizations, which are more often changed.

The third use of the metadata schema and indexing ontologies is the dynamic generation of the KASI, which allows users to browse through the metadata schema and specify their information needs step by step by articulating search constraints (i.e. metadata attribute values required for a relevant document or knowledge object) graphically in a point-and-click way of working.

While the user is specifying their information needs going through the metadata schema, each interface activity is directly handed over to the underlying search mechanism, which immediately updates the current result set corresponding to the actual information needs description. This *incremental update of retrieval results* allows for intertwining of the direct interaction with the documents considered (which can be opened for reading and editing in separate browser windows while the search goes on in another window) and the further specification of refined (in the case that document metadata or document source inspection of currently retrieved documents shows that the information need must be specified more specifically or in a slightly different way) or other, derived information needs (e.g. when the documents retrieved and read show that there are other topics that should also be considered).

The three main interface elements of this solution (Document Indexing Interface, Advanced Search Interface and the Ontology Editor) are discussed in more detail in the following sections.

4.9.3 The Document Indexing Interface

Since the main aim of this tool development is to integrate seamlessly the process view and the product view to KM support, the content-oriented indexing is directly integrated into the input forms of the Lotus Notes-based KM processes provided by the Know-Net KWN. This means, for example, that each document input form of a discussion or a library database as shown in Figure 4.12 contains not only the standard metadata input fields, e.g. for a short document description, but also additional fields for the metadata attributes holding graphically denoted index categories. In the current example, there is only one such metadata attribute, namely the Index-Categories field. For each such attribute, which has been provided with a concept map (also called indexing ontology, domain ontology or topic map), when defining the metadata schema, a link called "choose" has been added to the right of the input field. Clicking on this link opens the appropriate concept map as a clickable GIF image, as shown in Figure 4.12.

Clicking left on a concept in the window automatically inserts the respective index concept into the attribute field; deselecting a concept by clicking again removes it from the list of index terms. The example shows the indexing dimensions used in the knowledge object server of the Know-Net research project, namely the tangible "products" to be delivered by the project, the "document status" (draft, final, approved), the "content type" (idea, discussion entry, project deliverable, etc.), the "work-package" that a document is related to, "administrative" issues that the knowledge object is possibly related to (e.g. project contract, cost statements, intellectual property right agreement), "meetings" that a document or presentation relates to, and finally "external inputs" to the project that a knowledge object could come from (e.g. other research groups, relevant related work, basic technologies). The six dimensions currently not visible are accessible via the links at the top of the

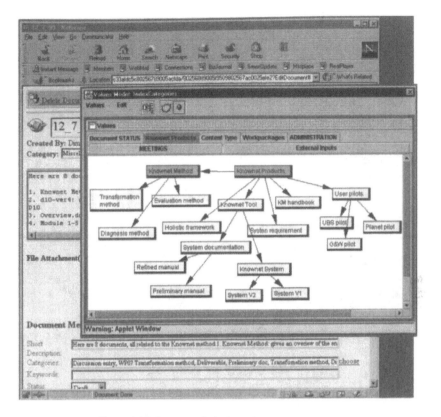

Figure 4.12 Document indexing using concept maps.

selection window. Often a knowledge object can be indexed with respect to several of these dimensions, which allows flexible usage of the tool and powerful search facilities.

4.9.4 The Advanced Search Interface

When the KASI is entered from any other navigator via the "Search" button, the user will reach a screen as shown in Figure 4.13. Basically, the screen is divided into three main areas. The upper part (region 1) contains control elements. The middle part (region 2 and 3) allows the user to specify their information needs graphically. The lower part (region 4) displays query results and other output streams if wished.

To ease the problems coming from complex, maybe underspecified or not initially fully specified searches in heterogeneous, big information spaces, three main ideas underlie the KASI search application: the metadata schema is browsable; attribute value models can be denoted for indexing and for querying in a graphical manner, which exploits people's ability to remember and deal with visual structures; and each user action gives immediate feedback in the result panel, thus a supporting sort of "iterative refinement" search.

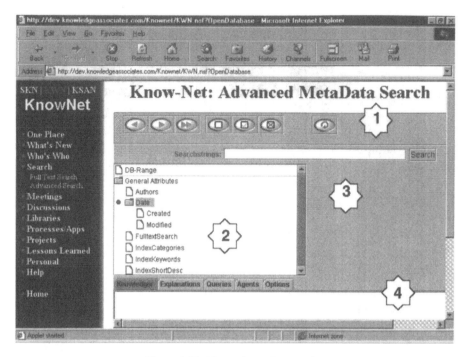

Figure 4.13 Advanced metadata search.

These ideas are reflected in the KASI as follows (Figure 4.13). First, in the interface region (2) the metadata schema is presented in a folder-like manner which can be folded and unfolded to reach the metadata attribute that the user wants to use to express an information need. If there is a large metadata schema which is difficult to oversee and uncomfortable to navigate, or the user does not know exactly which part of the metadata must be looked at in detail, the three buttons at the left of the navigation bar (1) can be used to unfold or fold together the whole folder tree level by level, or to unfold it completely with one click.

Another aid to navigation in the metadata schema is the text search field included in the control and navigation bar (1). Here, the user can type in an arbitrary string and if there is a metadata attribute or any possible value of some attribute containing this string, the metadata schema tree is opened up to this attribute, and the range of values of this attribute is shown on the right-hand side (3). Having found the appropriate metadata attribute in the schema, it can be marked by either clicking to select, clicking again to deselect, or using buttons in the control bar.

The interface region (3) on the right-hand side displays the possible values allowed for the attribute selected on the left-hand side. Having selected an attribute in the schema in panel (2) as interesting for characterizing the actual information need, the specific search condition can be formulated here. Three types of metadata attributes are available: date – the usual search conditions for dates can be expressed via pulldown menus; value lists – attributes the range of which has been declared as a value list are presented as lists with clickboxes (the "Authors" attribute in Figure 4.14); and index maps – some attributes can be graphically displayed by

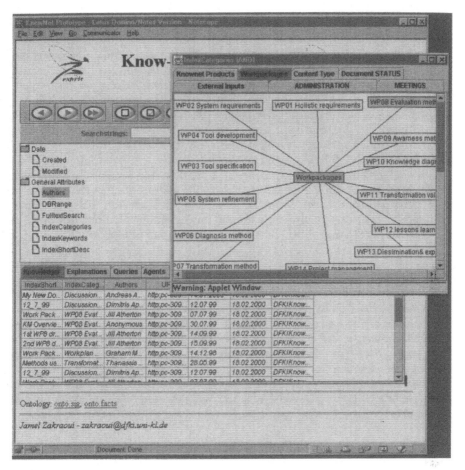

Figure 4.14 Use of the KASI.

clickable maps if they have been so defined during ontology building (the "Index-Categories" attribute).

The answer set resulting from the current query is always displayed in panel (3), in the lower part of the system interface (Figure 4.13). The other functionalities of this part (3) concern tool inspection and debugging and are less relevant in the context of this book.

4.9.5 Creating Personal Search Agents with KASI

A further service offered by the Know-Net platform is to define personal push agents that periodically (e.g. every hour, once a day, once a week) execute complex queries and actively deliver the search results to the user, by e-mail or in a "Personal What's New" space. To this end, the user enters his "Personal Agents Space", authenticates himself, specifies a search condition as discussed above, and then saves this query with a name, a timing condition and a delivery mode. Two important concepts underlie the push agents approach:

- *Two delivery modes*: as already mentioned, one possibility is to send an e-mail to the user whenever a push agent delivers new or modified information. In the case that this is not desired (e.g. because the push agents perform no very urgent searches, and the user just wants to check from time to time what happened in a specific area), the results are added to the list maintained in a personal "What's New" page. As the user reads the documents there, he can mark them to be removed for the next time he enters this personal web space.
- *Private and public queries*: since specifying the "right query" for a complex problem may be difficult, but interesting for more than one person in a knowledge network, queries can be marked 'public'. Public queries stand at the disposal of all users registered in the system for subscribing their services. The mechanism of public queries can also be used for implementing requirements such as "mandatory readings" which must be considered by all employees.

4.9.6 The Know-Net Ontology Editor

The Know-Net tool allows the system administrator to design and change the *metadata schema*, which describes the attributes and their respective value ranges that are used to annotate and index documents. These metadata attributes may not only have simple data types as their value range, but also hold graphically specified, ontology-based indices for describing document content from multiple viewpoints. The tool output is used to determine the outfit of the search interface, i.e. which metadata attributes are presented how, and holds the graphical representations of indexing ontologies (concept maps) for document categorization (Figure 4.15).

4.10 Summary and Related Work

In this chapter has presented the Know-Net software tool. This section summarizes some of the tool's most important features and compares them with related efforts of other researchers in the KM field.

The tool supports the Know-Net holistic framework and method for analyzing, planning, operating and evaluating the knowledge networks in an organization. Such a tool-supported method is quite unique in the KM area. Some examples of research in this area include the GPO-WM method by Fraunhofer IPK, which is based on comprehensive enterprise and process modelling (Mertins et al., 2000), the KODA method by IMS GmbH, which is based on a communication-oriented business-process analysis (Abecker et al., 2002), and the knowledge-oriented part of the ARIS business-process modeling method (Scheer, 2000). These efforts provide some tool-supported analysis and modelling. However, they tend to start with business processes, not with a dedicated KM strategy. Further, these approaches do not provide a link to KM measurement. The CommonKADS enterprise and knowledge analysis method (Schreiber, 1999) can be used together with UML modelling tools and simple template-based analysis support, but this approach is rather oriented towards business-process automation and support, e.g. in the best case an improved

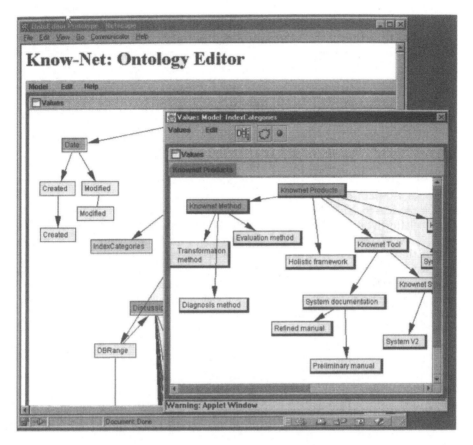

Figure 4.15 Sample screenshot of the Know-Net Ontology Editor.

information logistics, not so much embedding of KM processes into the business processes, and not the soft factors and non-technology issues of KM. All approaches focus mainly on business processes, which is not a bad idea, but they tend to neglect other areas, especially project work and process-independent knowledge networks in the company.

The installation and usage of the Know-Net tool is supported by the Know-Net method since the several browsers, applications and preinstalled libraries show the way to work optimally with the Know-Net tool. The above-mentioned business-process oriented methods also lead sometimes to implications for tool usage (e.g. GPO-WM offers best practice hints for specific business processes, ARIS helps to introduce workflow systems or the Hyperwave content management and portal technology). Recent research projects on business process-oriented KM, such as DECOR (Abecker and Mentzas, 2001), also pursue the goal of method-guided intro-duction of KM activities into business processes as well as the introduction of process-oriented content archives. However, they tend to neglect human factors, measurement and process-oriented knowledge. Hence these approaches are exten-sions in a specific direction rather than competitors of Know-Net.

A second unique feature of the Know-Net tool is that it supports the integration of process-oriented and product-oriented aspects of KM. This is done by the integration of communication- and collaboration-oriented technologies in one virtual space with the document- and knowledge object-centred approaches. This is supported by the KM applications, which stimulate the creation of explicit knowledge objects for best practices and best knowledge, such that knowledge objects can act as the common denominator between process view and product view. The software development was based on Lotus Domino for handling knowledge objects application development, providing intranet services and web hosting. The Lotus Sametime technology was integrated for giving comfortable communication and collaboration support. However, ideas like the ones presented in this book are not necessarily be based on the Know-Net tool, or even on Lotus software. Other commercial products such as Microsoft Net meeting or the ICQ free communication server provide similar services to Sametime. Moreover, commercial groupware products such as the BSCW platform or public domain products such as the Zope open source web application server (see http://www.zope.org) provide similar functionalities. It is important on the one hand to abstract from low-level software tasks such as file handling, user access rights, versioning, basic communication facilities, data security and mass storage, and also more difficult technical questions such as dealing with file attachments in different formats; and on the other hand to have a platform which allows the content-oriented and the process-oriented aspects to be integrated seamlessly.

A third unique feature of the Know-Net tool is the integration of KM-related applications to embed the generic knowledge creation process directly into the end user applications which, in turn, determine the knowledge workers' daily work, thus fulfilling one of the most important requirements, namely seamless integration with daily work and non-intrusive knowledge acquisition (Kühn and Abecker, 1997). This set of KM-enhanced applications is, to the authors' knowledge, not provided by other tools, although many of the basic applications (Yellow Pages, personal knowledge development plans, virtual group collaboration spaces, etc.) exist in abundance. Here the power really comes from the integration by settling upon the same software basis and working on the same knowledge objects, which also offers many extension possibilities for the future by deeper mutual integration of different applications.

The fourth unique characteristic of Know-Net refers to the ontology-based indexing and retrieval approach. Its uniqueness relates to its flexibility, power for complex search problems and extensibility for more intelligent search algorithms using, e.g. query expansion techniques (McGuinness, 1998; Guarino, et al., 1999). However, it is still at the experimental stage. Questions concerning the effort for manual indexing or roles and responsibilities for ontology creation and maintenance are subject to ongoing research. This work goes in the direction of: (1) ontology creation driven by process analysis (e.g. in projects such as PROMOTE, Karagiannis and Telesko, 2000; DECOR, Abecker et al., 2001a; or KDE, Jansweijer et al., 2000); (2) ontology creation supported by text analysis and machine learning (Staab et al., 2000); or (3) automatic classification of text documents in order to widen the metadata annotation bottleneck (Mladenic, 1999; Aas and Eikvil, 1999).

Figure 4.16 gives an overview of how the different elements of the Know-Net tool contribute to the several kinds of knowledge transfer in an organization.

Today's well-developed KM tools usually are very comfortable, web-enabled content management systems dealing with many types of document storage format,

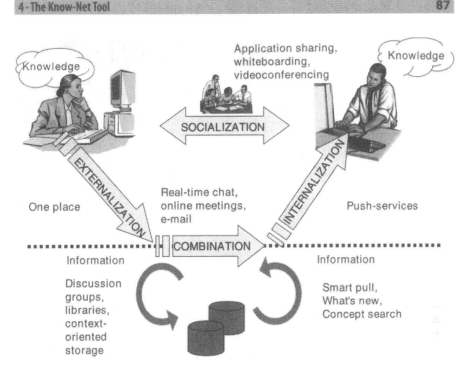

Figure 4.16 The Know-Net tool services support for the conversion modes.

often coupled with some agent technology for personalized push services and automated Internet search, and usually with sophisticated algorithms for extracting semantic content from text documents to allow for high-precision information retrieval. These products offer excellent services for what they promise, e.g. portals, content management or text mining. In this sense they could to some extent replace the Know-Net content-centric developments. However, they almost never offer the higher-level value-added services, which are at the core of the Know-Net approach: the KM-enhanced business process applications and the deep integration of process and product view.

To conclude, although words such as organizational KM vision, KM strategy and KM objectives are used throughout, they can equally refer to a team KM vision and objectives, a departmental KM vision and objectives, or a pilot KM vision and objectives. Furthermore, reference at the organizational level to a chief knowledge officer or director of knowledge management may not be appropriate to a team KM initiative, but the principles and responsibilities behind these new KM roles would still apply at any level, albeit to a lesser degree. In addition, the Know-Net tool approach equally applies to the personal, the team, the organizational and the interorganizational levels of knowledge networking.

5 Case Studies of the Know-Net Solution

5.1 Introduction

The applicability of the Know-Net knowledge management (KM) solution was tested in organizations that exhibit a high degree of knowledge utilization in their operations: knowledge-intensive organizations (KIOs). The term knowledge-intensive organizations has been recently introduced and reflects mainly the emergence of the post-industrial, knowledge economy, in which the traditional distinction between "manufacturing" and "services" is blurred, and where the role played by manufacturing is steadily being fused with new service industries and service professions. KIOs have the following characteristics: they are networked organizations, they are customer adapted and their most critical asset is their people.

The networked corporation is an idea that has arisen from the notion that the business environment has fundamentally changed from a straight competitive model based on price and economies of scale, to a new competitive environment based on knowledge, joint ventures, scope and scale of production, rapid technological development and increasing returns to scale. This change is spurring massive organizational changes, flattening hierarchies and opening them up, with team based rather than individual work, learning organizations and knowledge-based structures (see e.g. Tapscott and Caston, 1993, who have mapped this transformation to the networked corporation) (Table 5.1).

Table 5.1 Features of networked organizations (Tapscott and Caston, 1993)

	Closed hierarchy	Open networked Organization
Structure	Hierarchical	Networked
Scope	Internal/closed	External/open
Resource focus	Capital	Human, information
State	Static, stable	Dynamic, changing
Personnel/focus	Managers	Professionals
Key drivers	Reward and punishment	Commitment
Direction	Management commands	Self-management
Basis of action	Control	Empowerment to act
Individual motivation	Satisfy superiors	Achieve team goals
Learning	Specific skills	Broader competencies
Basis for compensation	Position in hierarchy	Accomplishment, competence level
Relationships	Competitive (my turf)	Cooperative (our challenge)
Employee attitude	Detachment (it's a job)	Identification (it's my company)
Dominant requirements	Sound management	Leadership

Figure 5.1 Customer adaptation. (Based on Sveiby, 1997b.)

Customer adaptation is a significant feature of KIOs (Figure 5.1) (Sveiby, 1992, 1997b). In companies that exhibit low levels of customer adaptation, the business logic is based on efficient, industrialized, preprogrammed production aimed at a mass market. The McDonald's fast-food chain exemplifies this type, where even the smile one gets as a customer is "preprogrammed" in the employee's manual. In contrast, in companies that exhibit high levels of customer adaptation, "service" provision emerges as an ongoing process of problem solving between the customers and teams of experts. They therefore have to treat their customers as individuals. Because the knowledge organization cannot force its customers to adapt to it, it must perforce adapt to them.

Provision of services in KIOs is related to solving problems that are hard to tackle in a standardized manner. People in KIOs have specific, service-delivery competencies, and they are highly educated, with long experience in a profession that often involves processing of information (Table 5.2). The business logic depends on how the managers of KIOs regard their assets, their key people and their customers, how they attract them and how they match their capacity for problem solving with the needs of the customers.

KIOs can be defined as organizations in which the products are intangible. They consist not of goods or services, but of complex, non-standardized problem solving; the end results usually consist of reports or processes delivered either orally or as hard copies. The production process of KIOs is non-standardized and highly dependent on teamwork, while the majority of their employees are highly educated and creative people. The customers of KIOs are treated individually and the products are adapted to them, rather than vice versa. Examples of such companies include advertising, management consulting, financial or legal advice, specialist nursing care, software programming and systems design.

Table 5.2 Principles of the knowledge organization (Sveiby, 1997b)

Item	The industrial perspective	The knowledge perspective
People	Cost generators or resources	Revenue generators
Managers' power base	Relative levels in organization's hierarchy	Relative level of knowledge
Main task of management	Supervising subordinates	Supporting colleagues
Information	Control instrument	Tool for communication
Production	Physical labour processing physical resources to create tangible products	Knowledge workers converting knowledge into intangible structures
Information flow	Via organizational hierarchy	Via collegial networks
Primary form of revenues	Tangible (money)	Intangible (learning, new ideas, new customers, R&D)
Production bottlenecks	Financial capital and human skills	Time and knowledge
Production flow	Machine-driven, sequential	Idea-driven, chaotic
Effect of size	Economy of scale in production	Economy of scope of networks
Customer relations	One-way via markets	Interactive via personal networks
Purpose of learning	Application of new tools	Creation of new assets
Economy	Of diminishing returns	Of both increasing and diminishing returns

This and the following chapter cover the application of the Know-Net KM approach in five KIOs: this chapter presents the application of Know-Net in four information technology (IT) service companies (Delta-Singular, AlphaNova, Debus I.T. and MDA), while Chapter 6 gives a detailed overview of the implementation of Know-Net in a management consulting company (Planet). The case of Planet covers the application of all aspects of the Know-Net methodology and aims to be a full example of the approach, while the four cases presented in this chapter highlight how the methodology has addressed specific but diverse KM undertakings in companies of the same industry sector.

5.2 Case Summaries of the Know-Net Application in IT Service Companies

In the following a brief description of Know-Net implementations in four companies is presented: Delta-Singular, MDA, AlphaNova and Debus I.T. These service companies experience the increased competitiveness and dynamism of their sector. Their objective was to undertake KM initiatives at the business unit, function or operational process level where they expected to have the most immediate impact on their performance. Within this context, the application of the Know-Net solution in each of the four companies focused on a specific area of the software development cycle, either in customized software projects or in the development of packaged software solutions (Figure 5.2).

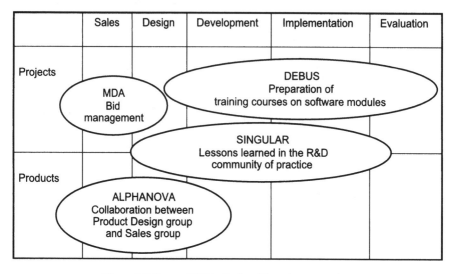

Figure 5.2 Focus of KM in the four IT service companies.

5.2.1 Debus I.T.

Debus I.T. specializes in the development, customization and training of Enterprise Resource Planning software and systems. It is a Czech company with Dutch management and investment. The specialist nature of the company's business requires that it gathers technical, marketing and other commercial information from diverse sources, to reconfigure and reuse that information for commercial and competitive advantage. Debus I.T. has acknowledged as critical factors for future success the potential ability to speed up the development and related cycle times through the application of KM principles. To do so there was a need for improved communication and collaboration between Debus I.T. and its customers and improved quality of Debus I.T. training courses.

The KM solution created and applied at Debus I.T. consisted of a number of interacting elements, all of which have been applied to the area of creating customized training courses. Debus had as its major objectives the ability to improve its communication and collaboration, and to reduce the cycle times associated with the delivery of customized training courses. This has been achieved through the following.

● The effective use of the contacts database has enabled the company to log key skills, knowledge and competencies.

● The application of ideas capture and management has enabled the company to aggregate critical skills and knowledge, leading to the creation of best practices and best knowledge databases, thereby leading to the reuse of knowledge.

● The knowledge asset measurement techniques incorporated within Know-Net allowed Debus I.T. to appreciate the value of its KM initiatives.

A distinct marketing advantage was gained through the use and application of various Know-Net components, as Debus I.T. has the potential to deliver better quality client/business solutions through the ability to access and evaluate a greater number of technical options, and the ability to access information from a wider and more diverse range of sources. Furthermore, the ability to integrate existing databases, marketing and sales records and information has been critical. Through having a central repository of marketing and sales intelligence the company is able to lever the business generation process.

Solution Highlight: Introducing KM to the Company

By applying the strategic planning stage of the Know-Net method a strong business case was developed to support and define the KM strategy for Debus I.T. The key to implementing KM successfully in Debus was to ensure that the KM strategy was able to manage knowledge to enhance product and service capability. Debus I.T. realized that as a consultancy/development company, it is driven by continuous market requests for technology and business knowledge. This knowledge is very dynamic, diverse and constantly expanding, therefore there was a clear need for a mechanism to collect, retrieve and share knowledge throughout the whole company.

- *Leadership.* Debus I.T. has successfully gained leadership support for the KM initiative. Management were educated of the need and the benefits of KM to gain buy-in from the top, before being presented at a company level. An initiation team, consisting of members from different departments, was created to introduce the KM solution and methodology to the rest of the company. The focus of these meetings and presentations was to ensure that all employees gained a clear understanding of the KM concepts and how KM could be integrated into their daily work. Gaining leadership support at this early stage gave the implementation of the KM initiative a smoother transition and made it more acceptable to the company.
- *Link KM strategy with corporate strategy.* Taking into account Debus I.T.'s mission to be both a technology- and consultancy-oriented company, and its objective to remain profitable in the emerging markets of central and eastern Europe, it is vital that it can constantly provide valuable solutions to meet market needs, and a KM strategy needs to be developed in line with this. Based on this, the critical success factors (CSFs) of the company have been identified as: recruitment and retention of the right people, business generation, new product development and management of technical knowledge.
- *Perform knowledge analysis.* A knowledge orientation analysis was undertaken and the results are shown in Table 5.3. The knowledge orientation matrix shows that Debus I.T. was quite knowledge aware in terms of KM. They had management support, a knowledge-sharing culture and some means to gauge how KM benefits the company. In terms of infrastructure, some level of strategy, processes and systems existed; however, there were no clear roles and responsibilities defined within the company to support these. The company as a whole was accustomed to sharing knowledge not just at an individual or a team level, but also at an organizational level.
- *Assess risk and change readiness.* As a company, Debus I.T. was not resistant to change and realized that to smooth the path to implementing KM, good

Table 5.3 Knowledge orientation matrix for Debus I.T.

	Still at base camp	Knowledge aware	Knowledge leveraging
Critical success factors			
Awareness		✓	
Senior management buy-in		✓	
Knowledge sharing culture			✓
Measures to gauge KM benefits		✓	
Incentives and rewards for knowledge sharing	✓		
KM infrastructure			
Strategy		✓	
Processes		✓	
Structure	✓		
Systems		✓	
Knowledge networking levels			
Individual		✓	
Team		✓	
Organizational		✓	
Inter–organizational	✓		

preparation for the base of change was required to improve and build upon the existing processes, rather than going for a radical change. To introduce and smooth the implementation of KM a gradual process of change was undertaken, through education, by gaining acceptance first from management, then from the project/department leaders. Once these people were on board, it was rolled out to the company staff. Debus I.T. continuously conducted education sessions for the whole company throughout the implementation stage. The change was also made more acceptable as Debus I.T. involved the whole company in KM and it was introduced almost simultaneously to all company staff. It was identified that KM would affect the majority of people within the company, due to its impact on existing information flow and processes. Debus I.T. ensured that any impact would be minimized through management support and training.

By applying stage I of the KM method to Debus I.T., a strong business case was put forward to senior management for the need for KM. In particular, it focused on the need to improve the existing tools and techniques, and on initiatives to improve the existing business processes.

5.2.2 Delta-Singular

Delta-Singular specializes in standardized business software covering market requirements in financial, accounting, distribution, logistics, retail, human resource management and e-commerce systems. In addition, the company provides solutions integration in large-scale projects for public utilities, telecommunication, aerospace and defence, transportation and public administration organizations. The company operates in all markets of southern and eastern Europe, the Middle East and Asia.

One of the most valuable commodities for Delta-Singular is the knowledge created within the R&D unit. The innovation originating from the R&D unit drives to a high degree the evolution of the company's products and services. Members of the

R&D unit as well as other employees from other units of the company form communities of practice (CoPs) that are formed dynamically to resolve specific technical problems. There was a need to develop a strategy for learning from the team experience, and to organize the knowledge created in a methodological manner. The challenge was to realize effective mechanisms for KM without imposing on these highly dynamic, highly creative teams. The technical infrastructure had to be highly dynamic and adaptable, integrating with existing systems and information repositories.

The solution focused on CoPs as a collaborative structure that facilitates the creation and transfer of knowledge. The project not only addressed the creation of new CoPs from the ground up but also it built on existing, informal, working networks. New roles, such as subject experts, have been assigned to take responsibility for providing expert opinion and identifying the knowledge assets stemming from the common effort. Mechanisms for information collection during the lifetime of the CoP were put in place, ensuring quality and consistent documentation of knowledge. These mechanisms provided for knowledge transparency, i.e. the ability to reuse knowledge identified in a specific project to other projects. Furthermore, the R&D unit put in place mechanisms and regulations for reviewing knowledge so that ageing knowledge items are collected and disposed of. The Know-Net methodology was used to support the launch of viable communities, the creation of relevant knowledge bases, and the provision of "care and feeding" for the communities' growth.

The Know-Net intranet-based KM tool facilitated CoP members' virtual collaboration. In particular, Know-Net provided for:

● real-time chat, person to person and in groups
● threaded discussion, for more focused, facilitated and contextual virtual meetings
● electronic white-boarding and sharing applications over the Internet
● storing, indexing and retrieval based on the developed ontology in addition to the full-text search option
● subscription service notifying users about new, or updated, information on topics that match their interests.

One year after the launch of the initiative, the creators are positive about their work, since KM has become an integral part of the strategy of Delta-Singular. The KM infrastructure put in place allowed for:

● savings in cost, e.g. by reusing knowledge on how to tackle specific software development problems
● increased returns, e.g. by maximizing reuse and exploitation of software approaches, components and products
● the alignment of R&D with product development requirements, by recognizing important trends and developments world-wide.

Solution Highlights: The R&D Community

Two levels of knowledge networking have been identified in the Singular R&D unit as pertinent to the proposal preparation process (Figure 5.3): at the unit level

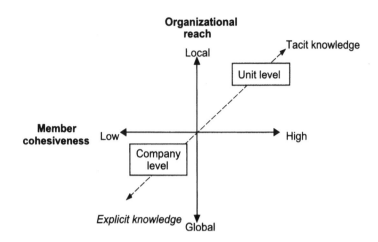

Figure 5.3 Networks related to the Singular R&D unit.

collaboration happens within teams that work in specific R&D projects and there is informal social networking based on common backgrounds; at the company level networking takes place between employees from other units who are considered subject matter experts.

Knowledge leveraging within the two types of network was addressed in two phases. At the R&D unit level during the first phase the team was organized around a common repository that was used as a place where information regarding the unit's work was stored and maintained. A procedure was adopted for users to deposit information that could be later retrieved from colleagues in accordance with their access rights to the document repository. A separate procedure was adopted for team members to ask questions for matters that were not found in the document repository. In this case, they sent their question to an e-mail account where the initiative coordinator assessed the question content and, if considered appropriate, forwarded it to the subject matter expert who was responsible for that thematic area.

For the mechanism to be of real value, a number of steps had to be taken before installing the process. These steps included the identification of the Singular universe of knowledge and the selection of a group of knowledge providers who would be responsible for answering questions in their specific thematic area. Department heads identified the Singular universe of knowledge within their departments and this knowledge segmentation was used for recognizing an expert in each field (i.e. a subject matter expert). Once a question had been submitted to the e-mail account the initiative coordinator forwarded it to the appropriate subject matter expert. The expert responded to the initiative coordinator who had the responsibility for forwarding the response to the person who asked the question, and simultaneously he or she updated the knowledge repository by posting the item in question or by making public the question published along with its response, in a frequently asked questions format. The initiative coordinator maintained a log-keeping mechanism that accounted for all knowledge requests submitted.

The subject matter expert provided descriptive keywords that were used from the initiative coordinator as file metadata for storing the information at the knowledge repository. The initiative coordinator updated the request database with the question submitted and its response according to the expert-provided keywords. Finally, the book-keeping mechanism was updated accordingly (i.e. response supplied within the preset time limit, etc.). Based on the information stored in the database during the first phase, the second phase was implemented in the following steps: a new knowledge brokering mechanism was established and the information recorded in the database was made available through a company-wide intranet that made use of the Know-Net tool.

The knowledge brokering system utilized in the second phase has the same general characteristics as those adopted during the first phase. The platform functionality was offered by the Know-Net tool that enhanced user access to the new corporate portal. The system general characteristics are briefly outlined as follows.

1. The knowledge stored in the database is placed in a company-wide intranet that is implemented with the Know-Net platform.
2. It is categorized according to knowledge assets identified through the implementation of the Know-Net method.
3. The identification of all subject matter experts along with their area of expertise has become available through the corporate portal.
4. Users who do not find the response to their request in the corporate knowledge base, are encouraged to submit it directly to the appropriate subject matter expert via e-mail.
5. Users are advised to consult the knowledge base before addressing questions to the subject matter experts.
6. Responses not existing in the knowledge base are deposited in it from the subject matter experts, who have the responsibility for maintaining the knowledge base content.
7. The need for a book-keeping mechanism has been eliminated.

Three roles have been assigned to the network members in relation to their normal activities. These roles include the author, who is a subject matter expert and is responsible not only for providing expert opinion but also for identifying the knowledge assets stemming from the common effort. All information collected is delegated to this person, who is in charge of documenting it according to pre-specified quality, consistency and design standards. Apart from authors there are also viewers who have the right to examine the documents deposited within the common workspace and receive messages every time the content of their interest has been updated. When they feel that certain pieces of information should be included in the repository they forward them to the author who is responsible for the specific thematic area and he or she decides upon publishing the document provided. There is also a system administrator who is responsible for maintaining the system integrity and ensuring its availability to the users.

The adopted approach facilitates the dynamic re-evaluation of the firm's knowledge assets. It introduces the notion of value-added processes that create experience (i.e. knowledge assets) to the company personnel. These elements are code samples, deliverables, technical troubleshoots, case studies, designs and methodology components that are applicable in various projects. Making these knowledge assets identified in a specific project reusable in other projects requires that the documented material is transparent.

The technical infrastructure implemented provides the technical means so that stored items can be indexed and retrieved using a full-text search option to retrieve content and any associated properties (metadata searching). In addition, a semi-automatic categorization process assists users in depositing and retrieving documents by associating them with specific categories that group similar documents. The same process was proven to be immensely useful when the documents already stored in the corporate file structure were moved to the web storage facility. It provided an automatic importation mechanism that expedited the migration process. Finally, a subscription service notifies users about new or updated information on topics that match their interests and have found their way into the corporate depository. This mechanism works through a user profile where the independent user declares his or her preferences.

5.2.3 MDA

MDA operates in Turkey and specializes in DBMS application development. MDA is a member of the Oracle Business Alliance Program as well as the value-added reseller of the Progres corporation. MDA is organized to deliver turnkey systems, and from this perspective it portrays a company that can be described as a systems integrator. MDA also provides IT consultancy services.

MDA wanted to improve the effectiveness of the bid preparation process. The company has been experiencing the "wheel reinvention" syndrome all too often during bid and proposal preparation. They needed a system to improve the collaboration and organization of bidding work.

The most important areas that MDA focused on were the effective capture and use of contacts from outside the company and the centralization and collaboration on new bids. The Bid Management System application of the Know-Net solution was used. This allowed for the effective capturing of contacts and it supported employees to work and collaborate centrally on bids. Furthermore, the Ideas Capture component was used. This allowed for new ideas on the best way to carry out the bid process to be logged and processed effectively. Also installed at MDA are Best Practices, Best Knowledge and a Knowledge Assets/objects directory.

The system put in place allows MDA quickly to match the requirements of its customers to the abilities of the staff and specialist associates across the strategic partnerships. Furthermore, the company has improved the bid preparation process effectively, reducing the time taken to prepare a bid and to locate a relevant bid, improving the success rate of bids, and reducing the time needed to train new employees participating in bid preparation.

Solution Highlights: The "Bid Preparation" Process

By applying the business process analysis module of stage II of the Know-Net method, the critical knowledge requirements of the Bid Preparation business process could be identified. Important information needed included financial data related to the funding of the project outlined in the bid, data related to people and external contacts, bid-specific information such as deadlines and official documentation, and information about previous bids that could assist in the preparation of the current bid. In considering an improved bid process, the following key areas for improvement were identified.

- *Knowledge about interest rates.* Knowledge about interest rates and the accurate forecast of interest rates are critical to this process, because they determine the safety and feasibility of borrowing money. To help with this problem area, web links were set up in the MDA Know-Net implementation to the best resources and knowledge bases on interest rates and interest rate forecasting. These include the national central bank or foreign exchange company sites that are being accessed regularly.

- *Speed of suppliers' response.* The speed of response to a bid by suppliers was usually too slow for the process to be carried out effectively. Suppliers put together the technical and marketing documents and these may take a long time to arrive. After the documents arrive, MDA often do not have enough time to study and prepare answers to specifications to the quality that they want to. To help speed up this communication with suppliers, a collaborative work area incorporating discussion forums and a central place for working on bids was utilized. The objective was to keep all of the work and communication with suppliers in one space and increase the speed of the supplier response. The common repository can be accessed easily through a web browser at any time, so suppliers can quickly access the main work area and current discussions on bids.

- *Reusing best practice knowledge.* In MDA there was no organized reuse of knowledge in the bid preparation process, so that no previous bids and experience were available in a codified, searchable format. To ensure that the company could start to manage their knowledge effectively in the bid process, a "best knowledge" process was introduced. The effective reuse of important knowledge in the process required a new role within the company in that, for this to be effective, a knowledge manager needed to be appointed and trained in the new KM processes. The knowledge manager oversees the harvesting of knowledge from within the system and ensures that it is transformed into best knowledge for effective reuse in the future. Harvesting is done by ordinary knowledge workers, who also make nominations for the best knowledge base.

Figure 5.4 depicts the "bid preparation" business process of MDA. The grey nodes are the knowledge leveraging steps that were introduced after the Know-Net implementation. These knowledge leveraging steps are described below.

At the start of any new bid process, the knowledge worker should review the best knowledge process for the current best available codified knowledge to conduct the bid process. If there is specific information or knowledge that the knowledge worker is looking for, then they can use the Search function to search the databases or the entire system. The point of this is to encourage the knowledge worker to access codified knowledge, rather than tie up the time of the experts. If none of these methods can help the knowledge worker, then as a last resort, they can access the best people/expert locator database to contact the relevant expert.

The next new step in the process is a "Bid/no bid" decision (step 4) just after the bids are reviewed. The advantage of this step, at this early stage, is to prevent any further work being carried out if the bid does not fall within the capability of MDA as a company (because of technical capability, financing, etc.). It is important to capture the reasons why the bid was not accepted, so that over time, a checklist for bid

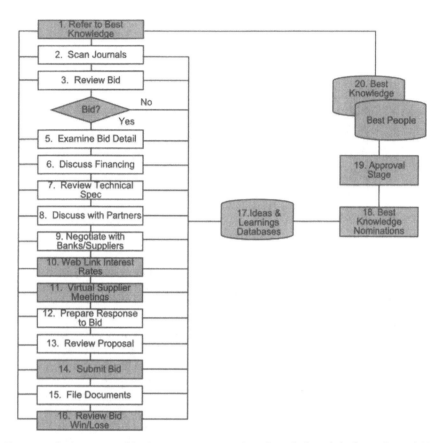

Figure 5.4 "Bid preparation" business process. Grey nodes refer to the knowledge leveraging activities.

acceptance can be defined. Therefore, at the review bid (step 3), a formal and knowledgeable process for decision making does not rest on the individual but comes from experiences of all workers.

The knowledge worker now has the ability to consult external web links for information on interest rates (step 10) and is able to make more informed decisions. It is vital that MDA incorporates this to ensure that workers know about interest rate status for the financing of bids.

Virtual meetings with suppliers can be carried out to speed up the response from suppliers (step 11). This stage is critical in that it helps both MDA and suppliers to have a central place to discuss and work on specific bids, to ensure that a thorough response to the bids can be created.

After the result of the bid is known and the bid has been completed, a review of the bid (step 16) carried out by the knowledge manager is a prerequisite for capturing learnings and ideas (step 17). A key part of introducing KM to the process is the continual capture of learnings and ideas at every stage of the process. With any new initiative, it is not a natural process for individuals to submit ideas and learnings into the ideas and learnings repositories as and when they conduct their work, therefore, formalized reviews need to be conducted in order for these valuable learnings and ideas to be captured.

At the end of each month, the knowledge manager is responsible for conducting a knowledge harvest of the KM system. The knowledge manager will review all ideas and learnings entered by the knowledge workers, as well as trawl the various discussion databases set up, to identify any valuable nuggets of information that may be useful ideas and learnings.

The knowledge manager is then required to submit all of the ideas, learnings and discussion nuggets (known as "best knowledge nominations", step 18) to the best knowledge owner of the process to improve the current best knowledge process.

The best knowledge owner reviews each knowledge nomination (step 19) and makes a decision as to whether it is a valuable contribution to improve the current best knowledge process. If not, the best knowledge nomination is rejected or returned to the knowledge worker for further clarification.

In addition to the best knowledge database, a best people (or "expert locator") database was introduced, to address the tacit dimension of knowledge. It is very difficult to be able to codify all knowledge in an organization and some knowledge will inevitably remain tacit. The best people/expert locator captures the expertise and skills of individuals and allows the knowledge worker to search for experts in order to contact them directly for further information.

The key for MDA is to always provide a current best knowledge bid process for knowledge workers to refer to. It is critical that the best knowledge bid process is always being reviewed and updated through the process described above. Knowledge workers need to contribute ideas and learnings actively, and to participate in collaborative discussions as part of their day-to-day work, in order for others to benefit accordingly. There must also be adequate systems and technology to support and facilitate the capture of ideas, learnings, collaborative discussions, and best knowledge and best people databases, so that knowledge workers can work effectively.

5.2.4 AlphaNova

AlphaNova is a global provider in customer relationship management software and solutions. AlphaNova supports companies to take advantage of the changing business environment by using alliances, multiple channels and customer focus to increase growth and profitability. Owing to rapid expansion and high employee intake, it has become imperative for AlphaNova that the knowledge of existing employees should be harnessed and maintained in an effective manner. AlphaNova has offices in the UK, Greece and Cyprus; communicating, collaborating and sharing knowledge within offices is critical to the success of the company. The company was faced with the challenge to facilitate and encourage employees to share their knowledge and adopt new methods of work practices in terms of collaboration.

The KM solution focused on the interaction and exchange of knowledge between the product design group and a selected team of people from the sales and consultancy groups. Using the Know-Net methodology, a formalized mechanism for managing the flow of knowledge was put in place to ensure that validated and quality knowledge is available to those who need it. The firm also used the Awareness

Creation modules of the methodology (which support education, workshops and presentations) to raise levels of awareness and knowledge among its employees.

AlphaNova used components of the Know-Net tool to develop their KM infrastructure. They used Discussion Forums and Libraries (to store commonly used information), AlphaNova Directory (containing information about employees contact details and, more importantly, key skills), Ideas Management, Learnings, Best Knowledge and Knowledge Assets Directory. The overall result was improved communications and collaboration due to the use of collaborative workspaces, shared discussion forums and learnings.

Solution Highlight: Measuring Knowledge Assets

AlphaNova applied the Know-Net knowledge measurement approach to investigate how KM is benefiting the company. Two levels of measures were identified and measured: business measures looking at the success of the KM initiative in terms of the company's business strategy, and knowledge asset measures of the company. This section will focus on the measurement of the knowledge assets of the KM initiative in AlphaNova, specifically on measuring the creation and sharing of the company's knowledge assets.

To derive the specific metrics and indicators a top–down approach was first used, identifying the organization's vision, strategy and CSFs, the business performance measurements for those CSFs and the key knowledge assets that should be associated with the CSFs. The process was then switched to a bottom–up one, starting with the knowledge assets identified for each of the key CSFs, the knowledge asset measurements were developed for them. The three CSFs for AlphaNova are: (1) improve the efficiency and effectiveness of cross-team communications; (2) improve the efficiency and effectiveness of interoffice communications; and (3) facilitate such communication with an overall KM system.

The analysis conducted during stage II helped to identify the human, structural and market knowledge assets involved in achieving each of the CSFs. When examining the enablers for improving the efficiency and effectiveness of cross-team communications, it was identified that key knowledge assets are the people. People, such as the product design consultants, software development team, and sales and marketing team, possess a lot of tacit knowledge. The ability to be able to get these people to communicate is key. The following KM tools and techniques were incorporated to facilitate communications: a who's who (of both internal and external people) identifying an individual's skill to point to the expert, discussion forums allowing for collaboration across the teams and library databases allowing for sharing knowledge and information. These human and structural knowledge assets apply equally to improving interoffice communications.

The knowledge assets associated with implementing KM focus not only on the technology structural assets but also on the KM processes of harvesting and improving best knowledge and best practice. These need to be measured to see whether KM is being implemented in the company. The measures should look at how frequently the knowledge harvesting process is being conducted, what is being harvested and how frequently the best knowledge is being improved.

The first stage of the measurements in any KM initiative is to take simple measures in terms of how many records are entered and how many of these records are

Table 5.4 Metrics for measuring the KM initiative in AlphaNova

	Measure 1	Measure 2	Measure 3
CSF	1, 2	1, 2	1, 2
Title of measurement	No. of knowledge workers	No. of knowledge workers with skills identified	No. of threaded discussions
Purpose	To identify who's who in the organization, allowing better access to colleagues	To identify which colleagues have what skills, so that individuals can approach the right person straight away	To identify the presence of cross-team communications
Target	To have all employees entered into the Who's Who database	To have all employees with skills attached to be entered into the Who's Who database	Five threaded discussions either initiated or continued
Calculation/approach	No. of entries in the Who's Who database vs no. of employees in organization	No. of entries into the "Skills" field entered	To count the number of new threaded discussions entries within the discussions database
Displayed as	Numerical count	Numerical count	Numerical count
Frequency of measure	Fortnightly	Fortnightly	Fortnightly
Frequency of review	Monthly	Monthly	Monthly
IC category	Human capital	Human capital	Collaboration
Is it calculated already?	Not formally	No	No
Who measures?	Knowledge manager	Knowledge manager	Knowledge manager
Source of data	Each individual	Each individual	Each individual
Ownership of measure	Each individual's responsibility	Each individual's responsibility	Knowledge manager
What do they do?	Not applicable	Not applicable	Monitor usage of discussions database
Who acts on the data?	All employees	All employees	Knowledge manager
What do they do?	Not applicable	Not applicable	Encourage usage of discussions
Notes and comments		This information will eventually lead to developing a competency management system	As KM progresses, there may be a need to start categorizing discussions in a more formal way to be able to capture meaningful results and measures to be defined to reflect this; also to analyze the location of participants. Can suggest the instigation of structured and unstructured discussions

Table 5.4 (Contd.)

	Measure 4	Measure 5	Measure 6
CSF	1, 2, 3	3	3
Title of measurement	No. of libraries	No. of ideas	No. of learnings
Purpose	To provide a central source of information for more efficient sharing of information	To start implementing KM by capturing ideas and to start analyzing for potential best practices and best knowledge definition	To start sharing learnings learnt by individuals through various projects and experiences
Target	To share all relevant documents related to the pilot team activities	To share all ideas generated to the pilot team	To share all learnings
Calculation/approach	No. of documents entered into the libraries and accessed	No. of new ideas entered and accessed	No. of learnings entered and accessed
Displayed as	Numerical count	Numerical count	Numerical count
Frequency of measure	Fortnightly	Fortnightly	Fortnightly
Frequency of review	Monthly	Monthly	Monthly
IC category	Structural capital	Structural capital	Structural capital
Is it calculated already?	Stored in MS Outlook, but not properly accessed	No, not formally	No, not formally
Who measures?	Knowledge manager	Knowledge manager	Knowledge manager
Source of data	Team members	Knowledge workers	Knowledge workers
Ownership of measure	Knowledge manager	Knowledge manager	Knowledge Manager
What do they do?	Identify types of documents that have been entered and maybe catergorize more logically	Review the ideas posted	Review the learnings posted
Who acts on the data?	Knowledge workers	Knowledge managers and process owners	Knowledge managers and process owners
What do they do?	Refer to see whether they can reuse any of the documents or their contents	Redefine processes to incorporate ideas where necessary	Redefine processes to incorporate learnings where necessary
Notes and comments	These should be reviewed and put into practice if applicable or will improve existing processes	These should be reviewed and put into practice if applicable or will improve existing processes	These should be reviewed and put into practice if applicable or will improve existing processes

Table 5.4 (Contd.)

	Measure 7	Measure 8	Measure 9
CSF	3	1, 2, 3	1, 2, 3
Title of measurement	No. of best practices/best knowledge	No. of feature requests	No. of bug reports
Purpose	To start building a knowledge base of best practice and best knowledge for users to refer to	To start logging and tracking feature requests. To provide a central source for all to access	To start logging and tracking bug reports. To provide a central source for all to access
Target	To share all agreed best practices and best knowledge	To encourage users to use this system	To encourage users to use this system
Calculation/approach	No. of best practices and best knowledge entered and accessed	No. of features entered and accessed	No. of bugs entered and accessed
Displayed as	Numerical count	Numerical count	Numerical count
Frequency of measure	Fortnightly	Fortnightly	Fortnightly
Frequency of review	Monthly	Monthly	Monthly
IC category	Structural capital	Structural capital	Structural capital
Is it calculated already?	None formally		
Who measures?	Knowledge manager	R&D	R&D
Source of data	Knowledge manager and process owners	Knowledge workers	Knowledge workers
Ownership of measure	Knowledge manager	R&D	R&D
What do they do?	Review best practice and knowledge together with ideas and learnings to identify whether improvements are required	Act on feature requested	Act on bug reported
Who acts on the data?	Knowledge workers	R&D, management	R&D
What do they do?	Refer to as a reference for best practice and best knowledge in conducting work	Consider whether the request is to be incorporated into the product as a new feature	Ensure that all reported bugs are removed from the software
Notes and comments	Iterative process. Over time a measure for the no. of improvements to a best practice should also be captured to understand the reasons why	Placing this on Knowledger will also improve communications, as a key for all knowledge workers to be up to date with the AlphaNova product development	Placing this on Knowledger will also improve communications, as a key for all knowledge workers to be up to date with the AlphaNova product development

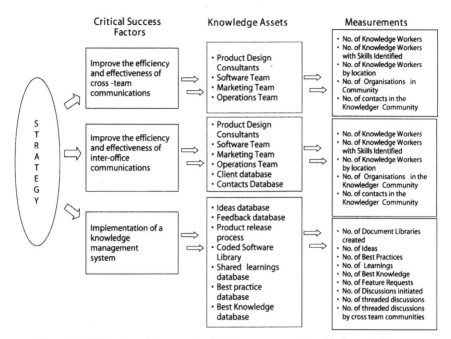

Figure 5.5 Linking knowledge assets and their measurements to critical success factors.

accessed. Each knowledge asset is then analyzed to identify the appropriate measure, the purpose of the measure, the target of a successful measurement and how it is to be calculated, based on frequency and method. Table 5.4 shows examples of some of the knowledge assets for AlphaNova and how they were measured. Knowledge assets should be dynamic in nature, e.g. library databases should be frequently populated and viewed and the measures used should reflect this. If there is no improvement in the use of knowledge assets, then the company should reassess the value and the need for each knowledge asset.

In the early stages of any KM initiative straightforward counting measures are usually taken to gain an understanding of how actively the knowledge assets are performing. Measures for AlphaNova were taken on a monthly basis to identify trends and performance of capturing and sharing of the knowledge assets. During the course of the KM initiative, AlphaNova have not yet had the opportunity to start measuring knowledge assets that indicate knowledge harvesting and improving best knowledge and best experts. As the KM initiative progresses more complex measures can be defined that reflect how the contribution of knowledge assets impacts on business measures, such as understanding the contribution of human knowledge assets in improving the communications process. Figure 5.5 provides a summary of some knowledge assets and links them to CSFs and measurements.

6 The Case of Planet S.A.

6.1 Context of the Case Study and the Company

6.1.1 The Case Study

Planet S.A. was established in 1987, in Athens, Greece, as a consulting company specializing in management consulting as well as development and engineering consulting. In 2000 Planet S.A. merged with the Ernst & Young management consulting practice for south-east Europe, thereby forming the first multinational consulting firm to provide both management and engineering consulting services in southeast Europe.

The company retains the values and traditions of both Planet S.A., which has been the leader in the Hellenic management consulting market for a number of years, and Ernst & Young, which is one of the leading international consultancy networks. Planet Ernst & Young is the first Greek company to provide management and engineering consulting services on a multinational basis.

In 2000, Planet Ernst & Young had revenues of approximately €14 million, with an estimated 26% yearly average growth rate projected for the years up to the Olympic Games of 2004. The company employs approximately 230 professionals and has established offices in Greece, Belgium, Cyprus, Albania, Bulgaria, the Federal Republic of Yugoslavia, the Former Yugoslav Republic of Macedonia and Romania. The company is also following business opportunities in other countries in the wider Black Sea area, mainly in Moldavia, Azerbaitzan and Russia.

Its affiliated companies include Planet Regional, which was established in 1993, has offices in Athens, Salonica and Patras, focuses on regional development and had revenues of €587,000 for 2000; Planner, which was established in 1993, has offices in Athens, Salonica and Patras, focuses on small and medium enterprises and had revenues of €352,000 for 2000; MDR, which was established in 2000, has offices in Athens and focuses on real estate; and Goverplan, which was established in 2001, has offices in Athens and focuses on policy advice.

The field of activities of Planet Ernst & Young extends to enterprises, organizations and agencies in both the public and private sectors. The company offers four core sets of services: management consulting services, information technology services, project and construction management services, and development consulting services (Table 6.1).

The case study in this chapter presents the knowledge management (KM) initiative of Planet S.A. The case study does not cover the postmerger period during

Table 6.1 Planet Ernst & Young's services

Management consulting services	Project and construction management services
Corporate and business strategy	Precontract support, tender documents, tender evaluation
Business process re-engineering	
Organizational development	Contract administration
Performance management	Environmental issues management
Postmerger integration	Project organization and management
Outsourcing·	Project planning and control
Knowledge management	Construction supervision and commissioning
Organizational and operational change management	

Information technology services	Development consulting services
Enterprise resource planning systems	Policy development
e-Business	Feasibility studies and cost–benefit analysis
IT strategy	Programme and project planning
IT project management	Programme management
Custom-made IT solutions	Development programmes assessment

which the new company consolidated the KM infrastructures of Planet S.A. with those of Ernst & Young in South-east Europe. The case study aims to provide a full, real-life example of an application of the Know-Net KM solution. The Know-Net implementation of Planet reported here was carried out during the 1998–1999 period.

6.1.2 Why Manage Knowledge in Planet?

> When one of our consultants shows up, the client should get the best of the firm, not just the best of that consultant.
>
> C. Paulk, CIO, Andersen Consulting

The global management consulting firms have been in the forefront of applying KM practices internally. They have embarked on large-scale, multi-year KM projects that attempt to cover both technical and organizational aspects. The efforts undertaken can provide the basis for drawing crucial inferences that could be extremely useful for similar KM efforts in any industrial setting (Apostolou and Mentzas, 1999). Tables 6.2 and 6.3 summarize the internal efforts of some consultancies as well as the exploitation paths of the developed competences.

Planet was a company that produced and sold knowledge. The company had been growing at a significant pace since its establishment. It was therefore imperative for Planet to invest in capturing and organizing newly acquired knowledge. The company's long-term KM goals included the establishment of concrete knowledge management and measurement systems, and the development of new capabilities and competences.

The following sections describe the KM initiative in Planet, following the stages and steps of the Know-Net method and presenting the application of the Know-Net tool as they were described in the previous chapters.

Table 6.2 Overview of internal KM efforts in global consultancies

Ernst & Young	Developed the Center for Business Knowledge (CBK) with more than 100 professionals; the CBK maintained a Notes database of key documents; by 1996 it was being accessed over 16,000 times a month
Booz, Allen & Hamilton	Created Knowledge On-Line (KOL), a web-based application that facilitates the sharing of information
KPMG Peat Marwick	Began a US-wide roll-out of Knowledge Manager, its information sharing and communication system. Proposals and reports, literature, industry data and methodologies are shared through the use of Knowledge Manager
Andersen Consulting (AC)	Established the Knowledge Xchange KM system, a shared repository of AC's best industry practices (industry visions, best practices and business process models), methods (set of methodology building blocks, work objects, job aids and other tools) and technology information
Arthur Andersen & Co.	Developed an intranet-based system called KnowledgeSpace

Table 6.3 KM services by global consultancies

Ernst & Young	Consulting assignments include tasks that follow an approach that examines "culture, infrastructure, knowledge content, and stewardship". Typical assignments last for 18 months and cost $2–3 million
Booz, Allen & Hamilton	Fees are about $20,000 for helping managers to set knowledge priorities in brainstorming sessions
Arthur D. Little	Its US subsidiary, Innovation Associates, claims to turn companies into learning organizations. Assignment duration is 2–3 years; fees can be as much as $10 million
Gemini Consulting	Assignments typically last for 3–6 months, with an emphasis on sharing intellectual capital as a competitive weapon
Arthur Andersen & Co.	Trademarked the Knowledge Management Assessment Tool, a survey that seeks to discover whether a company's employees are sharing intellectual capital. Assignments include the establishment of best practices and an intranet. Full knowledge consultancy fees are in the range of $1–2 million

6.2 KM Business Case: Applying Stage I of the Know-Net Method

6.2.1 Provide Leadership

The first internal presentation and a related discussion on the need explicitly to leverage knowledge within the company took place in February 1997. It was decided that the company should examine what could be done in the domain of KM, and analyze and learn from similar efforts.

KM in Planet has always been driven by senior management. A small number of senior managers formed the initial KM initiation team. After that, responsibilities were assigned to senior managers to assist the managing director in pushing the KM initiative forward. In the same year, training activities on KM services were initiated.

Table 6.4 Mission and strategy elements

Mission

Planet intends to be the leading Greek management consulting firm that:
- is continuously innovative, by leveraging its understanding of the local market needs and responding to them efficiently
- adapts dynamically to social evolution, by recognizing and accepting the social role of the modern enterprise and by establishing collective internal processes that are based on personal responsibility and continuous improvement of human communication
- transforms corporate knowledge into services in an efficient and effective manner

Strategy elements
- Market expansion and revenue growth
- Development of new service lines and practices
- Cost-efficient use of a combination of in-house resources and outsourcing

---

6.2.2 Link KM Strategy with Corporate Strategy

An internal analysis and investigation of the KM strategy by the KM initiation team of the company led to the identification of the KM-related mission and strategy elements (Table 6.4).

The first strategic goal of market expansion and revenue growth was to build on the company's experience. In the majority of existing services provided, Planet was the local market leader and exhibited a significant number of successful projects as well as accumulated know-how. It is characteristic that for some services, such as the IT Master Planning, Planet has developed its own methodologies. Its goal was to use this business maturity as a lever for expanding the current client base and increasing revenues.

The second goal was to develop new service lines and penetrate new market segments by entering into strategic alliances with international collaborators. The penetration in the market of banking organizations and the involvement in construction and environmental engineering projects following this approach are two successful examples of the results generated in this direction.

Finally, Planet set a concrete goal with relation to the use of in-house resources and outsourcing. It is a strategic decision of Planet to deal only with the knowledge-creating part of a given project. That means that it does not employ any professionals in non-knowledge-generating tasks; instead, these tasks are outsourced. Besides the cost efficiency, this strategic choice aims at the continuous improvement of the professionals employed – which is the main and most important asset of the company – through the acquisition of new skills and the enhancement of their knowledge.

To attain the goals outlined in the strategy, the management of Planet identified a set of five critical success factors (CSFs) (Figure 6.1).

- *Organization and sharing of existing knowledge.* This is probably the most critical success factor. Planet has accumulated useful knowledge and know-how, which may easily become useless, if not accessible. In order to be fully exploited, this knowledge should first be carefully organized and documented, and then be shared among the professionals. Sometimes, consultants may "reinvent the wheel" out of ignorance or an inability to gain immediate access to the information required. A centralized organization of all the available material will save a significant amount of time and facilitate an increase in effectiveness and efficiency.

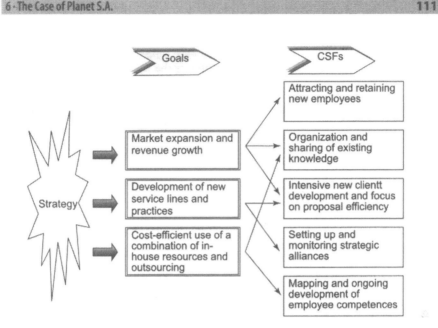

Figure 6.1 From strategy to critical success factors at Planet.

- *Attracting and retaining new employees.* To deal effectively with an increasing number of engagements, it is necessary to recruit new employees. It is crucial for Planet first to attract new competent employees and then to retain them. Planet invests constantly in its professionals through knowledge transfer and training. It would be a great loss if people were to leave once they had acquired useful knowledge, which they could use later in another company. Therefore, personnel retention is of equal importance with the recruitment of capable consultants.

- *Intensive new client development and focusing on proposal efficiency.* Having competent and skilled personnel is one factor that is required to achieve business growth. The other is attracting new customers. In a management consultancy company this calls for intensive new client development and proposal efficiency. The former involves mainly, if not exclusively, the top management level and is carried out through interpersonal contacts, while the latter requires the participation of professionals from all levels. Since the majority of projects result from tenders and not from direct assignments, the improvement of proposal efficiency is of vital importance.

- *Setting up and monitoring strategic alliances.* Strategic alliances with major international collaborators are critical for the achievement of deeper market penetration, since they provide the means for the involvement in new market segments, for which Planet does not have the required expertise. Selecting the "allies" as well as monitoring the progress of the established relationships should be handled with great care. Collaboration with image-enhancing partners results in the attraction of image-enhancing clients, boosting the public image and the reputation of the company. Image enhancement is a critical factor in maintaining a leading position.

● *Mapping and ongoing development of employee competences.* A full exploitation of existing employee competences presupposes the knowledge of those existing competences. Therefore, it is critical for Planet to map and monitor the competences of its professionals, in order to make optimal use of them and identify any possible inadequacies. The goal is the continuous improvement of employees through ongoing competence development in the form of training seminars and on-the-job training.

6.2.3 Perform Knowledge Analysis

The company initially identified eight core knowledge assets, as shown in Figure 6.2 and described in Table 6.5.

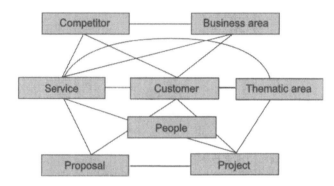

Figure 6.2 Planet's core knowledge assets.

Table 6.5 Description of Planet's knowledge assets

Practices/business areas	Represent the different target market segments of the company. The "Public Sector" business area, for example, should contain knowledge, best practices, etc., about this market segment
Customer	Specific client knowledge (e.g. history of Planet's contact with the client, background information) as well as contact information, "intelligence", etc.
Competitor/collaborators	Similar for competitors/collaborators/partners
Project	Knowledge related to specific assignments
Proposal	Knowledge gained/used for the preparation of bids to tenders
People	Detailed knowledge "owned" by company consulting staff and external consultants and partners, organized and linked to other knowledge assets such as projects (who knows what)
Service	Knowledge about key services that Planet provides to clients (e.g. project management services). It should include the way that these services have been provided in the past and/or should be provided in the future (know-how), learning histories from assignments, methodologies, etc.
Thematic area	Knowledge about key thematic (subject) areas that the company has experience in, or wants to develop, in order to incorporate them into services, e.g. specific knowledge about financial management (thematic area) that is useful in business plans (service)

Planet's strategic decision was to embed KM-related tasks into all existing business processes and roles, as well as to create new organizational roles that will exclusively perform KM-related activities. In the first respect, they already existed in organizational roles that had an indirect relation to KM. Such roles included the heads of business areas (senior managers who are involved in capturing market-related knowledge) and the service development or thematic area managers, (active consultants who are Planet's subject matter experts, in a specific service or subject area). The latter are responsible for collecting, storing, updating and advancing knowledge in their subject matter, and would be responsible for managing related content in the future KM system.

6.2.4 Assess Risk and Change Readiness

The results of the change readiness assessment in Planet indicated that the company needed to plan to deal with high resistance arising from shifts in communication patterns and changes in day-to-day working habits. Most people in the organization were familiar with the concepts of KM but the senior management felt that effective ways would have to be explored to ensure that the consultants and the support staff became habituated to the new environment. An important observation that emerged from the assessment of the ability to manage transformation is that the senior management considered active participation of all those directly or indirectly affected by the KM initiative to be a very high priority.

Integrating and coordinating the multiple activities that are being undertaken as part of KM is also a high priority and a focus for the effort. Business processes are clearly the high impact and high priority area. There also needs to be focus on communication and human resource management. The primary area of change of Planet's KM initiatives was in the daily job responsibilities of professionals (consultants). Table 6.6 summarizes the stakeholder analysis.

6.2.5 Develop the Case for KM

As already mentioned, the company saw KM as an ongoing activity and did not treat it as a one-off project. It had been experimenting with and piloting KM initiatives for several years, continuously reflecting on the lessons learned by each initiative, monitoring its success and modifying or fine-tuning these initiatives.

The focus of the KM initiative in Planet was on three areas. The first area concerned the "deliver services" business process, which is the primary business activity of Planet. Through the introduction of KM-related processes, the aim was to avoid "reinventing the wheel" and duplicating tasks during the planning and execution phase of a consulting assignment.

The second area dealt with the development and management of staff and organizational competences. A consultant should develop competences at four different levels: individual, project, business unit and corporate. The defined competences should be related to issues such as career paths, project planning and control, business planning and corporate level management. Therefore, there is a need to develop processes, systems and tools for competence development, which would meet various requirements at individual, project and company level.

Table 6.6 Stakeholder analysis

Area of change	Impact	Stakeholder	Anticipated reactions/ issues	Communication strategy and planned response
Daily activities of consultants	KM imposes overhead on daily activities	Consultants	Consultants do not consider KM an important part of their job responsibilities	(a) Extended communication on importance of KM from senior management (b) Incorporate KM contribution in consultants' appraisal system
			Consultants need more time to perform KM-related tasks	(a) Consultants' time allocated to KM to be included in timesheet (b) Project managers treat KM as one of the project deliverables
Job satisfaction of consultants	KM requires different skills/ expectations/ attitudes	Consultants	Consultants do not get personal or professional satisfaction by performing KM activities	Consider personal interest/habits/professional expectations of key individuals within the new KM responsibilities. Do not impose KM responsibilities but persuade consultants to participate. Exploit the capabilities of self-motivated communities of practice/interest

Finally, the third area referred to the development of thematic area networks, which were identified as the company's core knowledge networks. Knowledge areas (i.e. thematic or subject areas) comprise the cornerstone of Planet's business operations. The various services that the company provides to a number of practices are all based on a set of core knowledge areas. The knowledge required to support the services involves subject knowledge, industry knowledge and a knowledge of complex, large-scale programme management.

6.3 Developing a Knowledge Organization: Application of Stage II

This section presents the implementation of stage II of the Know-Net method in Planet. Stage II in Planet followed an iterative approach aiming at rapid learning from doing. Table 6.7 illustrates what has been done in the framework of each individual module.

6.3.1 "Deliver Services" Business Process

Initially, the "deliver services" business process was carried out in two basic steps:

1. *Plan project*: This step encompassed all of the planning activities, starting with the identification of the scope of the consulting engagement and the formation of

Table 6.7 Overview of modules of stage II as implemented in Planet

Module	Where has it been applied?	Who was involved?
1. Analyze Business processes	(a) Deliver services business process (b) Competence development business area	(a) Knowledge services group, selected project directors and project managers (b) Knowledge services group, consultants from human resource discipline
2. Leverage knowledge in business processes	As above	As above
3. Analyze knowledge networks	(a) Selected project teams (b) Selected thematic area networks	(a) Knowledge services group and selected project team (director, manager and consultants) (b) Knowledge services group and selected thematic area managers and participating consultants
4. Leverage knowledge networks	As above	As above
5. Analyze the technology	Company-wide	Knowledge services group
6. Leverage the technology	Company-wide	Knowledge services group
7. Develop the knowledge asset schema	(a) Organizational knowledge asset schema (used in the Know-Net tool) (b) Discipline ontologies	(a) Knowledge services group (b) Knowledge services group and selected discipline members
8. Integrate the KM architecture		Knowledge services group

the project team, and ending with the detailed project plan, including timeline and responsibilities of people. The project director held almost exclusive responsibility for this step.

2. *Execute project*: This was the actual implementation phase where the project team worked to deliver the system/study to the client.

During this process, several knowledge-related problems were identified. First, the phenomenon of reinventing the wheel was due primarily to ignorance. Consultants were duplicating work because they did not know that this piece of work had already been done for a previous engagement and therefore it was available. Moreover, knowledge sharing was limited within "people networks" and this was closely related to the lack of a systematic approach for capturing, organizing and sharing knowledge. In general, there was an explicit need for a KM system that would facilitate the capturing, organization and further dissemination of existing knowledge.

The new processes and system designed to support the "deliver services" business process exhibit explicitly the iterative approach suggested under stage II of the Know-Net method. During the first cycle (Figure 6.3), three specific actions were

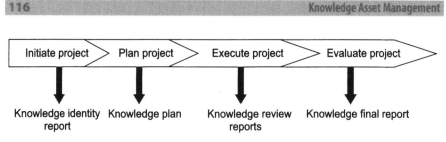

Figure 6.3 First cycle of knowledge leveraging within the "deliver services" process.

taken: introduction of two additional steps in the examined business process, introduction of KM processes, and activation of the "knowledge input-output" tables.

The four steps involve the following activities:

1. *Initiate project*: A project manager is assigned. The project manager identifies the scope of the consulting engagement, forms the project team, identifies the objectives of the assignment and works out an overall work plan for the project.

2. *Plan project*: A more detailed plan is developed. The plan includes timeline, responsibilities of people, specific tasks, software development/systems integration details and financial budgeting.

3. *Execute project*: This is the actual implementation phase where the project team works to deliver the system/study to the client.

4. *Evaluate project*: This is the closing phase of the project. The team evaluates the results, assesses the impact of the result, collects lessons learned and feedback from client, etc.

The newly introduced KM processes are:

● filling out the "knowledge identity" (i.e. practices/services/thematic areas, knowledge input, knowledge output, knowledge reviews) during the initiation project phase

● developing the "knowledge plan" during the planning project phase.

● generating knowledge review reports during the course of the project, which enhance, refine or correct the content of the knowledge plan

● formulating the knowledge final report, at the end of the project.

Although it was a significant step forward, introducing the new activities did not produce the expected results. The main cause of the problem was attributed to the strict implementation of this system-based approach to all projects, regardless of their importance or duration. There was a lot of work to be done and a number of forms to be filled out, and there was some resistance from the people that held the responsibility of carrying out these tasks.

Therefore, a second cycle of action was put forward (Figure 6.4), which was characterized by a loosening of the implementation of the four-step process. The process was followed strictly only for carefully selected projects. For the remaining, less important projects only filling in the knowledge identity report was mandatory. Moreover, an after-action review step was introduced, where the case summary for each project was formulated.

Figure 6.5 shows the knowledge assets and related objects and attributes that were identified during the analysis of the "deliver services" business process.

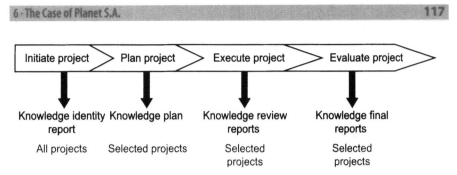

Figure 6.4 Second cycle of knowledge leveraging within the "deliver services" process.

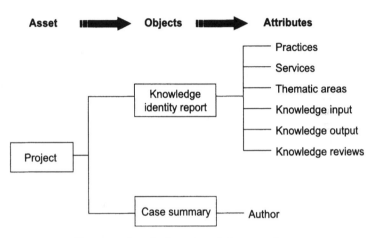

Figure 6.5 Contribution to knowledge asset schema.

6.3.2 Competence Development

During the implementation of stage I the need was identified to define the competences that a consultant should develop at four different levels: individual, project, business unit and corporate. The defined competences should be related to issues such as career paths, project planning and control, business unit planning and corporate level management. Therefore, there is a need to develop processes, systems and tools for competence development, which would meet various requirements at the individual, project and company level.

The requirements for individual competence development were identified as:

● the capability of mapping individual competences to a predefined structure of company-wide competences
● the possibility of grading individual competences against a predefined set of criteria
● the provision of a space for annotations, descriptions and comments on individual competences
● linking consultants' assignments, training seminars and learning experiences to their competences

- facilities for on-line availability of company training material, as well as information about other possibilities for enhancing of individual competences (e.g. from conferences and seminars)
- the development of personal plans for further competence development.

For a project-level competence management, facilities should be provided for finding consultants based on competence searches. The result of the search would ideally provide information about the current and previous assignments that a consultant has been involved in, the training seminars that he has attended, his personal development plan for enhancing competences, his preferences, etc. Moreover, the retrieval of information about the current and foreseeable availability of each consultant is required.

Finally, company-wide competence management, requires:

- the existence of an electronic space where the advisor and the "advisee" could collaborate in an unstructured way, i.e. arrange meetings, have discussions on-line (but not in real-time) concerning the consultant's development plan, monitor in a periodic manner the agreements they have reached concerning the consultant's core competences and critical skills, make changes and suggestions for revising the personal development plan, etc.;
- the capability of monitoring the overall current status of competences and skills and the expected organizational competence "map", based on the plans of each individual consultant;
- support for scheduling and monitoring the training requirements, providing on-line availability of the training material (mainly documents and presentations) and identifying requirements for further training;
- the capability of linking targets from business plans and foreseeable consulting assignments to the competence map of the company;
- the capability of evaluating the missing competences of current business unit competence maps and performing organizational "gap analysis" between the current state of competences and future requirements.

Consultants develop, apart from basic consulting skills, *discipline* (i.e. subject) knowledge, *service* knowledge and *practice* knowledge (Figure 6.6). Consultants are then evaluated accordingly based on an appraisal system that explicitly takes into account these three axes.

The competence development approach adopted by Planet is a combination of a top–down with a bottom–up approach (Figure 6.7). In the top–down approach, the company framework is developed. More specifically, the following activities are implemented:

- definition of a prestructured set of company-wide competences based on the formulated strategic objectives. In Planet, this set includes seven basic competences (Figure 6.8), which are further analysed into evaluation criteria;
- definition of levels to be developed for each competence. In Planet, there are five levels, from 0 to 4:

    0: is not aware of the key competence standards

    1: is aware of the key competence standards required

    2: can consistently achieve the required level of key competence

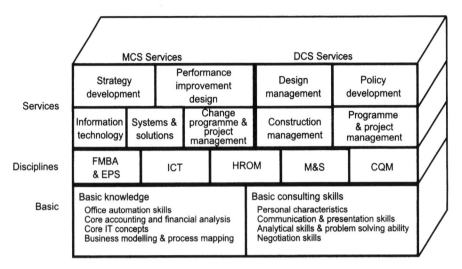

Figure 6.6 Competence development map.

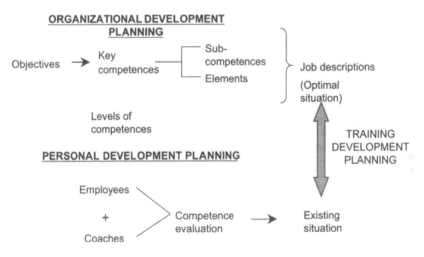

Figure 6.7 Approach to competence development.

3: can develop others in the key competence

4: can take corrective strategic action to redefine the key competence if necessary;

● matching of job titles to key competences and competence levels required. In Planet, there are five levels of seniority or job titles: analyst, consultant, senior consultant, manager and director. The assignment of key competences and competence levels to individual job titles was done on the basis of the significance that each key competence carries for each role. For example, basic consulting skills are regarded as highly important for analysts and of very low importance

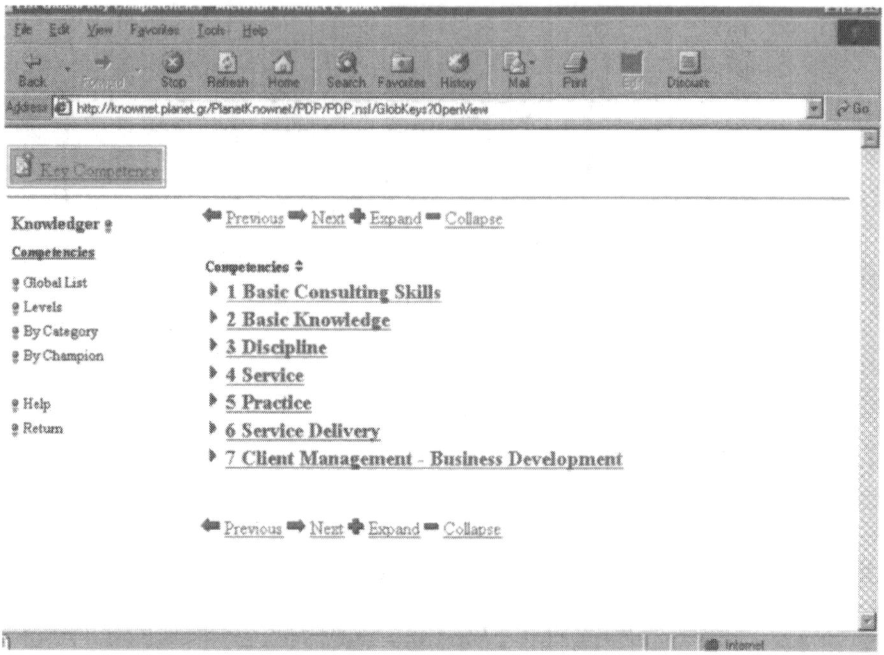

Figure 6.8 Planet's set of company-wide competences.

for managers and directors. The opposite applies to client management and business development.

Once the competence modelling for the company has completed, the focus shifts to the bottom–up approach; that is, the monitoring of the individual competences. This involves primarily the grading of individual competences against the predefined set of criteria and the formulation of personal development plans. This activity is carried out by each consultant (advisee) in cooperation with his or her coach (advisor). Advisor and advisee talk about the performance evaluation results, identify any existing areas of deficiency and set and prioritize future goals for improvement. Through the comparison of the current status of individual competences against the required status, the training needs can be identified and the company's training development plan can be formulated.

The contribution to the knowledge asset schema of leveraging knowledge in the "competence development" business area is shown in Figure 6.9.

6.3.3 Development of Thematic Area Networks

In Planet, three different levels of knowledge networking were identified, as presented in Table 6.8. The most active networks from those mentioned in Table 6.8 are the following:

● *Project teams*: These correspond to the work teams that work in consulting

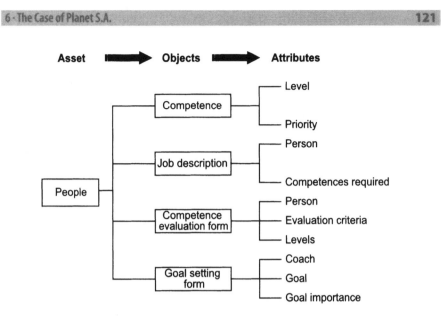

Figure 6.9 Contribution to knowledge asset schema.

Table 6.8 Levels of networking in Planet

Team level	Networking within the formal structure of disciplines
	Networking within teams that work in consulting assignments
	Informal social networking based on common background, interests, problems, etc.
Organization level	Networking across project teams
	Networking across disciplines (disciplines are groups of thematic areas)
	Networking across production departments
Interorganizational level	Networking with alliances
	Networking with affiliated companies
	Networking with competitors (in certain cases when Planet makes partnerships with them)

assignments and are characterized by high member cohesiveness and close social proximity.

● *Thematic Area Networks*: Although not identical, thematic area networks share some characteristics with communities of practice in terms of member cohesiveness and organizational reach. As their title implies, they are built around a thematic area or subject of interest.

● *Company alliances*: These are the knowledge networks formulated as a result of the cooperation or partnership of Planet with alliances, affiliated companies or competitors. In this case, the network members have similar business interests; therefore, company alliances could be regarded as communities of practice.

The main knowledge assets required to deliver the services consist of subject knowledge, industry knowledge and knowledge of management methodologies.

These three types of knowledge asset represent the cornerstone of Planet's business operations (Figure 6.10). All services that the company provides to a number of industries are based on these three types of knowledge asset, collectively called "thematic areas". The application of the Know-Net method focuses primarily on the thematic area networks, which were identified as the company's core knowledge networks.

The Know-Net methodology was used to leverage and further enhance the thematic area networks. More specifically, one thematic area manager (TAM) was appointed for almost every network. TAMs are active consultants who are regarded as subject matter experts and are responsible for collecting, storing, updating and advancing knowledge in their specific subject matter. A Know-Net web space was allocated for each network with document management facilities, discussion databases and real-time collaboration facilities.

The problems encountered during this implementation mainly involved the time required to play actively and effectively the newly introduced role of the TAM, which is regarded as a peripheral, not as a main activity. To solve these problems, senior management adopted a more formal approach to thematic area management, in order to promote it as a major business activity. As a first step, time has been explicitly allocated for carrying out this task, while contributions to the role of the TAM have been linked to the company's performance evaluation system.

Efforts have been made to create informal settings for member interactions. The emphasis is on open dialogue with no pressure to come to resolution. The TAM, as a key attendant in these meetings, personally invites prospective members and facilitates knowledge sharing. He or she is continually polling to identify new areas of interest or challenge for the community. A mechanism put in place for recognition of participation is for TAMs to inform senior management of success stories. This information is accompanied by a request for a personal note of appreciation from senior leadership to individuals, commending their work and acknowledging how their contribution has affected the bottom line.

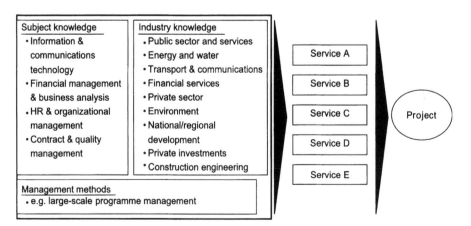

Figure 6.10 Knowledge required for service delivery.

6.3.4 Knowledge Asset Schema

Figures 6.11 and 6.12 outline the specifications of the knowledge assets, objects and attributes that were used in the business areas of the Know-Net implementation in Planet.

The development of the ontology of knowledge asset schema did not follow a formal, principled approach (Table 6.9). This was done for the following reasons.

● A decision was taken to limit the ontology subject matter to business concepts that were already defined and specified outside the Know-Net project. Having such a specification at hand there was no need for a formal procedure to model these concepts according to the Know-Net ontology requirements.

● The scope of the ontology implementation at Planet was prototyping. For prototyping reasons a non-formal approach is usually followed.

Table 6.9 Characteristics of case ontology

Level of formality	Structured informal
Purpose	To facilitate communication between members of the organization by giving a consistent terminology; to provide an infrastructure for indexing and searching based on common concepts and terms
Subject matter	Business environment (company practices, services and thematic areas)

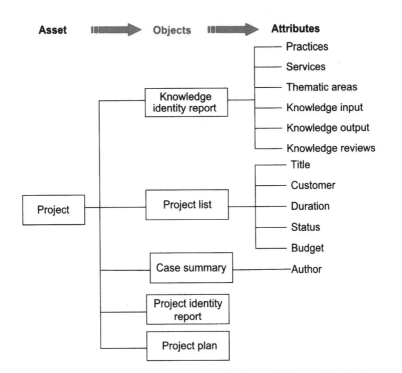

Figure 6.11 Objects and attributes related to the knowledge asset "project".

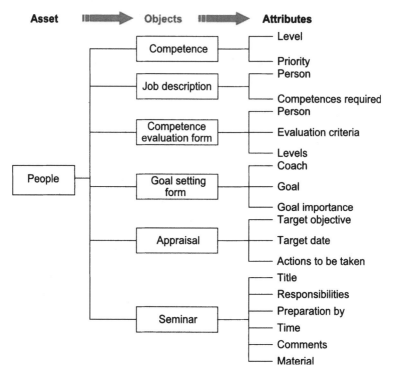

Figure 6.12 Objects and attributes related to the knowledge asset "People".

In choosing which terms to define first, the procedure went in a middle–out fashion rather than top–down or bottom–up. The choice of whether to go top–down, middle–out or bottom–up has a number of effects. The bottom–up approach results in a very high level of detail but can more easily adhere to some formal methodology, whereas middle–out usually involves a degree of iteration and thus a less formal approach is more suitable.

Figures 6.13–6.15 show the ontology developed to pilot the Know-Net tool in Planet.

6.3.5 Integration of the KM Architecture

The creation of new KM-related organizational roles was dictated by the introduction of new KM systems and the implementation of new KM processes.

To direct the cultural change and help the organization to adapt to the new knowledge structure, a knowledge officer (KO) was appointed, a knowledge services group (KSG) was formulated and TAMs (or subject matter experts) were identified (Figure 6.16).

The roles of the KO are:

● to provide a high-level, strategic view of the importance of KM to the company's business goals

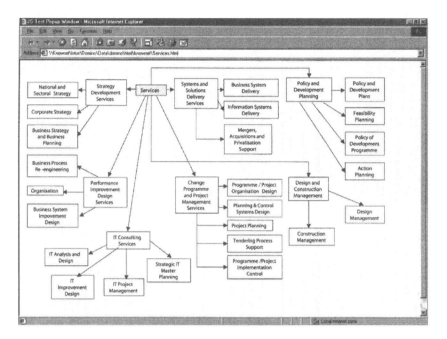

Figure 6.13 Planet's ontology (Services concept).

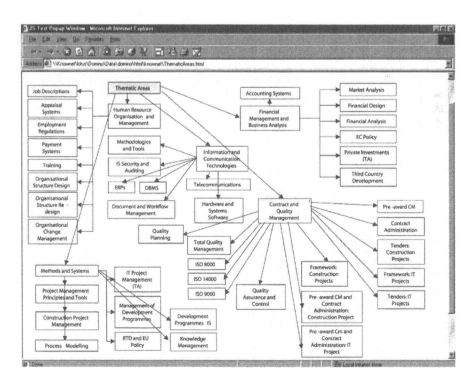

Figure 6.14 Planet's ontology (Thematic Areas concept).

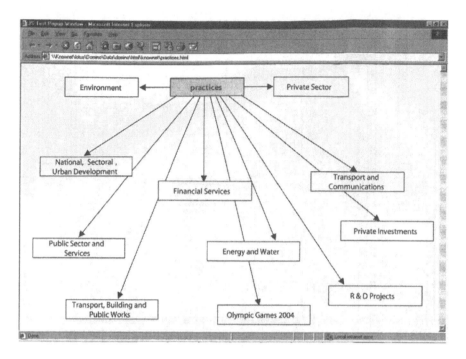

Figure 6.15 Planet's ontology (Practices concept).

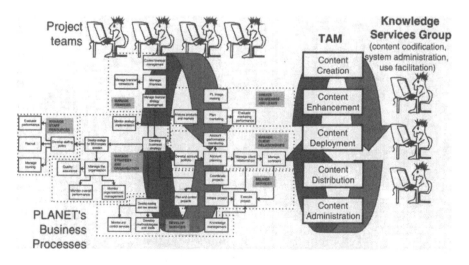

Figure 6.16 Planet's KM roles embedded into the actual business processes.

- to promote KM throughout the organization
- to act as a conduit between the board and the rest of the company so that the goals of KM are understood and shared across the organization
- to take responsibility for corporate initiatives, such as the development of corporate vocabularies and taxonomies, and provide a KM perspective on improvements to the corporate infrastructure
- to instigate and monitor measures and indicators of progress on KM
- to manage the KM specialists within the organization, providing training, ensuring cooperation and knowledge exchange between knowledge managers
- to manage knowledge creation within new projects and knowledge reuse from previous projects. In this context the KO has the overall responsibility of the new knowledge leveraging steps presented in the "Deliver services" business process (i.e. knowledge input–output forms for each project, case summary, etc.)
- to supervise and coordinate service development, discipline (thematic area) development and training activities.

The KSG is a team of active consultants with the expertise to hold the following responsibilities:

- to develop, package and maintain Planet's KM system
- to ensure that Planet's KM solutions are organized and accessible during consulting engagements and tender preparation
- to assist TAMs to structure information for input to the KM system.

TAMs are valued for their domain experience, which may involve a specific practice, service or thematic area. They are responsible for:

- collecting, storing, updating and advancing knowledge in their subject matter
- managing related content in the KM system
- carrying out knowledge reviews.

The new processes, systems and organizational structures that implemented the knowledge organization in Planet are summarized in Table 6.10, as related to the key knowledge assets used in the Know-Net pilot trial in Planet: projects, thematic areas and people.

6.4 Measuring the KM Initiative

To develop the knowledge asset measurements, the following procedure was undertaken. All the measures and indices comprising Planet's existing performance measurement system were reviewed in the light of the key knowledge assets; in other words, examining whether there were existing metrics for measuring each individual knowledge asset. For those knowledge assets captured by the existing set of metrics, the significance and the usefulness of each metric were reviewed to make sure that there was a point in making this measurement. For example, in the initial set of metrics, there was a measurement reflecting the mean duration of contracts. It was decided to exclude it from the revised set of metrics, since it did not provide any information vital for the business operations. At the same time, the introduction of new indicators was seriously considered. It was recognized from the very beginning

Table 6.10 Planet's KM architecture

Knowledge asset	Process	Systems	People		
			Knowledge officer	Knowledge services group	Thematic area manager
Project	Knowledge identity plan process	Knowledge input output tables Know-Net ontology	Responsible for: initial design of KIO tables modification of KIO tables	Responsible for: monitoring the use of KIO tables providing support when necessary	Responsible for: carrying out the knowledge reviews managing related content
Thematic areas	Informal meetings, day-to-day activities	Know-Net discussion databases	Responsible for: initial identification of thematic areas	Responsible for: providing support to thematic area managers	Responsible for: collecting, updating and advancing knowledge in their subject matter managing related content
People	Competence development	Know-Net's competences modelling module	Responsible for: supervising and coordinating training activities	Responsible for: providing support and system maintenance	

Table 6.11 Measures used per knowledge asset

Key knowledge asset	Metrics defined
Practice/business area	Number of projects per practice
	Percentage of revenues per practice
	Percentage share fees from new practice
Customer	Percentage of time allocated to customer development
	Number of new customers
	Revenues from new customers
	Number of image-enhancing customers
	Revenues from image-enhancing customers
	Win/loss tender index (success rate)
Competitor/collaborator	Number of projects with image-enhancing collaborators
Project	Reuse of project knowledge (qualitative)
Proposal	Percentage of time allocated to tender preparation
People	Proportion of professional staff
	Revenues/consultant
	Average level of experience/seniority
	Distribution of experience/seniority
	Percentage of time spent on training
Service	Percentage of time allocated to service development
	Percentage of share fees from new services
Thematic area	Percentage of time of personnel involvement in thematic area development

Table 6.12 Planet's stock and flow indicators

From: / To:	Human assets	Structural assets	Market assets	Financial assets
Human assets		Percentage of time of personnel involvement in thematic areas Percentage of time allocated to service development	Time allocated to client development	Revenues per consultant
Structural assets				
Market Assets		Number of projects with image-enhancing collaborators		Revenues from image-enhancing customers Revenues from new customers Percentage of share fees from new service/practice
Financial Assets		Investment in ICT		Percentage of revenues/practice
Stocks	Percentage of time spent on training Average level of seniority/experience Distribution of seniority/experience	Percentage of professional staff Reuse of project knowledge	Win/loss tender index Number of new customers Number of image-enhancing customers	Return on assets Earning power Sales rate of growth

of this review process that the existing set of metrics was neither comprehensive nor complete, although it contained a great number of indicators.

Table 6.11 summarizes the measures per key knowledge asset, while Table 6.12 classifies the identified measures into stock and flow indicators, as proposed by the Know-Net measurement method.

7 Knowledge Asset Management: Know-Net and Beyond

7.1 Introduction

The management of organizational knowledge has drawn the attention of academics, consultants and practitioners as a key lever for improving performance, boosting productivity and creativity, and facilitating innovation in organizational settings. The methods, tools and the actual knowledge management (KM) implementations in various companies have mainly followed one of two perspectives, which in this book are called the *process-centric* and the *product-centric* approaches. The former is primarily people-based and treats KM as a social communication process; the latter is mostly content-based and focuses on knowledge-related artefacts. This book presents a knowledge asset-based KM solution that attempts to fuse these two approaches in a balanced manner. The previous chapters of the book presented the individual components of the KM solution, i.e. a management framework, a knowledge leveraging method and an intranet-based tool, as well as their application in five companies.

This chapter explores the ways through which the components of the KM solution address the product and process perspectives to KM and analyzes the links and associations between these components. Finally, in the belief that the management of knowledge assets can be a key driver for organizational as well as societal performance, some avenues for future research and technological development are proposed, which build on and further exploit the basic conceptual structures.

7.2 Knowledge Assets as a Key Link for Holistic KM

7.2.1 Integrating the Product- and Process-centric Approaches in the Know-Net Solution

The three components of the Know-Net total KM solution – the framework, the method and the tool – have clear and consistent interdependences, which exploit the knowledge asset-centric nature of the solution and facilitate the amalgamation of the process- and product-centric perspectives to KM. Figure 7.1 highlights the overall interdependences of the Know-Net framework, method and tools.

The Know-Net framework can be used as an awareness tool as well as for developing a common language among the people of a company. By focusing on key

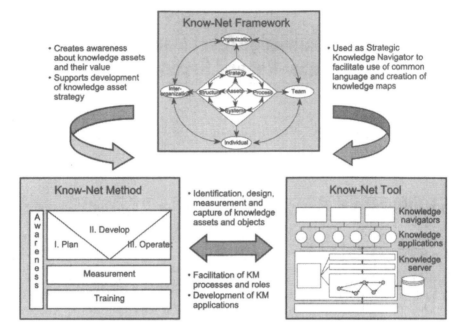

Figure 7.1 Interdependences of the Know-Net framework, method and tool.

knowledge assets the framework is useful as an enabler for discussing which are the critical knowledge areas, which ones are underdeveloped and should be further enhanced, and which are already valuable and should be protected and cultivated. In addition, the elements of the framework (strategy, structure, processes, systems) help to share a first draft picture of the level of knowledge awareness within the company. Finally, the first discussions about KM should focus on the various levels for leveraging knowledge assets (i.e. individual, team, organizational and inter-organizational levels) to help to identify possible areas for intervention. These rough analyses can provide useful input for the application of the Know-Net method (especially Stage I: Plan), as well as facilitate the smooth introduction of the concepts and terms used in the Know-Net tool.

The application of the method may be tightly linked to the use, customization and roll-out of the Know-Net tool. However, each one of the two (method and tool) is also self-sustained and can be independently applied: the method has already been applied to companies without the use of the tool.

The coupling between the method and the tool is mainly accomplished through the eight modules of stage II of the Know-Net method, as outlined in Table 7.1. As described in Chapter 3, each module of stage II is a self-contained, value-adding entity and therefore not all modules are mandatory in a KM effort. Ideally, however, just as the knowledge assets are the main unifiers of the approach, module 7 (develop the knowledge asset schema) acts as the frame of the Know-Net method that is being constructed with input from the "audit" modules (1, 3 and 5), while it supports the consistent execution of the "design/implement" modules (2, 4 and 6).

Table 7.1 Relation of stage II modules to the product- and process-centric views and support by the Know-Net tool

Module	Description	Relation to process and product integration	Relation to Know-Net tool
1. Analyze business processes	Helps the knowledge audit of business processes, in order to understand how business processes, people, systems and content are related, to reveal *who* needs *what* knowledge and *when* they need it	Detail identification of knowledge assets and objects involved in business processes (*product view*) Detail identification of knowledge flows within business processes (*process view*)	Provides requirements for the creation/ customization of KM applications (including functionality, user rights, etc.) Profiles people and roles involved in processes (to be used in personalized facilities of the tool) Provides a "first cut" of the knowledge objects that correspond to the knowledge assets
2. Leverage knowledge in business processes	Helps the enhancement of KM within existing business processes and the design of new business processes and corresponding roles for managing specific knowledge assets	Design of formal business processes and roles for KM (*process view*) Incorporation of knowledge objects, relations and attributes (metadata, classification, indexing, etc.) to business processes, e.g. who creates a knowledge object, which metadata should be used, how the indexing has been done (*product view*)	Definition of access rights for knowledge objects/applications Customization of KM applications to support business processes
3. Analyze knowledge networks	Helps to analyze the informal flow of knowledge within networks of people in the organization	Detail identification of knowledge assets and objects involved in informal communication/collaboration of employees (*product view*) Comprehension of patterns of informal knowledge flow, collaboration habits and requirements for improvement (*process view*)	Provides requirements for the creation/ customization of KM applications. Emphasis is on the groupware support of the tool, e.g. applicability of specific collaboration requirements such as video/audio conferencing, customization of community/ team support applications of the tool Profiles people and roles involved in networks (to be used in personalized facilities of the tool) Provides a "first cut" of the knowledge objects that correspond to the knowledge assets

Table 7.1 (Cont'd)

Module	Description	Relation to process and product integration	Relation to Know-Net tool
4. Leverage knowledge networks	Helps the design and stimulation of knowledge networks using a set of non-management techniques. The module addresses critical success factors for the network, content quality assurance issues, motivation and reward issues, etc.	Design of informal networks (communities of practice/interest) in support of KM (*process view*) Incorporation of knowledge objects, relations and attributes (metadata, classification, indexing, etc.) to knowledge networks, e.g. who has ownership of which knowledge object in the network, which metadata are suitable for the network, filtering rights (*product view*)	Definition of access rights for knowledge objects/applications Customization of KM applications to support knowledge networks. Emphasis on groupware applications
5. Analyze the technology	Assesses the current state of IT in the organization and identifies existing information sources	Mostly related to the *product view*, looks at knowledge artefacts that are stored in information systems	Examines the applicability of the Know-Net tool from a technical perspective (network bandwidth, geographical distribution, etc.) Identifies existing information sources within and outside the organization
6. Leverage the technology	Presents the technology element in KM	NA	NA
7. Develop the knowledge asset schema	Guides the design of the knowledge asset schema which comprises: ● the knowledge object store (for the formal knowledge organization) ● the knowledge ontology (for conceptual/logical structuring organization of knowledge objects)	*Product view* only, as discussed in Chapter 3	Direct mapping to the knowledge server. During this module the object store and the ontology are customized and configured for the organization
8. Integrate the KM architecture	Synthesizes and integrates all changes done in different modules in one working solution, seamlessly incorporated in the existing business environment	NA	NA

NA: not applicable.

All audit modules, among other issues aim to identify in detail the knowledge assets, and corresponding knowledge objects and their attributes. Module 1 (analyze business processes), for instance, produces processes maps that depict key knowledge assets that are being used or created in selected business processes. Module 7 (develop the knowledge asset schema) collects this information, along with similar information from modules 3 and 5, arranges possible overlaps, logically groups content and creates the formal schema (knowledge asset schema) on which the design/implement modules are based. Consider another example: module 4 (leverage knowledge networks) designs and organizes communities of practice and interest around the core knowledge assets of the organization and proposes the already specified knowledge objects as units for knowledge creation and sharing within these communities. Table 7.1 broadly describes how each module relates to the integration of the process- and product-centric approaches and to the functionalities and characteristics of the Know-Net tool.

7.2.2 Integrating the Product- and Process-centric Approaches in the Know-Net Implementations

The tight integration of the product- and process-centric approaches is also evident in the implementations of the Know-Net solution. The case of Planet (Chapter 6) demonstrates how both the process approach (i.e. dealing with communities of practice and facilitating competence development) and the product approach (i.e. dealing with knowledge as an object that is consumed or produced during consulting engagements) can interoperate in practice. For instance, one can see how knowledge developed during a proposal preparation by a business analyst can be codified so that it is accessible not only by another analyst during the same process but also by a subject matter expert participating in a thematic area network.

It is important to stress that this approach aims to ensure that the process-centric view and the product-centric perspective can interoperate, in the sense that they are not isolated from one another and one can make use of and add value to the other. The aim is not, and should not be, for all organizations to try to excel in both approaches in equal proportions. Such an attempt may not be in line with the business environment and could be overwhelming (in terms of resources and organizational and cultural changes needed) for an organization.

In the cases described in Chapter 5 it is evident that there is a varying emphasis on one of the two approaches. For instance, Delta-Singular focused on enhancing collaboration and knowledge sharing within informal networks of people that relate to the R&D unit (process approach), while MDA looked at the knowledge as an artefact produced during bid preparation. Nevertheless, the holistic approach followed during the design of the KM infrastructure ensures that any additional or future KM initiatives, no matter whether they lean towards one or the other approach, will not be independent of the existing KM infrastructure.

Some additional recommendations that were drawn from the five cases presented in this book include the following.

● *Focus on exploiting knowledge sources*: Fundamental to the principles of knowledge asset management is the utilization of existing knowledge sources. In keeping with this, Debus I.T. linked the KM tool with the existing software systems and a variety of external databases.

- *Facilitate knowledge exchange in communities*: Organizational structure, particularly geographical dispersion, exerts an effect on the management of knowledge. The bases for the transfer of rich, tacit knowledge are personal relationships and geographical proximity. KM seeks to extend the immediacy of this natural contact beyond its boundaries by taking advantage of technology. In so doing, it extends the formerly untapped and often invaluable benefits of local groups, to form communities of practice, unhindered by geographical boundaries, as was the case in Delta-Singular and AlphaNova.

- *Place emphasis on client needs and requirements*: For the successful implementation of KM projects in sales organizations or those that work closely with clients, such as Debus I.T., the needs and requirements of the clients must form the backdrop against which all other activities are performed. By paying close attention to the clients, high business value-adding KM solutions can be deployed.

- *Integrate KM within normal business processes*: To exploit fully the potential of KM environments, knowledge asset management has to be integrated into standard business processes, as in the case of Planet. At any point in a process, knowledge workers should be able to learn from the experiences of their colleagues, as well as to provide their own experiences as lessons from which others can learn.

Finally, the five cases verified the importance of finding the right balance between information technology (IT) solutions for capturing explicit codified knowledge and leaving enough room to allow for direct personal knowledge exchanges.

7.3 Knowledge Assets as a Concept for Future Research

The explicit treatment and leveraging of knowledge assets opens up a wealth of both basic research and action-oriented directions for further exploration. In the following paragraphs two main directions are sketched, which are currently being actively pursued. The first refers to knowledge-based process improvement and the second to knowledge asset trading.

7.3.1 Knowledge-based Improvement of Business Processes

Business processes embody knowledge as a form of codified know-how, since they reflect a certain perspective on the way to accomplish a task. In Chapter 3 it was shown how the Know-Net method facilitates the identification and leveraging of knowledge assets that may be found within business processes (see Modules 1, 2 and 7 of stage II of the method). Working from the idea that a specific business process, be it new product development or supply chain management, can be more effective if it captures and applies the most useful knowledge assets about how to achieve its objectives, a research programme has been initiated, which aims to facilitate weakly structured knowledge work and actively support knowledge workers through the explicit management of context-sensitive process-related knowledge assets (Abecker and Mentzas, 2001; Abecker et al., 2001b). This work builds on the artificial intelligence approach to organizational memories (Abecker et al., 2000a, b; Reimer et al., 2000) and extends the work of other researchers in the field of integrating organizational memories with workflow management (Staab et al., 2000; Van Kaathoven et al., 1999).

The starting point is that knowledge-intensive processes tend to be characterized by dynamic changes of goals, fluid information environment, unexpected constraints, and highly individual and ad hoc communication and collaboration patterns (Buckingham, 1998; Davenport et al., 1996). Such business processes have to be analyzed from a knowledge management perspective and knowledge-related tasks should be integrated in them. Support of this type of work seems difficult to achieve but is nevertheless desirable. Existing systems, such as project management and workflow management tools, present limitations that restrict their usability in such environments. However, a possible combination of the two types of system can potentially provide adequate support for knowledge-intensive processes.

The approach followed to weak workflow support combines a project management tool's flexibility with the complexity handling aspects of workflow management systems. It provides open points allowing for later process refinement at runtime and for flexible change possibilities that may facilitate on-the-fly adaptation of processes (see Klein et al., 2000, for a review of issues on adaptive workflow).

The introduction of such an IT solution in an organization should be done with appropriate methodological guidance and modelling tools. For this reason, a business process knowledge method is being developed that integrates the modelling and management of processes and knowledge assets. This method consists of the following steps: business process identification, business process analysis, task analysis, business process design, ontology creation and ontology refinement. The modelling tool extends the formalisms used in most existing business process modelling tools (see Yu and Wright, 1997, for a review of related tools), supporting the modelling of weakly structured processes and domain knowledge structures. It comprises five modelling perspectives: task specification, organization, data, process logic and knowledge perspectives (Papavassiliou and Mentzas, 2001).

The applicability of the IT solution and method is being tested on the business processes of IKA, the largest Greek social security organization. For example, work is ongoing on the process of granting full old-age pension to insured people which, as part of a normal administrative workflow, is to some extent a straightforward and well-defined business process. Nevertheless, it contains critical knowledge- and document-intensive steps for finding a decision (see Wenger, 1998, for similar forms-based knowledge-intensive processes). In this case, the steps of the process are often done under uncertainty, they are influenced by many legal regulations and they are vital for the correct result of the process. The preliminary application of the approach has shown a significant area for improving the performance of the business processes by capturing and sharing the knowledge assets involved.

7.3.2 Knowledge Asset Trading

This book has presented a total solution for leveraging a firm's knowledge assets; but how can a firm create the greatest market value, and therefore generate the greatest revenues, from these knowledge assets? Can firms sell knowledge assets, creating smart offerings that embed such assets, or develop knowledge-based products that embody knowledge assets? Which are the most appropriate pricing mechanisms for these offerings? How can they be promoted? How can they be organized and sold in an electronic marketplace? What are the points of view of the customer (needs met) and the supplier (return on investment), as well as the impacts of such an approach to products on its related processes?

These are some of the questions explored in a recent research programme on knowledge asset marketplace development (Mentzas and Abecker, 2001). This research attempts to extend the traditional Internet-based marketplaces (e-marketplaces), which improve overall market efficiency, reduce transactional costs by integrating sourcing, purchasing and billing; and provide wider choices of buying and selling trading partners, centralize access to information, and allow for pricing that better reflects supply and demand (Mohan, 2000; Archer and Gebauer, 2001; McKinsey, 2000; Aberdeen Group, 2000). The research explores the development of knowledge trading marketplaces, i.e. marketplaces that provide the digital community context where knowledge seekers can find knowledge providers (Kaieteur Institute, 2001).

Despite related research work, current virtual knowledge trading marketplaces have major limitations. They emphasize the explicit dimension of knowledge assets, thereby ignoring the complex context and content features, which determine the applicability and usefulness of knowledge in a given situation. Moreover, they do not consider the fact that the real power of electronic marketplaces lies not in copying ways of working already known from traditional business, but in exploiting the strength of synchronous and asynchronous community building. Finally, they limit their focus to the technical issues and do not take into account business matters such as customer relationships, advanced revenue models and alternative pricing mechanisms.

Further research should aim to address the above shortcomings. For instance, an effort has been initiated to build a solution for knowledge trading, which gives due attention to both technological and methodological developments and investigates long-term issues such as the creation of trust and customer satisfaction.

The first research statement in this effort is that in an interorganizational knowledge trading scenario the pivotal role of community building cannot be overemphasized. Hence, the process builds upon and extends the concepts and methods for building virtual communities of transaction that provide the necessary features for the trustworthy commercial and social environments needed for shared community knowledge trading. Such communities extend electronic product catalogues into participatory electronic product catalogues, which combine aspects of product information and community building (Schubert, 2000; Schubert and Ginsburg, 2000).

A second research stream refers to the explicit description of supply and demand, and the matchmaking between the two. Since knowledge is by definition highly context dependent, all explicit representations (on the seller's side) will necessarily decontextualize it to some extent. In addition, in a knowledge e-marketplace sophisticated representations of products and customer needs are needed, which should also express aspects such as knowledge quality and knowledge actuality, which can hardly be dealt with in a general manner. In this approach we use a knowledge-rich, ontology-based formalization of knowledge objects and the domain of application as the backbone of the matchmaking system (McGuinness, 1999). Although there already exist proposals for specific types of knowledge assets, such as lessons learned, best practices or expert knowledge, there has been neither a generally agreed upon proposal on any of these object types, nor a unifying view of all of them. To cope with the difficulties of clearly stating a knowledge demand or the content of a knowledge object, an ontology modelling tool is being developed that also exploits case-based similarity, building upon the REFSENO methodology (Althoff et al., 1999).

A final research direction in the knowledge asset trading programme refers to the analysis and evaluation of alternative trading mechanisms and models for price setting and negotiating (e.g. auctions and exchanges) and the role and functions of knowledge infomediaries. This builds on and extends the business media framework of Schmid and Lindemann (1998).

7.4 Leveraging Knowledge Assets for k-Business

Chapter 1 outlined the need for managing knowledge as an enabler for organizational growth. Throughout the book it has been shown how the management of an organization's knowledge assets can be developed, nurtured and facilitated by the Know-Net solution. It is the authors' belief that the knowledge asset-based line of thinking may also assist in exploring the current evolution of society towards a knowledge society and the progress from e-business towards k-business.

k-Business can be defined as any professional activity that generates value to the consumer by enhancing the usefulness of the knowledge assets used and by improving the ways to find, share and use them. Many different knowledge businesses are possible. These include being a knowledge portal, a knowledge aggregator, a knowledge refiner or a knowledge franchiser (Skyrme, 2001). New knowledge mechanisms and models for k-business are continually emerging as innovators combine elements from knowledge assets in a myriad of different ways. The number of different pathways through a knowledge value system multiplies as knowledge moves from person to person, and changes between explicit and tacit. A k-business can focus on specific knowledge domains or applications, on specific knowledge processes, or on any of the infinite number of possible combinations.

The shift towards k-business is also evident from the change of emphasis in companies from a predominantly inward-looking perspective to an external one. Most knowledge initiatives start with a focus on reusing existing knowledge assets to improve internal processes. The next logical move is to extend the scope of knowledge asset management beyond the enterprise (Holger Rath, 2001). As organizations start to recognize their internal knowledge as a valuable asset, they then examine how to exploit it externally. Creating knowledge products and services is only one aspect of creating a profitable knowledge business. The way in which knowledge products are marketed and traded is fundamentally different to that of traditional products.

e-Business opens up new channels of distribution, marketing, trading and networking. The power of e-business is that it offers much more than the mere handling of online transactions. First, it offers a wealth of information and knowledge that can help buyers to assess their requirements, identify suitable products and suppliers, and receive online after-sales support. Multimedia can further enrich the buying experience. Second, the Internet is an effective communications medium, where all kinds of one-to-one, one-to-many and many-to-many communications are possible. Third, because of global connectivity, the Internet opens up worldwide electronic marketplaces, which are a hotbed of innovation in new ways of trading.

On the other side of the coin, knowledge asset management can help companies to progress along the e-business path, from "brochure-ware" and on-line interaction, to trading and full integration with back-office systems. E-business processes require input from knowledge assets, perhaps much of it initially from outside. Technical, e-business, market and competitive knowledge assets need to be acquired and regularly updated. The accumulated knowledge needs to be managed and accessible. Each step of the progression should be treated as a learning exercise, with the repository of knowledge assets being refined and updated in the light of new experiences.

So, there is a natural link between KM and e-business, and a wealth of both applied research areas and business opportunities that are at the intersection of the two. This fusion of KM and e-business perhaps represents the true value creation opportunities of managing knowledge assets.

Appendix

Knowledge Orientation Matrix

A.1 Overview

The knowledge orientation matrix is a simple tool to assess the knowledge orientation of an organization and determine how advanced an organization is in knowledge management (KM) (Figure A.1, Table A.1).

There are three distinct stages in the KM journey of an organization: still at the base camp, knowledge aware and knowledge leveraging. Each stage has its own characteristics and resource requirements.

A.1.1 Still at the Base Camp

This stage is characterized by little interest among the senior management for managing knowledge. The organization is unaware of the importance of knowledge to the achievement of its goal. There is no clear KM strategy. Knowledge is created, shared, used and organized in an ad hoc manner with no clear structure, systems and processes in place. Accessing and retrieving information is time consuming

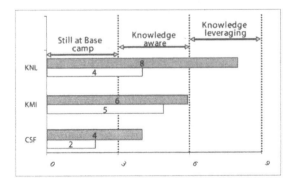

KNL :   Knowledge Networking Level
KMI :   Knowledge Management   Infrastructure
CSF :   Critical Success Factors

Figure A.1 Typical output of knowledge orientation matrix.

Table A.1 Tabular form of the knowledge Orientation Matrix

	Still at the base camp	Knowledge aware	Knowledge leveraging
Critical success factors			
Awareness			
Senior management buy-in			
Knowledge-sharing culture			
Measures to gauge KM benefits			
Incentives and rewards for knowledge sharing			
KM infrastructure			
Strategy			
Structure			
Processes			
Systems			
Knowledge networking levels			
Individual			
Team			
Organizational			
Interorganizational			

because of difficulty in identifying sources of knowledge. The level of collaboration and communication between individuals and teams is low.

A.1.2 Knowledge Aware

In this stage the organization is aware of the need to harness knowledge and senior management, though not completely convinced, is willing to experiment with the concept. A beginning has been made to consolidate the KM infrastructure and improve collaboration within the organization. Sources of knowledge within the organization have been identified and documented. The awareness across the organization is not uniform, and the processes, structure and systems for KM have still not been implemented.

A.1.3 Knowledge Leveraging

KM is beginning to benefit the business. Senior management is committed to providing the resources and time for explicitly managing knowledge assets in the organization and there is a clear KM strategy and direction. Knowledge resources have been inventoried, evaluated and classified. The organization is attempting to network with customers, suppliers and competitors.

A set of questions is posed to assess where you might be positioned in this model. The questions are divided under three broad headings based on the Know-Net holistic framework: critical success factors (CSFs) KM infrastructure and knowledge networking levels. The presence or absence of these three parameters tells a lot about the extent to which an organization is leveraging its knowledge. A company that has the technology for KM but very low awareness is not optimally leveraging its knowledge. It can improve further by increasing the awareness about KM in the organization. The model is designed to indicate the areas in which the company should focus.

A.2 Questionnaire for Developing the Matrix

A.2.1 Critical Success Factors

The questionnaire for the CSFs is given in Table A.2.

A.2.2 KM Infrastructure

The questionnaire for the KM infrastructure is given in Table A.3.

Table A.2 Questionnaire for critical success factors

Awareness	
People at all levels in the organization have a general understanding of the concept of "knowledge management"	NA ○ 1 ○ 2 ○ 3 ○
People at all levels recognize knowledge as a key resource	NA ○ 1 ○ 2 ○ 3 ○
People in the organization are aware of the need to manage knowledge assets proactively	NA ○ 1 ○ 2 ○ 3 ○
Senior management buy-in	
There is a board-level representation for KM	NA ○ 1 ○ 2 ○ 3 ○
Top management in the firm is committed to KM	NA ○ 1 ○ 2 ○ 3 ○
Top management recognizes KM as an important part of the business strategy	NA ○ 1 ○ 2 ○ 3 ○
Knowledge-sharing culture	
Recording and sharing knowledge is routine and second nature	NA ○ 1 ○ 2 ○ 3 ○
Failure is seen as an opportunity to learn	NA ○ 1 ○ 2 ○ 3 ○
Change is accepted as part of working life	NA ○ 1 ○ 2 ○ 3 ○
All employees are cooperative and helpful when asked for some information or advice	NA ○ 1 ○ 2 ○ 3 ○
Knowledge sharing is seen as strength and knowledge hoarding as a weakness	NA ○ 1 ○ 2 ○ 3 ○
Measures to gauge knowledge management benefits	
Intellectual assets are recognized and valued	NA ○ 1 ○ 2 ○ 3 ○
There is a senior-level ongoing review of the effectiveness of KM to the whole company	NA ○ 1 ○ 2 ○ 3 ○
Intellectual assets are recognized and valued	NA ○ 1 ○ 2 ○ 3 ○
Incentives and rewards for knowledge sharing	
Good KM behaviour such as sharing and reusing knowledge is actively promoted on a day-to-day basis	NA ○ 1 ○ 2 ○ 3 ○
Bad KM behaviour is actively discouraged	NA ○ 1 ○ 2 ○ 3 ○
Individuals are visibly rewarded for knowledge sharing and reuse	NA ○ 1 ○ 2 ○ 3 ○

Table A.3 Questionnaire for the KM infrastructure

Strategy	
KM is a vital part of the business strategy	NA ○ 1 ○ 2 ○ 3 ○
There is a vision for how KM should integrate into the business	NA ○ 1 ○ 2 ○ 3 ○
There are defined responsibilities and budget for KM initiatives	NA ○ 1 ○ 2 ○ 3 ○
There is a clear ownership of KM initiatives either by business units or by the whole business	NA ○ 1 ○ 2 ○ 3 ○
The organizations hones its skills for generating, acquiring and applying knowledge by learning from other organizations' learning processes	NA ○ 1 ○ 2 ○ 3 ○
The organization systematically assesses its future knowledge requirements and executes plans to meet them	NA ○ 1 ○ 2 ○ 3 ○
Processes	
Key knowledge assets such as customer knowledge are identified, preserved and maintained	NA ○ 1 ○ 2 ○ 3 ○
Effective cataloguing and archiving procedures are in place for document management (not necessarily electronic)	NA ○ 1 ○ 2 ○ 3 ○
Intellectual assets are legally protected	NA ○ 1 ○ 2 ○ 3 ○
Training and development programmes in KM behaviour are undertaken from the point of recruitment	NA ○ 1 ○ 2 ○ 3 ○
There is hardly any duplication of effort in the organization	NA ○ 1 ○ 2 ○ 3 ○
In the day-to-day work, it is easy to find the right information	NA ○ 1 ○ 2 ○ 3 ○
When a team completes a task, it distils and documents what it has learned	NA ○ 1 ○ 2 ○ 3 ○
Structure	
There are specified roles and responsibilities for KM activities in the organization	NA ○ 1 ○ 2 ○ 3 ○
Formal networks exist to facilitate dissemination of knowledge	NA ○ 1 ○ 2 ○ 3 ○
Internal staff rotation is actively encouraged to spread best practices and ideas	NA ○ 1 ○ 2 ○ 3 ○
Systems	
Technology is a key enabler in ensuring that the right information is available to the right people at the right time	NA ○ 1 ○ 2 ○ 3 ○
There are systems in place to facilitate effective communication across boundaries and time zones	NA ○ 1 ○ 2 ○ 3 ○
Information retrieval is effective	NA ○ 1 ○ 2 ○ 3 ○
There are complete IT security procedures in place (backup, recovery, etc.)	NA ○ 1 ○ 2 ○ 3 ○

A.2.3 Knowledge Networking Levels

The questionnaire for the knowledge networking levels is given in Table A.4.

A.3 Evaluating the Knowledge Orientation Matrix

Assign a value of 0 to the NA (not applicable) entries and add the total for each sub-section (awareness, senior management buy-in, knowledge-sharing culture, etc.). Use the following guide to determine where you are and where you want to be in what timeframe (Table A.5).

Table A.4 Questionnaire for the knowledge networking levels

Individual	
Individuals are committed to continual improvement and are constantly generating new ideas within the organizational context	NA O 1 O 2 O 3 O
Resources are committed for ongoing training and development of individuals	NA O 1 O 2 O 3 O
Team	
The teams in the organization are effective, self-managed teams composed of individuals capable of learning from each other	NA O 1 O 2 O 3 O
There is good intrateam communication and sharing of knowledge	NA O 1 O 2 O 3 O
Organizational	
Virtual or remote teams are supported effectively in terms of access to networks or knowledge	NA O 1 O 2 O 3 O
Multidisciplinary teams are effectively formed and managed	NA O 1 O 2 O 3 O
There is participative goal setting, measurement and feedback	NA O 1 O 2 O 3 O
Interorganizational	
Technology is shared with clients and suppliers where appropriate to enhance relationships	NA O 1 O 2 O 3 O
Ideas for alliances and joint ventures are constantly reviewed and acted on when necessary	NA O 1 O 2 O 3 O

Table A.5 Knowledge orientation matrix assessment

	Still at the base camp	Knowledge aware	Knowledge leveraging
Critical success factors			
Awareness	< 5	5–7	> 7
Senior management buy- in	< 5	5–7	> 7
Knowledge-sharing culture	< 6	6–9	> 9
Measures to gauge KM benefits	< 3	3–4	> 4
Incentives and rewards for knowledge sharing	< 5	5–7	> 7
KM infrastructure			
Strategy	< 7	7–14	> 14
Processes	< 10	10–14	> 14
Structure	< 4	4–7	> 7
Systems	< 5	5–8	> 8
Knowledge Networking Levels			
Individual	< 3	3–4	> 4
Team	< 3	3–4	> 4
Organizational	< 4	4–7	> 7
Interorganisational	< 3	3–4	> 4

Analyze and Leverage Knowledge in Business Processes

This appendix gives detailed guidelines for implementing modules 1 and 2 of stage II of the Know-Net method.

B.1 Module 1: Analyze Business Processes

B.1.1 Purpose of Module

- To analyze selected business processes in order to understand how *business processes, people, systems* and *content* are related, and reveal *who* needs *what* knowledge and *when* they need it.
- To identify the knowledge gaps within the execution of the business process and elicit requirements for knowledge management (KM) within the business process.
- To provide input to the knowledge asset schema by identifying knowledge *assets, objects* and their attributes.
- To understand and depict the knowledge *flow* within the business process.

B.1.2 Where to Start From

Start from the Identified Key Business Areas

Based on the high-level identification of strategic knowledge assets and business areas, review key business processes that support them. Understanding the objectives of the organization (enterprise, department, division, workgroup) allows you to focus on small KM projects without losing sight of the big picture. Based on the key business areas, review the key business processes that are executed within each business area.

Base the Analysis on what Stage I Identified as of Strategic Importance

It is advisable to look for documentation of the business processes under examination before you start. If the organization has recently undergone a re-engineering project, for instance, there should exist analyses of the business processes. In most cases, however, these business processes may not be formalized or explained anywhere. Set up small meetings with process experts or people who can steer you in the right direction. If the strategic orientation of stage I stresses quality and the organization's customers have a low tolerance for defects, focus on the quality management business process. If the organization's revenue over the next few years will be driven less by new sales and more by selling to the existing customer base, you need to focus on the customers' value. You may even need to evaluate suppliers' business processes.

Go through the steps presented below. You can use a flowcharting tool to visualize the process maps. Depicting the business processes in charts is not compulsory, however. Alternatively, you can use Table A.1 (module template) as a way to report on the business process analysis.

Example

Suppose we are focusing on the service delivery business process of an IT consulting company. Such companies usually operate on a project-based approach. The service delivery business process for a technical product such as an integrated IT system comprises the following steps and activities.

1. *Initiate project*: A project manager is assigned. The project manager identifies the scope of the consulting engagement, forms the project team, identifies the objectives of the assignment, and works out an overall work plan for the project.
2. *Plan project*: A more detailed plan is developed. The plan includes timeline, responsibilities of people, specific tasks, software development/systems integration details and financial budgeting.
3. *Execute project*: This is the actual implementation phase in which the project team works to deliver the system/study to the client.
4. *Evaluate project*: This is the closing phase of the project. The team evaluates the results, assesses the impact of the result, collects lessons learned and feedback from client, etc.

B.1.3 Things to Look for when Analyzing the Business Processes

- Understand where, when and what type of knowledge is needed within the business process.
- Add the knowledge workers: what personnel are involved in the business process? What are their job descriptions and responsibilities? You may need to consult the human resources department.

Figure B.1 Sample "deliver services" business process.

- Are there documents and expertise regarding the business process that are currently scattered around the company?
- How important and how feasible is it for this information to be collected at an easy-to-access place?
- How can the needed information be delivered ideally to help those involved in the business process to do their jobs better? Through a web page, e-mail, personal agent, new reports or better use of existing databases?

B.1.4 Identify the Knowledge Objects Involved

This step helps you to understand how information, tacit and explicit knowledge are used in the chosen business process (Figure B.2). Start by identifying those events where people need to act effectively to move the process along. This step shows how content fits into each part of the business process and how to prioritize it.

Example

Continuing from the previous example, the focus is on the first step/activity, namely "initiate project". When preparing the initial plan of the project the project manager:

- looks for consultants/developers based on their competences; the project manager is looking for information about the current and previous assignments in which the consultant has been involved, the training seminars that he or she has attended, his or her personal development plan for enhancing competences, his or her preferences, etc.
- analyzes how the company delivers such services, by looking at service/methodology descriptions, handbooks, etc.

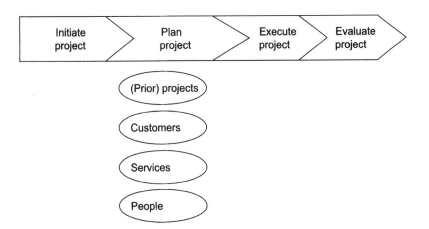

Figure B.2 Identifying the knowledge objects involved.

- refines the time, activity and resource plan for the new assignment based on the contract with the client and the previous experience within the company (if any), by looking at similar past assignments, locating their project plans, locating the people responsible for such plans, talking to these people, etc.
- examines the resource availability of people in order to make staff allocations and define the consulting assignment project team, by defining the required competences for the specific assignment, searching across the people competences, and checking their current and planned availability
- analyzes previous company "knowledge" experience, e.g.:
  - how have similar assignments been carried out by the company in the past?
  - what were the major problems (if any)?
  - what were the major results?
  - what "traps" may a project director fall into when defining the plan?

B.1.5 Things to Consider in Identifying Knowledge Objects

- Do not hung up on perfection. Most business processes are not precise.
- Focus on a consensus or a general understanding.
- Interview key people involved. Ask about inefficiencies in the business process. Many people have a good understanding of where they succeeded or failed in such processes.

B.1.6 Add the People

This step identifies the people who "consume" or "generate" knowledge at each step/activity of the business process (Figure B.3). Who is responsible for executing

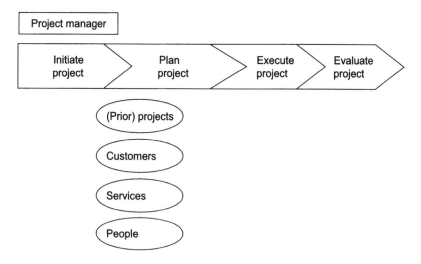

Figure B.3 Adding the people.

each task? What are the relevant job titles? Write them on the map showing how they connect to the different steps and knowledge objects. You may need to talk to people who are recognized performers in the business process. What can they tell you about who is involved? Interview these people if necessary to obtain insight on their knowledge requirements.

Example

As discussed above, the project manager is the main person involved in the first step/activity, namely "initiate project". You simply add the project manager to the map.

Things to Consider when Adding the People

● Consult the human resources department. They can provide you with useful information such as job descriptions or point you to the right people involved in the business process.
● Talk to mangers who govern the business process. They will also be able to point you to the people who are involved.
● Do not narrow your focus to people in the organization alone. Consider people outside the organization.

B.1.7 Identify Detailed Content

Having identified the people and knowledge at each step in the process, you will need to identify in more detail the information and knowledge that they need (Figure B.4). This step normally involves interviews with the people who were identified in the previous step. They are the best source for discovering what information they need to be successful.

An even better way to search for insight is to organize facilitated workshops with a small number of employees. These workshops may even include partners, customers or people who can make suggestions that lead to a successful audit. It is advisable to set up focus groups with the people who were identified in the previous step. You, as a facilitator, can elicit knowledge requirements by assisting and guiding people to identify the real knowledge needs within their everyday work. Devise interview questions that help you to determine what information is necessary for them to act.

Example

The knowledge objects are refined based on a more detailed analysis of the task or an interview with project managers. For instance, as discussed above, the "service" knowledge object includes knowledge of company-used methodologies, e.g. the Structured Systems Analysis and Design Method (SSADM), the Unified Modelling Language (UML) and service descriptions.

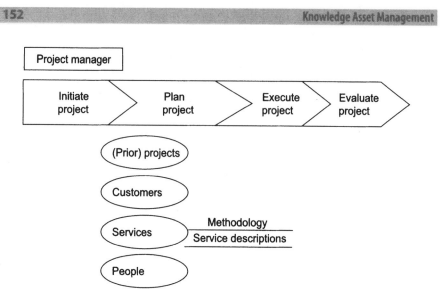

Figure B.4 Identifying detailed content.

Things to Consider in Identifying Detailed Content

● Talking to the people involved in the business process allows you to refine your entire picture of the business process.
● Focus on understanding the content that helps people to act.

B.1.8 Map the Systems

This is the final step during which you identify the systems used to support the detailed content (Figure B.5). These could be IT-based systems such as a web server, a file or a database, or non-IT systems such a report or a document stored in the library.

Let us assume that descriptions of the company services are currently stored on the "seminars database" of a Lotus Notes server.

Things to Consider in Mapping the Systems

● Do not start from the IT department. Although people in the IT department know better the IT infrastructure of the organization, they are not the ones who are using the information and therefore they do not know exactly where and how people are looking for information. This is even more true when people make heavy use of the Internet.
● Having mapped the systems, talk to the IT department and have them verify that what you have recorded is in accordance with to the existing IT infrastructure.

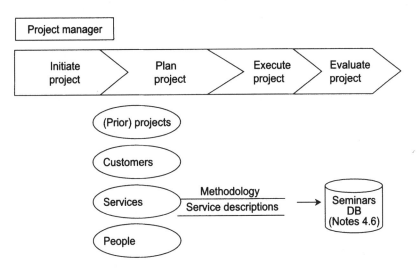

Figure B.5 Mapping the systems.

B.1.9 Sample Questionnaire

This section contains indicative questions for interviewing people involved in steps/activities of business processes under examination. The goal of this set of questions is to find out what knowledge needs people have when executing a specific step/activity within a business process.

● What are the knowledge-centred characteristics of these steps/activities?
● What should KM activities focus on?
● What kind of KM support could be appropriate?

Whom do you Ask the Questions?

Ideally, you should interview the people identified during the analysis of the business processes. They are the key stakeholders and they know first hand what they need to perform. If practical limitations prevent you from profiling all of the people involved, you can focus on the few people who "govern" the business process, i.e. those who really understand it. For instance, you can ask the manager who is responsible for the outcome of the process. If possible, though, do not limit the interviews to veterans or long-term business partners. Some of the greatest knowledge seekers within the process are people who are new to the organization and are trying to get up to speed with their new tasks.

How do you Ask the Questions?

Profiling can be accomplished in many different ways. An effective way is to watch a day in the life of the employee. What are the employee's sources of frustration?

Where do processes seem to go very smoothly? Finding this information may involve travelling to remote offices to observe people's daily lives.

Do not rely on sending out e-mail surveys and expect people to answer them in a way that helps you; it is likely that people will not give you the information you need. A good way to search for insight is to conduct focused interviews with a small group of key people who are involved in the business process. These people could also be outsiders (clients, suppliers, etc.).

Sample Questions

- What are the three or four typical situations in which lack of information affects you or hinders your ability to do the specific step/activity effectively?
- How often do you perform the step/activity? Is it possible that it is not clear when a certain step/activity is finished, or that a finished step/activity must be considered again after some time?
- How important is the step/activity? Is it "mission critical"?
- What potential for improvement is there within the step/activity? Which things could be done better? Could be done more easily? Could be done more safely? Are things often done wrongly, insufficiently, or inefficiently? Are there obvious errors because certain documents, rules, information sources, old experiences, experienced colleagues, etc., were not regarded?
- How repetitive or how formal is the step/activity under consideration? Can you build a task list saying what things must be done, and partly, in which order? Would such a structure be useful (e.g. for tracing open business processes)?
- How knowledge intensive is the step/activity under consideration? Does it require much personal knowledge? Tacit knowledge, experience, social or communication skills, factual expert knowledge? Is the processing of internal or external knowledge sources (persons, databases, documents, archives, etc.) important and central? Is it useful to have access to knowledge, artefacts or documentation from older, similar business cases in order to reuse or adapt older decisions and experience?
- How document intensive is the step/activity under consideration? Are many paper-based or electronic inputs needed or outputs created? Are formal documents in use to support the business process, communication or documentation? Is it usual to employ personal archives, memos, notes and annotations to perform and document the process?
- How communication oriented is the step/activity under consideration? Why? How many people work together? Where are they working? How often do they communicate? Always the same people? Do they share knowledge? Why is communication required? Via which media do they communicate? Would it be possible and useful to have an archive of such communication?
- How collaboration oriented is the step/activity under consideration? How many people with which specific expertise and competences collaborate? How important are the different contributions for the end result? Is the collaboration process in some way structured or organized? Are specific ways for collaboration required or would they be useful, such as shared document editing, shared

design editing, shared artefact repositories, video conferences, telephone conferences and live meetings?

● What about change management? How stable is the step/activity, its input/output, constraints (market situation, competitors, legal restrictions, suppliers) and results? How are changes noticed and what effects do they have on the tasks and the knowledge required? Are there specific knowledge and information sources to be constantly watched for changes? Are there specific procedures to deal with change?

B.2 Module 2: Leverage Knowledge in Business Processes

B.2.1 Purpose of Module

● To enhance KM within existing business processes.
● To design new business processes and KM organizational roles for explicitly managing specific knowledge assets.
● To support the new design with IT (Know-Net or not) applications and services.

B.2.2 Where to Start From

Start from the Identified Key Business Areas

You may start from the knowledge asset schema. Using the process map developed with module 1, decide whether it is possible to enhance the management of a particular knowledge asset by improving existing business processes or by designing completely new processes explicitly to support management of the specific knowledge asset.

Improve the Existing Process ...

If you have undertaken module 1, you may use the process maps created and think of new steps or activities that, if added, would enhance the management of the knowledge assets in question. Think also of new organizational roles that may be required to undertake the new steps. Alternatively, assign responsibilities of new steps to existing organizational roles.

... or Design a New Process

To design a new process for managing a knowledge asset there must exist a clear need for that, as well as an initial vision. A clear need may mean that management of a particular knowledge asset cannot be facilitated within existing processes or that it is considered so important that it requires special handling. The clear vision should include answers to how, in broad terms, the process will work and what it will achieve.

In the design of the new process you should perform similar steps to those followed in modifying an existing one. You should, however, pay additional attention to identifying critical success factors for the new process, potential barriers to implementation of the new process, and other similar issues that are related to the introduction of changes in the organization.

In any case, it is likely that you will need to perform a short stakeholder analysis. Stakeholders are individuals or groups who, at some time during the implementation of this module, will affect and be affected by what is happening. Depending on the scope of the change the stakeholder population could include customers, employees, process owners, business partners, etc.

B.2.3 How to Design the New Activities/Steps/Process

Design the added activities/steps or the entire new process based on the knowledge asset schema, developed in module 5. Work around the knowledge assets and their attributes. In any additions or modifications to the business processes that you design, make sure that all metadata, classification and indexing information required by the system are fulfilled in these steps.

The design of the new activities/steps or process must aim towards the following outcomes.

Introduction of Knowledge Leveraging Steps Within Existing Business Process

The following questions need to be addressed for each knowledge asset.

1. What knowledge is required to execute the process? Design steps that clearly take into consideration existing knowledge, e.g. for sharing knowledge on the subject that already exists in the organization. Establish organizational roles with clear responsibilities for the execution of the new steps, e.g. a *topic expert* who can direct people to the right sources of knowledge.
2. What knowledge is produced within this process? Design steps that clearly capture new knowledge produced, e.g. for *distributing* knowledge created within the process. Establish roles with clear responsibilities for the execution of the new steps, e.g. a *topic expert* who develops competences and experiences in this subject.
3. Is any knowledge produced as a by-product of this process? Design mechanisms to capture it.
4. What IT or other systems are going to be used in the new activities/steps?

The example presented in Figure B.6 is based on the process analysis example of module 1. There is a need to capture some project knowledge early, even before the project has actually started. This is a simple task and can be undertaken by someone in an existing organizational role, the project manager. The information will be stored on the existing file server of the organization.

Simplification and Improvement of Existing KM in Business Process

1. Are many people involved in existing KM in the business process? Try allocating resources more efficiently.

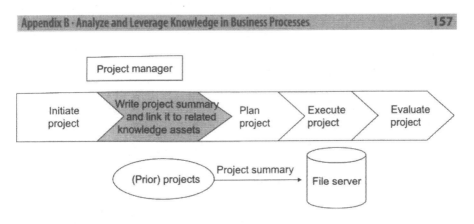

Figure B.6 Add new steps in the business process.

2. Are many different systems or documents used? Are there any documents used that are stored locally? Design a centrally managed repository. Assign resources to manage this repository.
3. Is there a need for better managing existing KM in the business process? For instance, is there duplication of KM activities (different people doing similar knowledge-related tasks, e.g. searching the same Internet sites for similar information)? Assign clear responsibilities as to who does what, where information should be stored, when tasks should be done, consideration of review processes for knowledge created/consumed, etc.

Integration of KM Activities Within Daily Work Practices

1. Can existing, non-KM steps/activities be slightly altered so that they accommodate the knowledge-leveraging steps? For instance, can you supplement an existing report that is an outcome of an existing step with a section that reports on knowledge generated in this step?
2. Can you assign KM responsibilities and ownership of specific content to people who are performing related activities as a standard work practice?

Automation of the New KM Steps/Activities

1. Which of the Know-Net applications are suitable for supporting the redesigned process?
2. How will this technology complement the present IT infrastructures, as depicted in the maps of module 1?
3. How will it be integrated and managed?
4. Will a new set of IT development skills be required?
5. Will automating the KM steps provide long-term leverage?
6. With respect to automation, a word of caution: automating processes for the sake of automation will not lead to significant improvement. It is not necessary for the

new KM steps to be supported by IT, as this may be overwhelming. Often a good archiving mechanism is all that is required.

B.2.4 Example Knowledge Leveraging Steps

The following are examples of modules that can be introduced within the business process to enhance knowledge creation and sharing. The list illustrates the different possibilities of knowledge leveraging modules that can be used.

- Lessons learned databases provide an effective and powerful approach to learning from noteworthy situations. Lessons learned are prepared by individuals who are familiar with the situation and its setting, as well as the management, business and technical perspectives. An effective lessons learned report must include a structural set of worksheets, which guide the process and document the situation and the associated learnings.
- Knowledge elicitation mechanisms help individuals to explain and explicate what they know so that others can use it. Knowledge elicitation can be performed ad hoc or by a designated team of competent professionals who systematically elicit knowledge for inclusion in the KM system.
- Linkage to knowledge networks in the form of formal referral paths provides backup and support within the areas of expertise.
- Training activities periodically communicate what has been learned.
- Job rotation of non-experts to learn from experts in particular business processes.
- Paper-based training manuals document in writing the process-related know-how.
- Case-based reasoning techniques utilize valid knowledge documented in cases for known or correct conditions.

B.2.5 Things to Consider

Any additional tasks assigned to existing organizational roles should be done very carefully. You should try to embed these "overhead" tasks in the existing work practices. Technology can be a significant enabler towards achieving this goal. Define in detail any customization that needs to be done to Know-Net applications or services. If required, document user requirements for completely new applications or agent functionality and discuss with the KM team the feasibility of developing them specifically to support the business process.

Any modifications to existing business processes will almost certainly impinge on authority, power and culture. Such implications can present considerable barriers to the successful implementation of change initiatives, which is why top management sponsorship is essential.

Establishing a steering committee of senior board members is a requirement. The steering committee will have responsibility for:

- defining the scope and initial vision of the business redesign

- defining the key process characteristics and critical success factors
- giving direction and guidance
- appointing process design teams
- approving plans and providing resources (labour and cash)
- tracking usage and performance.

C Analyze and Leverage Knowledge Networks

This appendix gives detailed guidelines for implementing modules 3 and 4 of stage II of the Know-Net method.

C.1 Module 3: Analyze Knowledge Networks

C.1.1 Purpose of Module

● To identify whether knowledge networks exist within the organization.
● To identify the requirements for better knowledge management (KM) within knowledge networks.
● To identify inefficiencies in the knowledge flow within the knowledge networks.
● To understand the basic patterns of informal knowledge flow needed in order to design and moderate knowledge networks (module 4).

C.1.2 Where to Start From

To identify existing knowledge networks, you may start from the high-level strategic business areas where the KM initiative is going to focus. Figure C.1 shows how knowledge networks are linked to business areas.

Alternatively, if the high-level audit has revealed strategic knowledge assets or core competences of the organization, you may start directly from there and work to identify knowledge networks that embody the organization's knowledge assets and core competences.

Conduct a Network Survey

In a second phase the knowledge networks that embody the organization's knowledge assets should be identified. The consultant in collaboration with the change agent can analyze networks in three steps. The first step is to conduct a network survey using interviews with employees. The survey is designed to solicit responses about who talks to whom about work, who advises whom on technical matters, etc. It is important to pre-test the survey on a small group of employees to see whether

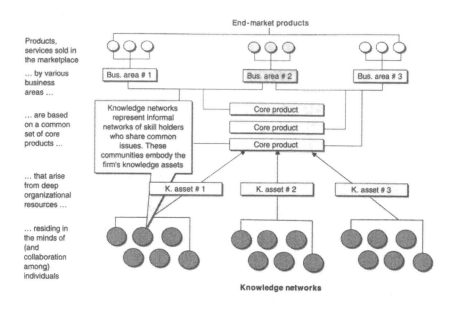

Figure C.1 From business areas to knowledge networks.

any questions are ambiguous or meet with resistance. The following are among the questions that should be asked.

- Whom do you talk to every day concerning knowledge asset n?
- Whom do you go to for help or advice at least once a week concerning knowledge asset n?
- With one day of training, whose job could you step into?

It is very important that such interviews with employees *should be focused around the knowledge asset under examination*, and not general discussions regarding internal communication patterns.

Cross-check Responses

Once the interviews are completed, the second step is to cross-check the responses. Some employees, worried about offending their colleagues, say that they talk to everyone in the department on a daily basis. The final map should be based not on the impressions of one employee but on the consensus of the group.

Draw a Map

The third step is to process the information using one of several commercially available flowcharting computer programs. The consultant, with maps in hand and in

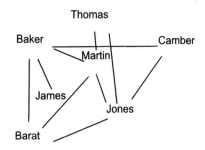

Figure C.2 The knowledge network reveals the informal knowledge flow.

close collaboration with the change agent and other managers, can devise a strategy that plays on the strengths of the informal organization (Figure C.2).

C.1.3 Profile People in the Network

Profiling people who participate in knowledge networks is the key to leveraging knowledge creation and management successfully within these networks. People usually become members of knowledge networks not because they are obliged to do so but mostly because they receive personal satisfaction by being part of these communities. Because this is a fundamental driving force of knowledge networks, understanding and supporting the human factor is imperative. Profiling of people should therefore be done in this context and should be aimed primarily at understanding issues such as "meaning in the workplace" for the people involved in the networks. Therefore, questions to be asked should aim to identify personal interests, job satisfaction factors, personal ambitions and expectations, but also personal competencies, experiences, skills, etc.

Indicative questions include the following.

- What are your personal interests? In which one of the knowledge assets described above would you be more interested in actively participating? With which people would you like to collaborate on this?
- If you need to call someone informally for information regarding this knowledge asset, how do you know whom to call? What do you do if you don't know? Why do you call this particular person?
- What do you best like to do when you informally collaborate with other people from the knowledge network?
- What do you do in your free time regarding this knowledge asset?
- What are you favourite sites/journals/newspapers regarding this knowledge asset? Which ones do you read in your free time?
- What are the factors that hinder/encourage you to contact someone from the same/a different department?
- What do you think could be improved in the network? Would you like to have someone facilitating communication and collaboration in the network? Who would be ideal for this?

- What about technology? Would you use Internet forums, for instance, to communicate? Is a more specialized application required?
- What experience/competences/skills do you have with respect to these knowledge assets?

It is important to note that such questions or interviews should focus on the key knowledge assets that the network deals with, and should not be a general discussion about all personal interests and habits.

C.1.4 How to Identify Knowledge Networks

There are several ways to identify knowledge networks in an organization. The following three characteristics make a knowledge network.

- *Mutual engagement*: This is the combination of what we do, what we know, and the ability to connect meaningfully to the contributions and knowledge of others. In these communities, it is important to give and receive rather than to try to know everything yourself. Furthermore, each participant in a community of practice finds a unique place and gains a unique identity, which is defined in the course of engagement.
- *A joint enterprise*: The enterprise of a knowledge network refers to a statement of purpose, and also includes a sense of mutual accountability among those involved. Accountability includes a shared understanding of what matters, what does not, what is important and why it is important, what to do and what not to do, what to pay attention to and what to ignore, what to talk about and what to leave unsaid, what to justify and what to take for granted, what to display and what to keep in, when actions and artefacts are good enough and when they need improvement or refinement.
- *A shared repertoire*: The repertoire of a knowledge network includes routines, words, tools, ways of doing things, stories, gestures and symbols. The community has either adopted these or produced this repertoire in the course of its existence and they have become part of its practice. Further, communities develop a sense of identity. This identity may be reflected in how the members dress or even in how they maintain their desks.

C.1.5 Types of Network

Knowledge sharing takes place between informal networks of people who share similar goals and interests. Such informal networks or communities vary depending on the geographical distribution of their members and the social proximity of people participating in them. Ernst & Young, for example, recognizes five types of community (Figure C.3). These are characterized in two dimensions: organizational reach (global versus local) and community member cohesiveness (low versus high).

At one end we have economic webs. These are networks with wide geographical distribution (could be nation-wide or even world-wide) and very low social cohesiveness (typical members have not even met each other in person). An economic web may be formed by companies that participate in a supply chain (e.g. main

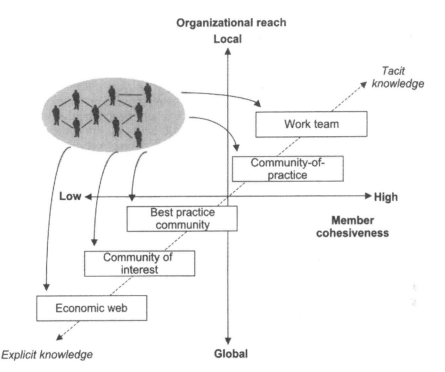

Figure C.3 Types of network. (Source: Ernst & Young.)

manufacturers, subcontractors and suppliers). At the other end we have work or project teams of people who know each other quite well, meet regularly face-to-face and share professional as well as social encounters. In the middle there are communities that have similar interests, professional experience, etc., or communities of interest (e.g. professional chambers or associations).

Alternative categorization of knowledge networks can be based on the purpose of the network.

● Helping networks provide a forum for community members to help each other to solve everyday work problems.

● Best practice networks develop and disseminate best practices, guidelines and procedures for their members' use.

● Knowledge stewarding networks organize, manage and steward a body of knowledge from which members can draw.

● Innovation networks create breakthrough ideas, knowledge and practices.

Determining the primary intent for a knowledge network will help to determine how the community will be organized in terms of key activities that it will undertake, community structure and leadership roles. Although communities may serve more than one of these purposes most communities focus on one type and develop their structure with that specific intent in mind.

C.1.6 Things to Look For

- *Fit between networks and business objectives*: Determine whether networks are in sync with the identified strategic knowledge assets and key business areas.
- *Imploded relationships*: Communication maps often show networks of people within departments that have few links to other groups. In these situations, employees in a department spend all their time talking among themselves and neglect to cultivate relationships with the rest of their colleagues. Frequently, it is only the most senior employees who have ties with people outside their areas.
- *Irregular communication patterns*: The opposite pattern can be just as troubling. Sometimes employees communicate only with members of other groups and not among themselves. A lack of cohesion resulting in factionalism suggests a more serious underlying problem that requires bridge-buildling. Initiating discussions among peripheral players in each faction can help to uncover the root of the problem and suggest solutions.
- *Fragile structures*: Sometimes group members communicate only among themselves and with employees on one other division. This can be problematic when contribution in several areas is necessary to accomplish work quickly and spawn creativity.
- *Holes in the network*: A map may reveal obvious network holes, places you would expect to find relationship ties but do not.
- *"Bow ties"*: Another common trouble spot is the bow tie, a network in which many players are dependent on a single employee but not on each other. Individuals at the centre knot of a bow tie have tremendous power and control within the network.
- *Geographical distribution*: Assess the geographical distribution of the network. This element will be useful at a later stage when you decide which of the Know-Net tool applications will best support the network.

C.2 Module 4: Leverage Knowledge Networks

C.2.1 Purpose of Module

- To design and moderate knowledge networks that manage identified knowledge assets.
- To support existing knowledge networks of people, through management and non-management as well as through technology.

C.2.2 Where to Start From

You should start from the detailed description of the knowledge asset schema. As a rule of thumb, one knowledge network should be built for each core knowledge asset. Additional knowledge networks can act as satellites and serve subsets of knowledge (i.e. specific attributes of a core knowledge asset).

In the product knowledge network, for example, the satellites could be networks that deal with technical specifications, training material, product best practices, etc.

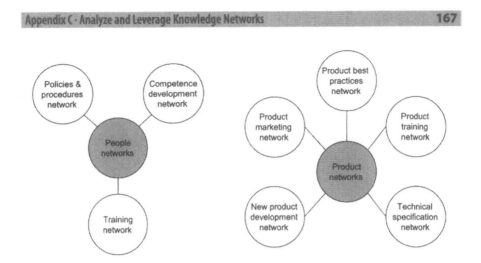

Figure C.4 Knowledge networks should map the knowledge asset schema.

Ideally, this organization of the knowledge networks should map directly to the already developed knowledge asset schema (Figure C.4). It is important to stress that the point is to organize knowledge networks around the core knowledge assets of the organization and not to replicate the existing departments and organizational structures.

C.2.3 Things to Consider

● Rely on the already developed knowledge asset schema. If necessary, make required adjustments to it.
● As a rule of thumb, each network satellite should be a manageable domain for a single person who can oversee the content.
● Build on existing knowledge networks. Go through the knowledge networks report. See whether there are already knowledge networks that deal with the knowledge asset under examination.

C.2.4 Create the Knowledge Network Blueprint

The knowledge network blueprint aims to support the entire process of creating a knowledge network, from design to implementation.

Although typically knowledge networks are self-organized groups that naturally communicate with one another because they have common work practices, interests and aims, the Know-Net methodology aims to formalize the internal dynamics of the community by establishing the "knowledge interchange system".

This includes not only the definition of community roles and responsibilities, but also technological support for collaboration. The knowledge network blueprint comprises six main steps (Figure C.5).

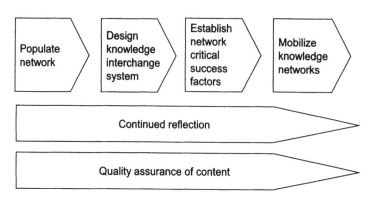

Figure C.5 Main steps for creating the knowledge network blueprint.

Populating Knowledge Networks

Individuals who could learn form each other and have a stake in the network's success should be welcome as network members. The essence of these networks is their members. Members are self-organizing and participate because they gain value from their participation. Participation is voluntary and employees are encouraged to participate only if they see the network purpose to be meaningful and believe that they could gain from or contribute to the community.

- Build on existing networks of people as much as possible. It is much easier to make minor shifts to the focus of an existing network (where people know each other and the trust and political issues have been balanced out) than to put the effort into establishing a new community.
- When populating a new knowledge network around a knowledge asset consider the people profiles as identified with the diagnostic tools. Try to match, as much as possible, people's interests and experiences with the knowledge assets and content satellites.
- Involve people with overlapping personal goals.
- Network membership should span the corporate organization chart both laterally and vertically. It may contain individuals dispersed throughout the organization and in different departments (Figure C.6).
- Each knowledge network should involve approximately 5 to 15 professionals. Too large networks can hinder effective communication and collaboration.
- There should be a mix of people in the network, including experts in the area, professionals who have working experience and others who are just interested in the area. You may also consider involving outsiders, such as academics, vendors, former employees and even competitors (with limited access) (Figure C.7).

Designing the Knowledge Interchange System

The knowledge interchange system includes the following factors.

- *Definition of network identity*: A collective understanding of the purpose of the

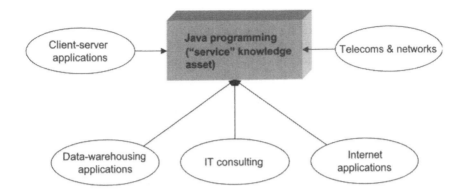

Figure C.6 Knowledge network participants span the organization.

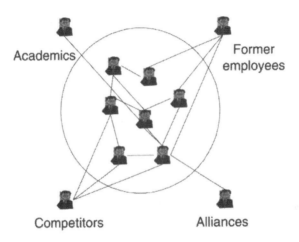

Figure C.7 Knowledge networks extending beyond company borders.

network is useful in having people working together in a collaborative environment. The identity should address the network's purpose, how the network supports the business objectives, how the network determines whether or not it is adding value, what members need from the network, and what cultural norms and conventions will be honoured.

● *Definition of roles and appointment of new roles to support the network*: Networks may be supported by "corporate roles" that provide resources and infrastructure support, or the network may provide these roles internally to its own organization. Such roles are useful when getting a community up and running, creating or capturing knowledge, and providing continuous focus and support. Roles may be associated with a specific network or support and link multiple networks and/or other KM initiatives (such as knowledge-intensive business processes). Roles do not equate to job positions; they can be viewed as responsibilities within the context of the team. Typical network roles include:

   – *leader*, who sets direction and provides guidance, resolves issues, ensures that the network receives the support needed, tracks the progress of the network, plans and coordinates the allocation of resources, resolves problems and spreads the word throughout the organization;

- *facilitator*, who energizes the process and provides continuous nourishment for the network. The facilitator typically tries to connect members with each other, manages day-to-day activities of the team, helps to create and foster a collaborative environment, recognizes contributions and provides support on network infrastructure (tools, processes, group dynamics);

- *subject expert*, who serves as a subject matter expert on the focus of the community. The subject expert brings in new ideas when the community starts to lose energy, has recognized competences on specific areas related to the network, harvests and creates new knowledge, and acts as a champion for the team.

The above roles also ensure that the network infrastructure is in place to meet the requirements, build community expertise, locate or foster the collaborative environment and provide crucial input for the design and management of the infrastructure (e.g. establish the network ontology).

Additional roles are those responsible for *quality assurance, brokers* who connect people and information across network boundaries, *administrative coordinators* who coordinate meetings, events and schedules, documenters who document network proceedings, librarians, etc.

- *Definition of expectations within the network*: Different people join knowledge networks for different reasons. Some want to learn from others, others to establish personal relationships with people working in similar areas. Different purposes yield different expectations. These expectations should be taken into account separately and should be monitored through the evolution of the network. If personal expectations are not met, it is likely that people will start losing interest and eventually will dissociate themselves from the network.

- *Assignment of ownership for content*:
  - Owners of information should be management-level people.
  - Owners provide a contact point for the clarification and validation of content.
  - Without ownership at the network satellite level, it is difficult to enforce discipline in terms of ensuring the quality of information.
  - No matter how well the collection and presentation of useful information is done, people need to know who they can call or e-mail for more.

- *Tool application selection and customization*: The network will need an operational environment in which to collaborate. This should address practical requirements (e.g. geographical distribution of network) as well as cultural and habitual requirements (e.g. is the team Internet literate or used to using the phone). Alternative strategies for capturing knowledge should be revised ad hoc, depending on the peculiarities. For instance, if the network rejects the idea of an Internet discussion forum and prefers to use the phone, it should be ensured that there is a mechanism or a person that captures the essence of the communication, so that this is reusable by others. As another example, if the network communicates via high-bandwidth Internet access then audio or video conferencing could be used. At this phase any customization required to the agent's facilities should be addressed, as well as the assignment of filtering and access rights for Know-Net applications.

Establishing Network Critical Success Factors

Examples of knowledge network success criteria are:

● personal satisfaction and fulfilment
● organizational knowledge management and advancement
● satisfaction of specific knowledge goals
● reduction in hours needed to solve problems
● number of innovative ideas
● member satisfaction survey results
● success stories
● transfer and adoption of best practices
● sustained mutual relationships
● decrease in effort required to accomplish specific tasks.

Mobilizing Knowledge Networks

● *Introduce members*: Introduce individuals (especially those in different locations) facing similar issues to one another, perhaps by sponsoring an internal symposium addressing large common problems.
● *Provide resources*: Give resources, such as a small budget or a conference location, to network members as requested; do not require specific deliverables or "payback" for resources allocated.
● *Allow slack time*: Create time for network members to interact, perhaps by including the creation of slack time. Talk to members' managers about the need for slack time!
● *Provide visibility*: Publicize the network to ensure that all potential members are aware of its existence; encourage participation based on the desire to attract senior management's attention.
● *Recognize output*: Acknowledge the output of the network to encourage continued creation of collaborative solutions over time.

Ensuring Improvement and Progress (Continuous Reflection)

The following is a checklist of the issues that should be addressed periodically to ensure the success of the knowledge network. Solutions should be developed and implemented to address potential problems.

● Is the network purpose aligned with the business objectives?
● Is there a critical mass of experts or content to provide perspective and meaning to the membership of people?
● Is there a shared environment for people to collaborate as a team?
● Are there enough members to keep the network alive?
● Are needed resources available?

● Is there enthusiasm between the members?

● Does management agree that "employee time away from the job" is valuable?

● Another valuable exercise would be for the network members loosely to evaluate their participation. Collecting lessons learned from network members provides a tool for obtaining feedback on the value and the meaning of the knowledge network.

Techniques for Enhancing KM Within Networks of People

The purpose of this section is to suggest techniques for generating ideas, building relationships and promoting knowledge flow and transfer. The following is an overview of the techniques included in the *Community of Practice Practitioner's Guide* (NAVSEA, 2001) that aim to support the creation, capture and sharing of knowledge.

● *Group sessions*: These range from spontaneous, ad hoc sessions that serve primarily as brainstorming or sounding boards, to host-facilitated, problem-solving meetings, which are an excellent approach to creating and sharing knowledge about best practices. These forums serve many purposes:
  – they solve relevant, day-to-day problems
  – they build trust among network members by enabling them to help each other
  – they solve problems in a public forum, thereby creating a common understanding of tools, approaches and solutions.

  Often during problem-solving discussions, members will discover areas where they need to create common standards or guidelines. These discoveries may lead to the formation of smaller, more focused work groups to develop detailed standards for incorporation into best practice recommendations.

● *Lessons learned*: People learn by reviewing their successes and failures, accessing them systematically, and recording the lessons in a form that employees find open and accessible. Recording network members' experience with projects, work operations, client engagements, site visits, etc., can help to ensure that useful knowledge is shared and that mistakes are not repeated. Regardless of the medium in which the lessons learned are stored, it is important that a record is made while events are still fresh. In effect, this allows access to accumulated hindsight, as opposed to hindsight that has been tempered by poor memory recall and defensive reasoning (Kransdorff and Williams, 1999).

● *Storytelling*: The construction of fictional examples to illustrate a point can be used to transfer knowledge effectively. An organizational story is a detailed narrative of management actions, employee interactions or other intraorganizational events that are communicated informally within the knowledge network. Conveying information in a story provides a rich context, which remains in the conscious memory longer and creates more memory traces than information out of context. Storytelling, whether in a personal or an organizational setting, connects people, develops creativity and increases confidence. The use of stories in knowledge networks can build descriptive capabilities, increase organizational learning, convey complex meaning, and communicate common values and rule sets.

● *On-the-job learning*: This involves the formation of a small group of people who share common issues, goals or learning needs. This group works to resolve issues and achieve these goals together, meeting regularly, about once a month, to reflect on progress, issues and solutions, and refine the way forward. The team can brainstorm on alternative approaches or offer advice to an individual on how to proceed in achieving specific goals. Emphasis is on trying new things and evaluating the results.

Develop the Knowledge Asset Schema

This appendix gives detailed guidelines for implementing module 7 of stage II of the Know-Net method.

D.1 Purpose of Module

- To finalize the identification of the knowledge assets and related knowledge objects, and their characteristics (attributes).
- To design the metadata, or properties, of knowledge assets, such as ownership and tags.
- To develop a common ontology that will allow employees to search accurately across many sources of information.
- To design corporate classification schemata based on the common ontology.

D.2 Knowledge Object Store and Knowledge Ontology

A knowledge object store is required to support the disciplined, formal and, in some cases, mandatory archiving of knowledge objects. Such a disciplined approach ensures that all information collected or distributed adheres to some department or company standards, e.g. has the name of the author on it. Having such structured mechanisms in place reduces the noise in knowledge distribution and will simplify the passing of information from creators to users. The price that the organization has to pay for these advantages is the overheads that are required first to design the knowledge object store for organizing knowledge objects (which also includes metadata, content types, etc.), and second to package and store knowledge objects according to the schema.

Nevertheless, presentations of and queries about information content must be allowed in many ways that need to be independent of the way in which information was provided originally. In this context there does not exist only one, uniform model for information structuring and storage. In order to have a more effective knowledge organization that supports different conceptual levels for structuring information, alternative classification mechanisms are used (such as ontologies). These mechanisms allow employees to organize their knowledge objects according to their conceptual understanding of the business, and then retrieve information by making use of the facilities that these mechanisms provide.

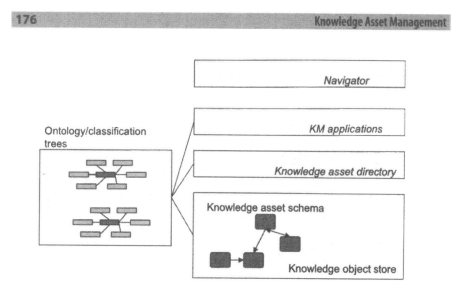

Figure D.1 Two sides of knowledge organization in Know-Net.

For the first feature (formal knowledge organization according to a data model), Know-Net provides the knowledge object store, which is the storage mechanism for the collection of knowledge assets and their attributes (including metadata). For the second feature, Know-Net provides mechanisms for building ontologies and classification schemata, as described below. In brief, an ontology is a centrally managed taxonomy of terms, while classification schemata are used to provide different views on the same information according specific users' needs. Figure D.1 illustrates this schematically.

D.3 Development of the Knowledge Object Store

Mapping knowledge to business processes has helped to identify the important pieces of information that need to be captured and delivered to the key knowledge workers and in critical business processes. You can start from the description of the knowledge assets and their attributes that are part of the output of module 1.

Mapping knowledge to networks helps to locate information within human networks and to identify the life cycle of informal knowledge. This step will design the knowledge architecture, creating a common vocabulary and well-defined content types. Before proceeding to the actual design of the knowledge object store an additional refinement process is needed, which includes:

● the identification and arrangement of possible overlap. This exercise is of significant importance if you have undertaken both modules 1 and 3. It is practically certain that you will have identified the same knowledge assets twice during the work done for these modules.

● logical grouping of knowledge assets into high-level categories and grouping of lower level of knowledge assets into subcategories. For instance, "product" knowledge would be a high-level knowledge asset, while "technical specifications" or "training material" would be subcategories of "product" (secondary knowledge asset in the Know-Net terminology; please refer to the Know-Net tool documentation for more information).

If you are starting directly from this point you need to focus on the high-level identification of strategic knowledge assets and business areas, as this was done in stage I of the Know-Net method. Here, you have to work in more detail and produce a formal specification of the knowledge assets, objects and attributes that are going to become the elements of the Know-Net knowledge object store. The Know-Net knowledge object store has a built-in default collection of knowledge objects and attributes. It is advisable to go through this collection and compare it with the one that you produced. It may be easier for you to keep the default collection and make changes and additions as appropriate.

D.4 Development of the Knowledge Ontology

D.4.1 What is an Ontology?

An ontology is a shared and common understanding of some domain that can be communicated across people and computers. (The definition given builds on definitions by Gruber, 1993; Guarino, 1995; and Benjamins et al., 1998.) An ontology can be defined as a formal, explicit specification of a shared conceptualization.

- *Conceptualization*: an abstract model of some phenomenon in the world produced by identifying the relevant concepts of that phenomenon.
- *Explicit*: the type of concepts used and the constraints on their use are explicitly defined.
- *Formal*: the ontology should be machine readable.
- *Shared*: an ontology captures consensual knowledge, that is, it is not private to some individual, but accepted by a group.

An ontology describes the subject matter using the notions of concepts, instances, relations, functions and axioms. Concepts in the ontology are organized in taxonomies through which inheritance mechanisms can be applied. To come up with a consensual ontology of some domain, it is important that the people who have to use the ontology have a positive attitude towards it. Dictating the use of a particular ontology to people, to which they have not contributed, is not likely to succeed. Preferably, an ontology is constructed in a *collaborative effort* of domain experts, representatives of end users and IT specialists.

D.4.2 How do you Build the Ontology?

This section draws from Uschold (1996). It applies the methodological advice given there to the Know-Net solution.

Purpose

Ideally, an ontology builder should first have a clear idea of why the ontology is wanted, what it will be used for and possible mechanisms for its use. In practice, this is not always easy to achieve.

Ways to proceed include the following.

- Identify and characterize the range of intended users (e.g. managers, technical people, consultants).
- Identify motivating scenarios and competency questions and use these to help to clarify specific uses and mechanisms (see below).

Subject Matter

The subject matter that an ontology characterizes can be anything at all. Three widely accepted categories are:

1. subjects such as IT or finance, considered separately from the problems or tasks that may arise relevant to the subject
2. the subject matter of problem solving
3. the subject matter of knowledge representation languages.

An ontology in the first category is frequently called a domain ontology; an ontology for the second is usually called a task, method or problem-solving ontology. The terms representation and meta-ontology are used to refer to ontologies in the third category.

This is by no means intended to be a complete characterization of how subject matter may differ; in particular, the first category is very fuzzy and organization- and context-specific. Many subdimensions are possible, such as uncertainty or impression in the domain.

Level of Formality

A prospective ontology builder must also decide how formal the ontology needs to be. This is determined in large part by the purpose and users of the ontology. For example, if the users are non-technical people and the primary purpose is to provide a shared vocabulary to facilitate communication between them, then an informal glossary may suffice. In general, the degree of formality required increases with the degree of automation in the tasks that the ontology will support. For example, if the intended use is to support interoperability or reuse and sharing of knowledge bases, then a more formal representation will be required.

In some cases both an informal and a formal ontology may be required to satisfy both technical and non-technical users. Where there are only technical users, it may still be useful to generate a complete informal ontology, which can serve both to document and to specify a subsequent formal encoding. There may be good reasons for any or all of these approaches depending on the specific circumstances.

Purpose of the Ontology in Know-Net

The primary, expected purposes and uses of an ontology in the Know-Net context are to facilitate communication between people and to enable a common indexing and searching infrastructure.

As such, the purpose and formality of the Know-Net ontology can be characterized as:

- *level of formality*: Structured or informal
- *purpose*: To facilitate communication between members of the organization by giving a consistent terminology; to provide an infrastructure for indexing and searching based on common concepts and terms
- *subject matter*: Organization environment (i.e. subject matters, services, products, structure, external environment).

Scope: Subject Matter

Once the purpose and level of formality of the ontology have been fairly well determined, the next step is to identify the scope. The output for this phase is a set of concepts and terms covering the full range of information that the ontology must characterize to satisfy the requirements already identified. There are two main ways to proceed with this process.

- *Motivating scenarios and informal competence questions*: One excellent way to gain a clear picture of the scope of the ontology is to create detailed scenarios that arise in the applications. These correspond to story problems and the scenarios should include possible solutions to the problem. This may have been done at a high level previously to help to clarify the purpose of the ontology. At this stage, more detail and more coverage are appropriate. Ideally, exemplary scenarios for all envisaged situations and uses should be identified.

    It may be that the concepts and terms defining the scope of the ontology can be gleaned directly from the scenarios themselves, by casual inspection. However, this is somewhat ad hoc. A more thorough approach is to use the scenarios as the basis for defining a complete set of competence questions.

    Competence questions are based on the scenarios and express different reasoning problems that must be supported. A set of questions is complete in the sense that if the ontology can provide answers to all of the questions, then the ontology can serve its intended purpose. In other words, the set of competence questions collectively specifies the expressive and reasoning requirements of the ontology.

    Thus, we know what must be *in* the ontology. However, scoping also entails knowing what must *not* be in the ontology. The competence questions can also be used for this. Very simply, if there is no competence question that requires the use of a term or concept, then that term or concept is not included.

    Competence questions should be devised in a hierarchical manner, starting with general ones, which in turn give rise to more specific ones.

    The most adequate context in which to create the scenarios is during the application of the audit–leverage pairs of modules of stage II of the Know-Net method.

    For instance, specific scenarios can be formulated during the analysis and design of a business process. The scenario should correspond to alternative steps/actions that are performed by the different organizational roles/actors in the context of the business processes under examination.

● *Brainstorming and trimming*: Motivating scenarios and competence questions are not always ready to hand, or they may not sufficiently cover the expected requirements. This may arise if no clear purpose emerged in the initial step. In this case, brainstorming could also be used effectively instead of or in conjunction with motivating scenarios and competence questions to do a more thorough and accurate job of scoping.

Brainstorming can take place during the focused workshops of modules 1–6 of stage II of the Know-Net method, during which the performance indicators are also identified.

Proceed as follows.

- First brainstorm to produce a list of all potentially relevant concepts. If, collectively, the people involved possess insufficient expertise, then another body of knowledge may need to be consulted to ensure adequate coverage. The nature of brainstorming is that initially, nothing is excluded. Therefore, some way to trim the set of concepts down to size is required. There are two reasons for removing terms: lack of relevance and duplication [i.e. (near) synonyms].
- To determine relevance, compare with the output of the previous stages, which should have identified one or more of: purposes, a requirements document, motivating scenarios and/or competence questions.
- For each and every term you should make a conscious decision as to whether to keep it or get rid of it. To make the task more manageable, it may help to *group* the terms into semantically similar categories. This will also facilitate identifying duplicate terms, which can be eliminated, as well as form a basis for organizing the ontology in later stages of development.

Scoping: Concluding Remarks

The primary and necessary output of the scoping phase is a set of concepts and terms that must be included in the ontology. The concepts may or may not have been structured in some way, e.g. into groups, or perhaps implicitly by inheriting a hierarchical structure that may have existed in the set of competence questions from which the terms were derived.

As indicated above, the degree to which there is confidence in these terms being the right ones varies according to how they were identified. In all cases, however, it should be expected that there will be some later modification and fine-tuning. This will be the result of the careful analysis required to produce the definitions and structure the ontology as it was being designed and built, as well as during the evaluation phase.

The need for refinement and fine-tuning is true for all aspects of analysis and modelling performed with the Know-Net methodology, and it is accommodated by the cyclic approach of the whole method.

D.4.3 Building the Ontology

To illustrate the steps needed an example is given of the development of an ontology for an IT consulting company. This section restricts the ontology development to the level of detail required by the Know-Net tool.

Develop a Glossary

The first step is to build a glossary of terms that includes all of the terms (concepts, instances, attributes, verbs, etc.) of the domain (department, network of people or company) and their description, as shown in Table D.1.

Note that this step is important for resolving ambiguities between ontology terms. It is, however, not used by the Know-Net tool, therefore it is up to the knowledge management (KM) team to decide whether they will undertake this step, since it can be laborious.

Table D.1 Glossary

Name	Synonyms	Description
Practice	Know-how	The core competence or expertise that is underneath a wide variety of services or products that the firm offers to its clients
Maritime industry	Shipping industry	
Publication	Article	
Market analysis	Market research	
Deliverable	Report	
Proposal	Tender, bid	

Table D.2 Example Concept Classification Trees

Industry
  Automotive
  Energy
  Financial services
    Banking
    Insurance
    Credit institutions
  Health care
  Insurance
  Life sciences
  Manufacturing
  Retail
  Transportation
Services
  IT consulting services
    Strategic IT master planning
    IS analysis and design
    IT improvement design
    IT project management
  Systems and solutions delivery services
    Client-server systems development
    Web-based systems development
Document
  Deliverable
  Proposal
    Proposal presentation
    Tender
  Marketing material
  Training material
  CV
  Internal document

Develop Classification Trees

The second step is the development of concept classification trees. Each concept classification tree represents a taxonomy for the domain. Taxonomies can be also seen as different views for presenting the same information. For example, for the IT consultancy the concept classification trees in Table D.2 were identified.

The third step is to build ad hoc binary relations diagrams between concept classification trees (Figure D.2). The goal of these diagrams is to establish relationships between concepts of the same or different ontologies.

D.4.4 Testing and Maintaining the Ontology

During testing checks are made as to whether the developed ontology satisfies the requirements set during the planning phase. In this step the ontology is also tested in the target application environment. Feedback from pilot testing may be valuable input for further refinement of the ontology.

The ontology often needs to be changed to reflect changes in the business environment. To reflect these changes ontologies have to be maintained frequently. This will be the responsibility of a knowledge professional (i.e. the knowledge manager), who will gather feedback and thoroughly test possible effects on the applications before committing to any changes.

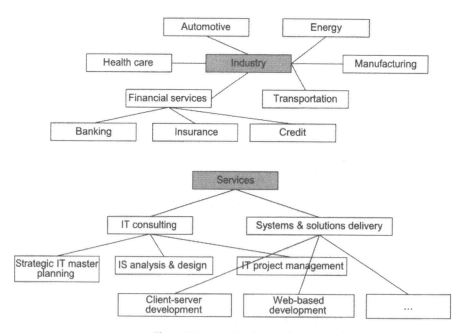

Figure D.2 Example of an ontology.

General Criteria

Various general criteria should be borne in mind when creating definitions and organizing an ontology. These can also be used after-the-fact as evaluation criteria.

● *Clarity*: Definitions should be maximally clear and unambiguous, whether expressed in natural language or formally encoded. Use examples where possible to illustrate what is intended; negative examples can also be useful to clearly show what is *not* intended and where mistakes may be anticipated. In addition, state all underlying assumptions, especially where they are not explicitly formalized as axioms.

● *Consistency and coherence*: An ontology should be internally consistent; circularity should be avoided, especially if a formal encoding is desired. It should also be externally consistent, so that terms conform to common usage. Avoid introducing new terms by consulting dictionaries, thesauri and technical glossaries.

● *Extensibility and reusability*: An ontology should be designed in such a way as to maximize subsequent reuse and extensibility. This can be achieved by getting the right balance between its being specific enough to perform the required tasks, but not so specific that it will be of little use to others. During formal coding, symbol-level biases should be avoided, e.g. those made purely for the convenience of notation or implementation. It also helps to be very careful to avoid introducing several terms that mean roughly the same thing; instead, identify the key underlying term and reuse it to define other terms. This achieves parsimony, which in turn facilitates reusability.

Other Guidelines

Some specific guidelines are provided to assist in identifying terms and producing definitions.

● *Go middle–out*: In choosing which terms to define first, proceed in a middle–out fashion rather than top–down or bottom–up. The choice of whether to go top–down, middle–out or bottom–up has a number of effects. A bottom–up approach results in a very high level of detail. This, is turn:
  – increases overall effort
  – makes it difficult to spot commonality between related concepts
  – increases the risk of inconsistencies, which leads to
  – reworking and yet more effort.

● *Handling ambiguity*: To reach agreement when terms are used ambiguously, concentrate on the underlying ideas first, ignoring the terms. Define each related idea, inventing meaningless labels for each, then decide on the most important idea(s) and, *lastly*, choose appropriate terms.

● *Tailoring*: The intention is not for all departments to have a single, inflexible schema. Rather, the ontology needs to be tailored for each knowledge network. There should, however, be an overall consistency, at least as far as the high-level categories are concerned. Each network should adopt these terms when appropriate, while continuing to use their own classification scheme for specialized information and knowledge.

● *Structure*: KM ontologies often have some similar high-level structure for different organizations; for instance, customer, competitor, product, technology and sales operations branches of the hierarchy are commonly used, though with very different topics at the narrower levels.

● *Quality*: the quality of an ontology depends on:
  - its structure (whether it parallels business processes)
  - the use of concise and familiar terminology
  - the lack of synonyms that confuse usage
  - the lack of orphan topics (those not part of the structure)
  - its evolution to cater for new issues and entities.

● *Stability of ontology structure*: This is important so that users can find their way around. Changing it regularly, say every time an analysis of documents is made, will be counter-productive.

● *Location of topics*: Some narrow topics naturally exist in multiple branches of the hierarchy (i.e. they have more than one parent), because they belong to more than one part of the business structure.

References and Further Reading

Aas, K. and Eikvil, L. (1999) *Text Categorisation: A Survey*. Technical Report 941, Norwegian Computing Center.

Abecker, A. and Mentzas, G. (2001) Active knowledge delivery in semi-structured administrative processes. In: M. Wimmer (ed.), *Knowledge Management in Electronic Government, KMGov-2001*, 2nd International Workshop organized by IFIP WG 8.3 and 8.5, 22–24 May 2001, Siena, Italy, pp. 47–57.

Abecker, A., Bernardi, A., Hinkelmann, K., Kühn, O. and Sintek, M. (1998a) Techniques for Organizational Memory Information Systems. DFKI Document D-98-02. Kaiserslautern, Germany: DFKI.

Abecker, A., Bernardi, A., Hinkelmann, K., Kühn, O. and Sintek, M. (1998b) Towards a technology for organizational memories. *IEEE Intelligent Systems*, 13 (3).

Abecker, A., Bernardi, A., Maus, H., Sintek, M. and Wenzel, C. (2000a) Information supply for business processes – coupling workflow with document analysis and information retrieval. *Knowledge-Based Systems*, 13 (5): 271–284.

Abecker, A., Decker, S. and Maurer, F. (eds) (2000b) Special Issue on Knowledge Management and Organizational Memory. *International Journal on Information System Frontiers*, 2 (3/4).

Abecker, A., Bernardi, A., Ntioudis, S., Herterich, R., Houy, C., Legal, M., Mentzas, G.N. and Müller, S. (2001a), The DECOR toolbox for workflow-embedded organizational memory access. In: *ICEIS 2001, 3rd International Conference on Enterprise Information Systems*, Setúbal, Portugal.

Abecker, A., Mentzas, G., Legal, M., Ntioudis, S. and Papavassiliou, G. (2001b) Business-process oriented delivery of knowledge through domain ontologies. Presented at the *DEXA Conference, TAKMA-2001, 2nd International Workshop on Theory and Applications of Knowledge Management*, Munich, 3–7 September 2001.

Abecker, A., Hinkelmann, K., Maus, H. and Müller, H.J. (eds) (2002) *Geschäfts prozessorientiertes Wissensmanagement*. Berlin: Springer, Series xpert Press. (In German.)

Aberdeen Group (2000) *The e-Business Marketplace: The Future of Competition*. April.

Althoff, K.-D., Birk, A., Hartkopf, S., Müller, W., Nick, M., Surmann, D. and Tautz, C. (1999) Managing software engineering experience for comprehensive reuse. In: *11th International Conference on Software Engineering and Knowledge Engineering (SEKE'99)*.

Amidon, D. and Skyrme, D.J. (1997) *Creating the Knowledge-based Business*. London: Business Intelligence.

Angus, J. and Patel, J. (1998) Knowledge management cosmology. *Information Week* (http://techweb.cmp.com/iw/673/73olkn2.htm).

Anon. (2000) *Building and Sustaining Communities of Practice*. Final Report. American Productivity and Quality Center.

Apostolou, D. and Mentzas, G. (1999) Managing corporate knowledge: a comparative analysis of experiences in consulting firms. *Knowledge and Process Management*, 6, 3.

Applehans, W., Globe, A. and Laugero, G. (1999) *Managing Knowledge. A Practical Web-based Approach*. Addison-Wesley Information Technology Series.

APQC (1997) *Using Information Technology to Support Knowledge Management*. Consortium Benchmarking Study: Final Report.

Archer, N. and Gebauer, J. (2001) B2B applications to support business transactions: overview and management considerations. In: M. Wakerntin (ed.), *Business to Business Electronic Commerce*, Chapter 10. New York: Idea Group Publishing (forthcoming).

Argyris, C., Ruggles, R. and Seemann, P. (1997) *Leveraging Knowledge for Business Value*. Managing the Knowledge Organisation Working Group.

Arthur, W.B. (1990) Positive feedbacks in the economy. *Scientific American*, (February), pp. 80–85.

Arthur, W.B. (1996) Increasing returns and the new world of business. *Harvard Business Review*, (July–August), pp. 100–109.

Barchan, M. (1999) Measuring Success in a Changing Environment. *Strategy and Leadership*, May/June, pp. 12–15.

Barney, J. (1991) Firm resources and sustained competitive advantage. *Journal of Management*, 17, 99–120.

Benjamins, V.R., Fensel, D. and Gomez-Perez, A. (1998) Knowledge management through ontologies. In: U. Reimer (ed.), *Proceedings of the 2nd International Conference on Practical Aspects of Knowledge Management (PAKM-98)*, Basel, Switzerland. (http://sunsite.informatik.rwth-aachen.de/Publications/CEUR-WS/Vol-13/)

Bettoni, M., Ottiger, R., Todesco, R. and Zwimpfer, M. (1998) KnowPort – a personal knowledge portfolio tool. In: U. Reimer (ed.), *Proceedings of the 2nd International Conference on Practical Aspects of Knowledge Management (PAKM-98)*, Basel, Switzerland.

Blair, M.M. (1995) Corporate "Ownership". *Brookings Review*, (Winter), pp. 16–19.

Bontis, N. (1996) There's a price on your head: managing intellectual capital strategically. *Business Quarterly*, (Summer), pp. 41–47.

Bontis, N. (1998) Intellectual capital: an exploratory study that develops measures and models. *Management Decision*, 36 (2), pp. 63–76.

Bontis, N. (1999) Managing an organisational learning system by aligning stocks and flows of knowledge: an empirical examination of intellectual capital, knowledge and business performance. Unpublished doctoral dissertation. London, Canada: Ivey School of Business, University of Western Ontario.

Bontis, N., Dragonetti, N.C., Jacobsen, K. and Roos, G. (1999) The knowledge toolbox: a review of the tools available to measure and manage intangible resources. *European Management Journal*, 17 (4), pp. 391–402.

Brennan, J. (2001) Monitor for Government Agency. Paper posted on the web (http://www.sveiby.com.au/IntangAss/Brennan/intellectual_capital_barometer.htm).

Buckingham, S.S. (1998) Negotiating the construction of organisational memories. In: U.M. Borghoff and R. Pareschi (eds), *Information Technology for Knowledge Management*. Berlin: Springer, pp. 55–78.

Cap Gemini (1999a) *Managing your Knowledge for Sustainable Competitive Advantage*. White Paper.

Cap Gemini (1999b) The Cap Gemini Approach (www.capgemini.co.uk/challenge/kmm/kmm.htrm).

Coleman, J.S. (1990) *Foundations of Social Theory*. Cambridge, MA: Harvard University Press.

Computerworld Enterprise Business Solutions (1999) *Making Connections with Enterprise Portals*. White Paper.

Conner, K.R. and Prahalad, C.K. (1996) A resource-based theory of the firm: knowledge versus opportunism. *Organization Science*, 7 (5), pp. 477–501.

Cook, S. and Brown, S.J. (1999) Bridging epistemologies: the generative dance between organisational knowledge and organisational knowing. *Organization Science*, 10 (4) pp. 381–400.

Cusumano, M.A., Mylonadis, Y. and Rosenbloom, R.S. (1992) Strategic manoeuvring and mass-market dynamics: the triumph of VHS over Beta. *Business History Review*, 66 (Spring), pp. 51–94.

Davenport, T. (1996) Knowledge roles: the CKO and beyond. *CIO Magazine*, (April 1).

Davenport, T. and Prusak, L. (1998) Working knowledge: how organisations manage what they know. Boston, MA: *Harvard Business School Press*.

Davenport, T., Javenpraa, S. and Beers, M. (1996) *Improving Work Processes*. Center for Business Innovation, Ernst & Young.

Day, J. and Wendler, J. (1998) The new economics of organisation. *McKinsey Quarterly*, 1 (19).

De Long, D., Davenport, T. and Beers, M. (1997) *What is a Knowledge Management Project?* Center for Business Innovation, Ernst & Young.

Delphi Group (1998) *Best Practices in Knowledge Leadership, A Survey of 25 Organisations*. Boston, MA: Delphi Group.

Delphi Group (1999) *Knowledge Management. Enterprise Portals Shape Emerging Business Desktop*. White Paper.

Dierickx, I. and Cool, K.O. (1989) Asset stock accumulation and sustainability of competitive advantage. *Management Science*, 35 (12), pp. 1504–1511.

Dolmat-Connell, J. (1999) Developing a reward strategy that delivers shareholder and employee value. *Compensation and Benefits Review*, (March/April).

Drew, S.A.W. (1997) From knowledge to action: the impact of benchmarking on organizational performance. *Long Range Planning*, 30 (3), pp. 427–441.

Drucker, P. (1994) *Knowledge Work and Knowledge Society: The Social Transformations of this Century.*
Transcript of the Edwin L. Godkin Lecture delivered at Harvard University's John F. Kennedy School
of Government.

Drucker, P. (1997) The future that has already happened. *Harvard Business Review*, (September–
October).

Duffy, D. (1998) Knowledge champions. *CIO Enterprise Magazine*, (15 November).

Edvinsson, L. and Malone, M.S. (1997) *Intellectual Capital: Realising Your Company's True Value by
Finding its Hidden Roots.* Harperbusiness.

Epstein, M. and Manzoni, J.-F. (1997) The balanced scorecard and tableau de bord: translating strategy
into action. *Management Accounting*, (August), pp. 28–37.

Epstein, M..J. and Manzoni, J.-F. (1998) Implementing corporate strategy: from tableaux de bord to balanced scorecards. *European Management Journal*, 16 (2), pp. 190–203.

Fensel, D. (2001) *Ontologies: A Silver Bullet for Knowledge Management and Electronic Commerce.* Berlin:
Springer.

Glazer, R. (1991) Marketing in an information-intensive environment: strategic implications of knowledge as an asset. *Journal of Marketing* 55 (October), 1–19.

Grant, R. (1991) The resource-based theory of competitive advantage: implications for strategy formulation. *California Management Review*, 33 (3), pp. 114–135.

Grant, R.M. (1996) Prospering in dynamically-competitive environments: organizational capability as
knowledge integration. *Organization Science*, 7 (4), pp. 375–387.

Gruber, T.R. (1993) A translation approach to portable ontology specifications. *Knowledge Acquisition*, 5,
pp. 199–220.

Guarino, N. (1995) Formal ontology, conceptual analysis and knowledge representation. Special Issue on
the Role of Formal Ontology in the Information Technology. *International Journal of Human-
Computer Studies*, 43 (5/6), pp. 625–640.

Guarino, N., Masolo, C. and Vetere, G. (1999) Ontoseek: content-based access to the web. *IEEE Intelligent
Systems*, 14 (3), 70–80.

Hagel, J. III (1998) Shaping collaboration webs. Workshop: Knowledge networks: do we and our customers know what we know. Project: *Inventing the Organisations of the 21st Century*, (February)
(http://www.siemens.com/public/uk_sys/future/21cen/).

Hansen, M.T., Nohria, N. and Tierney, T. (1999) What's your strategy for managing knowledge? *Harvard
Business Review*, (March–April), pp. 107–116.

Hartigh, E. den and Langerak, F. (2001) Managing increasing returns. *European Management Journal*,
19 (4), pp. 370–378.

Havelock, E. (1976) *Origins of Western Literacy.* Toronto: Ontario Institute for Studies in Education Press.

Heijst, G. van, Spek, R. van der and Kruizinga, E. (1998) The lessons learned cycle. In: U.M. Borghoff and
R. Pareschi (eds), *Information Technology for Knowledge Management*, Berlin: Springer.

Holger Rath, H. (2001) e-Commerce powered by knowledge technologies. Presentation at the Conference
Knowledge Technologies 2001, 4–7 March 2001, Austin, TX, USA.

Huang, K.-T. (1997) Capitalizing collective knowledge for winning, execution and teamwork,
(http://www.ibm.com/services/articles/intelcap.html)

Illich, I. (1986) On literacy. Annual Meeting of the American Educational Research Association, San
Francisco, CA, USA.

Ives, W., Torrey, B. and Gordon, C. (1997) *Knowledge Management is an Emerging Area with a Long
History*, Working Paper, Andersen Consulting.

Ives, W., Gifford, T. and Hankins, D. (1999) *Integrating Learning Through Knowledge (and Skills)
Management*, Working Paper, Andersen Consulting.

Jansweijer, W., Stadt, E. van de, Lieshout, J. van and Breuker, J. (2000) Knowledgeable information brokering. In: B. Stanford-Smith and P.T. Kidd (eds), *E-business: Key Issues, Applications and Technologies.*
Amsterdam: IOS Press, S. 402–408.

Junker, M. (2000) Symbolisches Regellernen für die Textkategorisierung. PhD Thesis. Kaiserslautern:
University of Kaiserslautern and DFKI. (In German.) (forthcoming).

Kaieteur Institute for Knowledge Management (2001) *e-Knowledge Markets*. Toronto: Advanced Research Working Group, Kaieteur Institute.

Kaplan, R.S. (1996) *Mobil USM&R (A): Linking the Balanced Scorecard*. Boston, MA: Harvard Business School, 9-197-025.

Kaplan, R.S. and Norton, D.P. (1992) The balanced scorecard – measures that drive performance. *Harvard Business Review*, (January–February), pp. 71–79.

Kaplan, R.S. and Norton, D.P. (1993) Putting the balanced scorecard to work. *Harvard Business Review* (September–October), pp. 134–142.

Kaplan, R.S. and Norton, D.P. (1996a) *The Balanced Scorecard: Translating Strategy into Action*. Boston, MA: Harvard Business School Press.

Kaplan, R.S. & Norton, D.P. (1996b) Using the balanced scorecard as a strategic management system. *Harvard Business Review*, (January–February), pp. 75–85.

Karagiannis, D. and Telesko, R. (2000) The EU-Project PROMOTE: a process-oriented approach for knowledge management. In: U. Reimer (ed.), *PAKM 2000, 3rd International Conference on Practical Aspects of Knowledge Management*.

Kim, W.C. and Mauborgne, R.A. (1997) Fair process: managing in the knowledge economy. *Harvard Business Review*, (July–August), pp. 65–75.

Kingston, J. and Macintosh, A. (1999) Knowledge management through multi-perspective modelling: representing and distributing organisational memory. In: B.R. Gaines *et al.*, (eds), *12th Workshop on Knowledge Acquisition, Modeling and Management (KAW'99)*. Knowledge Science Institute, University of Calgary.

Klein, M., Dellarocas, C. and Bernstein, A. (2000), Introduction to the Special Issue on Adaptive Workflow Systems. *Computer Supported Cooperative Work*, 9, pp. 265–267.

Knapp, E. (1998) Knowledge management: the key to success in the 21st century. *European Business Information Conference*.

Know-Net Consortium (1999a) Refinement of the Knowledge Diagnosis Method D 6.1.

Know-Net Consortium (1999b) Stage 2: Developing the Knowledge Organisation D7.1.

Know-Net Consortium (1999c) Tool Documentation D4.2.

Know-Net Consortium (1999d) The Know-Net WWW site (www.know-net.org).

Kogut, B. and Zander, U. (1996) What firms do? Coordination, identity and learning. *Organization Science*, 7 (5), pp. 502–518.

KPMG (1999) *The Knowledge Journey*. White Paper (www.kpmg.com).

Kransdorff, A. and Williams, R. (1999) Swing doors and musical chairs. *Business Horizons*, 31 (May–June).

Kühn, O. and Abecker, A. (1997) Corporate memories for knowledge management in industrial practice: prospects and challenges. *Journal of Universal Computer Science*, Special Issue on Information Technology for Knowledge Management. 3 (8) (http://www.iicm.edu/jucs_3_8).

Kühn, O., Becker, V., Lohse, G. and Neumann, P. (1994) Integrated knowledge utilization and evolution for the conservation of corporate know-how. *Proceedings of ISMICK'94: International Symposium on the Management of Industrial and Corporate Knowledge*.

Leonard-Barton, D. (1995) *Wellsprings of Knowledge: Building and Sustaining the Sources of Innovation*. Boston, MA: Harvard Business School Press.

Lever Consortium (2001) The Lever WWW site (www.kmlever.com).

Lotus (1998) *Lotus, IBM and Knowledge Management*. White Paper (http://www.lotus.com).

McGuinness, D.L. (1998) Ontological issues for knowledge-enhanced search. In: *Proceedings of Formal Ontology in Information Systems*. Also in: *Frontiers in Artificial Intelligence and Applications*. Washington, DC: IOS Press.

McGuinness, D.L. (1999) Ontologies for electronic commerce. In: *AAAI-99 Workshop on Artificial Intelligence for Electronic Commerce*, Orlando, FL, USA.

McKinsey and Company (2000) *B2B e-Marketplaces*. McKinsey and Company and CAPS Research.

Manville, B. and Foote, N. (1997) Strategy as if knowledge mattered. *Fast Company* (2), p. 66.

Marwick, A.D. (2001) Knowledge management technology. *IBM Systems Journal*, 40, (4).

Mentzas, G. and Abecker, A. (2001) Inter-organizational knowledge asset trading in virtual marketplaces. Working paper.

Mentzas, G. and Apostolou, D. (1998) Towards a holistic knowledge leveraging infrastructure: the KNOWNET approach. *2nd International Conference on Practical Aspects of Knowledge Management*, 29–30 October 1998, Basel, Switzerland.

Mentzas, G.N., Apostolou, D., Young, R. and Abecker, A. (2000) Knowledge networking: a holistic approach, method and tool for leveraging corporate knowledge. *Journal of Knowledge Management,* **5** (1), pp. 94–106.

Mertins, K., Heisig, P. and Vorbeck, J. (2000) *Knowledge Management: Best Practices in Europe.* Berlin: Springer.

Mintzberg, H. (1994) *The Rise and Fall of Strategic Planning.* Hertfordshire: Prentice-Hall International.

Mintzberg, H., Pascale, R.T., Goold, M. and Rumelt, R.P. (1996) The "Honda effect" revisited. *California Management Review,* **38** (4), pp. 78–117.

Mladenic, D. (1999) Text-learning and related intelligent agents: a survey. *IEEE Intelligent Systems,* **14** (4).

Mohan, R. (2000) *Electronic Marketplaces.* TJ Watson Research Center, New York: Institute for Advanced Commerce, IBM.

Naval Sea Systems Command (NAVSEA) (2001) *Community of Practice Practitioner's Guide,* Version 1.0a (May).

Neely, A., Richards, H., Mills, J., Platts, K. and Bourne, M. (1997) Designing performance measures: a structured approach. *International Journal of Operations & Production Management,* **17** (11), pp. 1131–1152.

Newbern, D. and Dansereau, D.F. (1995) Knowledge maps for knowledge management. In: Wiig, K. (ed.), *Knowledge Management Methods.* Arlington, VA: Schema Press.

Nonaka, I. (1988) Toward middle–up–down management: accelerating information creation. *Sloan Management Review,* **29** (3), pp. 9–18.

Nonaka, I. (1991) The knowledge-creating company. *Harvard Business Review,* (November–December), pp. 96–104.

Nonaka, I. (1994) A dynamic theory of organisational knowledge creation. *Organisation Science,* **5** (1), pp. 14–37.

Nonaka, I. and Ray, T. (1993) *Knowledge Creation in Japanese Organizations: Building the Dimensions Of Competitive Advantage.* First Theory-Oriented Research Group, National Institute of Science and Technology Policy Science and Technology Agency (September).

Nonaka, I. and Takeuchi, H. (1995) *The Knowledge-Creating Company: How Japanese Companies Create the Dynamics of Innovation.* Oxford: Oxford University Press.

Noy, N. and McGuinness, D.L. (2001) *Ontology Development 101: A Guide to Creating Your First Ontology.* SMI Report Number SMI-2001-0880. Stanford University.

O'Leary, D. (1998) Using AI in knowledge management: knowledge bases and ontologies. *IEEE Intelligent Systems,* (May/June), pp. 34–39.

Olson, D. (1976) Toward a theory of instructional means. *Educational Psychologist,* **12**, pp. 14–35.

Omelayenko, B. (2001) Learning of ontologies for the web: the analysis of existent approaches. In: *Proceedings of International Workshop on Web Dynamics, In Conjunction with the 8th International Conference on Database Theory (ICDT'01),* London, UK.

Ovum (1998) *Knowledge Management Applications, Markets and Technologies.*

Ovum (1999) *Knowledge Management: Building the Collaborative Enterprise.*

Papavassiliou, G. and Mentzas, G. (2001) Knowledge modelling in weakly-structured business processes. Special Issue on Knowledge Management and Organizations: Process, Systems and Strategy. *Business Process Management Journal* (submitted).

Porter, M.E. (1980) *Competitive Strategy: Techniques for Analyzing Industries and Competition.* New York: Free Press.

Porter, M.E. (1985) *Competitive Advantage.* New York: Free Press.

Porter, M.E. (1992) Capital disadvantage: America's failing capital investment system. *Harvard Business Review,* (September–October), pp. 65–82.

Provenzo, E. (1986) *Beyond the Gutenberg Galaxy: Microcomputers and the Emergence of Post-typographic Culture.* New York: Teachers College Press.

Prusak, L. (1999) What's up with knowledge management. In J.W. Cortada and J.A. Woods (eds), *The Knowledge Management Yearbook 1999–2000.* Woburn, MA: Butterworth-Heinemann, pp. 3–7.

Polanyi, M. (1966) *The Tacit Dimension.* London: Routledge & Kegan Paul.

Quinn, J.B. (1992) *The Intelligent Enterprise.* New York: Free Press.

Reimer, U., Margelisch, A. and Staudt, M. (2000) EULE: a knowledge-based system to support business processes. *Knowledge-based Systems Journal,* **13** (3).

Rockart, J.F. (1979) Chief Executives define their own data needs, *Harvard Business Review*, 57, March–April, pp. 81–93.

Romhardt K. and Probst, G. (1997) Building blocks of knowledge management – a practical approach. Paper presented at the seminar *Knowledge Management and the European Union*, 12–14 May 1997, Utrecht.

Roos, G. and Jacobsen, K. (1999) Management in a complex stakeholder organisation. *Monash Mt. Eliza Business Review*, (July), pp. 83–93.

Roos, G. and Roos, J. (1997a) Measuring your company's intellectual performance. *Long Range Planning*, 30 (3), pp. 413–426.

Roos, J. and Roos, G. (1997b) Intellectual capital: the next generation. *Financial Times Mastering Management*, 1 (1), pp. 6–10.

Roos, J., Roos, G., Dragonetti, N.C. and Edvinsson, L. (1997) *Intellectual Capital: Navigating in the New Business Landscape*. Houndmills, Basingstoke: Macmillan.

Rumelt, R.P. (1984) Towards a strategic theory of the firm. In: R. Boyden Lamb (ed.), *Competitive Strategic Management*. Englewood Cliffs, NJ: Prentice-Hall, pp. 556–570.

Sackmann, S., Flamholz, E. and Bullen, M. (1989) Human resource accounting: a state of the art review. *Journal of Accounting Literature*, 8, pp. 235–264.

Saint-Onge, H. (1996) Tacit knowledge: the key to the strategic alignment of intellectual capital. *Strategy and Leadership*, (March–April), pp. 10–14.

Scheer, A.-W. (2000) *ARIS – Business Process Modeling*. 3rd edn. Berlin: Springer.

Schmalensee, R. (1989) Inter-industry studies of structure and performance. In: R. Schmalensee and R.D. Willig (eds), *Handbook of Industrial Organization*. Amsterdam: Elsevier.

Schmid, B.F. and Lindemann, M.A. (1998) Elements of a reference model for electronic markets. In: Sprague, E. (ed.), *Proceedings of the 31st Hawaii International Conference on Systems Science (HICSS'98)*, pp. 193–201.

Schreiber, G. (ed.) (1999) *Knowledge Engineering and Management: The Common KADS Methodology*. Cambridge, MA: MIT Press.

Schubert, P. (2000) The participatory electronic product catalog: supporting customer collaboration in e-commerce applications. *Electronic Markets Journal*, 10 (4).

Schubert, P. and Ginsburg, M. (2000) Virtual communities of transaction: the role of personalization in electronic commerce. *Electronic Markets Journal*, 10 (1).

Skyrme, D. (2001) *Capitalizing on Knowledge: From e-business to k-business*. London: Butterworth-Heinemann.

Skyrme, D.J. and Amidon, D.M. (1997) *Creating the Knowledge-based Business*. London: Business Intelligence.

Sonnenberger, G. and Wolf, M. (1999) User requirements of UBS/CRV: metadata for document management. Internal document of the Know-Net project. Zürich: UBS AG.

Spek, R. and Spijkevert, A. (1997) *Knowledge Management, Dealing Intelligently With Knowledge*. The Knowledge Management Network, Kenniscentrum CIBIT and CSC.

Staab, S. and Schnurr, H.-P. (2000) Smart task support through proactive access to organizational memory. *Knowledge-based Systems*, 13 (5), 251–260.

Staab, S., Maedche, A., Nedellec, C. and Wiemer-Hastings, P. (eds) (2000) *ECAI'2000 Workshop on Ontology Learning*, Berlin, Germany.

Staab, S., Studer, R., Schnurr, H.-P. and Sure, Y. (2001) Knowledge processes and ontologies. *IEEE Intelligent Systems*, (January/February).

Stewart, T.A. (1997) *Intellectual Capital: The New Wealth of Organisations*. London: Nicholas Brealey.

Sveiby, K.-E. (1992) The knowhow company: strategy formulation in knowledge-intensive industries. *International Review of Strategic Management*.

Sveiby, K.-E. (1997a) Knowledge management and EU: challenging the perspective. *Seminar on Knowledge Management and the European Union*, 12–14 May, Utrecht, The Netherlands.

Sveiby, K.-E. (1997b) *The New Organisational Wealth: Managing and Measuring Knowledge-based Assets*. Berrett-Koehler, 275 pp.

Sveiby, K.-E. (1998) Measuring intangibles and intellectual capital – an emerging first standard. Paper posted on the web, 5 August (http://www.sveiby.com.au/EmergingStandard.htm).

Tapscott, D. and Caston, A. (1993) *Paradigm Shift – The New Promise of Information Technology*. New York: McGraw-Hill.

Thompson, J.D. (1967) *Organizations in Action*. New York: McGraw-Hill.

Tschaitschian, B., Abecker, A. and Schmalhofer, F. (1997) Information tuning with KARAT: capitalizing on existing documents. In: E. Plaza and R. Benjamins (eds), *10th European Workshop on Knowledge Acquisition, Modeling, and Management (EKAW-97)*, Sant Feliu de Guíxols, Catalonia, Spain. LNAI 1319. Springer.

Tschaitschian, B., Sintek, M., Abecker, A., Hackstein, J. and Bernardi, A. (1999) Using ontologies for advanced information access. Internal document of the KonArc project. Kaiserslautern, Germany: DFKI GmbH (September).

Tushman, M.L. and Nadler, D.A. (1978) Information processing as an integrating concept in organizational design. *Academy of Management Review*, 3, pp. 613–624.

Uschold, M. (1996) Building ontologies: towards a unified methodology. *Proceedings of Expert Systems 96, 16th Annual Conference of the British Society Specialist Group on Expert Systems*, Cambridge, UK, 16–18 December 1996.

Van Kaathoven, R., Jeusfeld, M., Staudt, M. and Reimer, U. (1999) Organisational memory supported workflow management. *Electronic Business Engineering*. Physica Verlag, pp. 543–563.

Weber, A. (1993) What's so new about the new economy? *Harvard Business Review*, (January–February).

Weber, A. (1994) Surviving in the new economy. *Harvard Business Review*, (September–October).

Wenger, E. (1998) *Communities of Practice*. New York: Cambridge University Press.

Wenger, E. (1999) *Communities of Practice: Learning, Meaning and Identity*. Cambridge: Cambridge University Press.

Wenger, E. and Snyder, B. (2000) Communities of practice: the organizational frontier. *Harvard Business Review*, 78 (1), pp. 139–145.

Wernerfelt, B. (1984) A resource-based view of the firm. *Strategic Management Journal*, 14, pp. 4–12.

Wiig, K. (1993) *Foundations of Knowledge Management*. Arlington, VA: Schema Press.

Wiig, K.M. (1995) *Knowledge Management Methods*. Arlington, VA: Schema Press.

Wiig, K. (1998) Perspectives on introducing enterprise knowledge management. In: U. Reimer (ed.), *Proceedings of PAKM-98: Practical Aspects of Knowledge Management*.

Williamson, O.E. (1985) *The Economic Institutions of Capitalism*. New York: Free Press.

Young, R. (1998) Knowledger. *Knowledge Management*, 1 (4, February/March), pp. 21–25.

Yu, B. and Wright, T.D. (1997) Software tools supporting business process analysis and modeling. *Business Process Management Journal*, 3 (2), pp. 133–150.

Index